ESTATE PUBLICA...

EAST SUSSEX

Street maps with index
Administrative Districts
Population Gazetteer
Road Map with index
Postcodes

COUNTY RED BOOKS

This atlas is intended for those requiring street maps of the historical and commercial centres of towns within the county. Each locality is normally presented on one or two pages and although, with many small towns, this space is sufficient to portray the whole urban area, the maps of large towns and cities are for centres only and are not intended to be comprehensive. Such coverage in Super and Local Red Books (see page 2).

Every effort has been made to verify the accuracy of information in this book but the publishers cannot accept responsibility for expense or loss caused by any error or omission. Information that will be of assistance to the user of these maps will be welcomed.

The representation of a road, track or footpath on the maps in this atlas is no evidence of the existence of a right of way.

Street plans prepared and published by ESTATE PUBLICATIONS, Bridewell House, TENTERDEN, KENT, and based upon the ORDNANCE SURVEY mapping with the permission of the Controller of H. M. Stationery Office.

The Publishers acknowledge the co-operation of the local authorities of towns represented in this atlas.

Estate Publications 519 C   ISBN 0 86084 966 X

COUNTY RED BOOK

EAST SUSSEX

contains street maps for each town centre

SUPER & LOCAL RED BOOKS

are street atlases with comprehensive local coverage

BRIGHTON

including: Hove, Lewes, Newhaven, Portslade,
Seaford, Shoreham etc.

EASTBOURNE

including: Lewes, Hailsham, Bexhill, Seaford,
Cooden, Polegate, Pevensey etc.

HASTINGS & BEXHILL

including: Rye, Battle, Winchelsea, Camber,
Fairlight, St. Leonards etc.

CONTENTS

LEGEND TO STREET MAPS

One-Way Street	→	**Post Office**	●
Pedestrianized	▨	**Public Convenience**	C
Car Park	P	**Place of Worship**	+

Scale of street plans: 4 Inches to 1 mile (unless otherwise stated on the map).

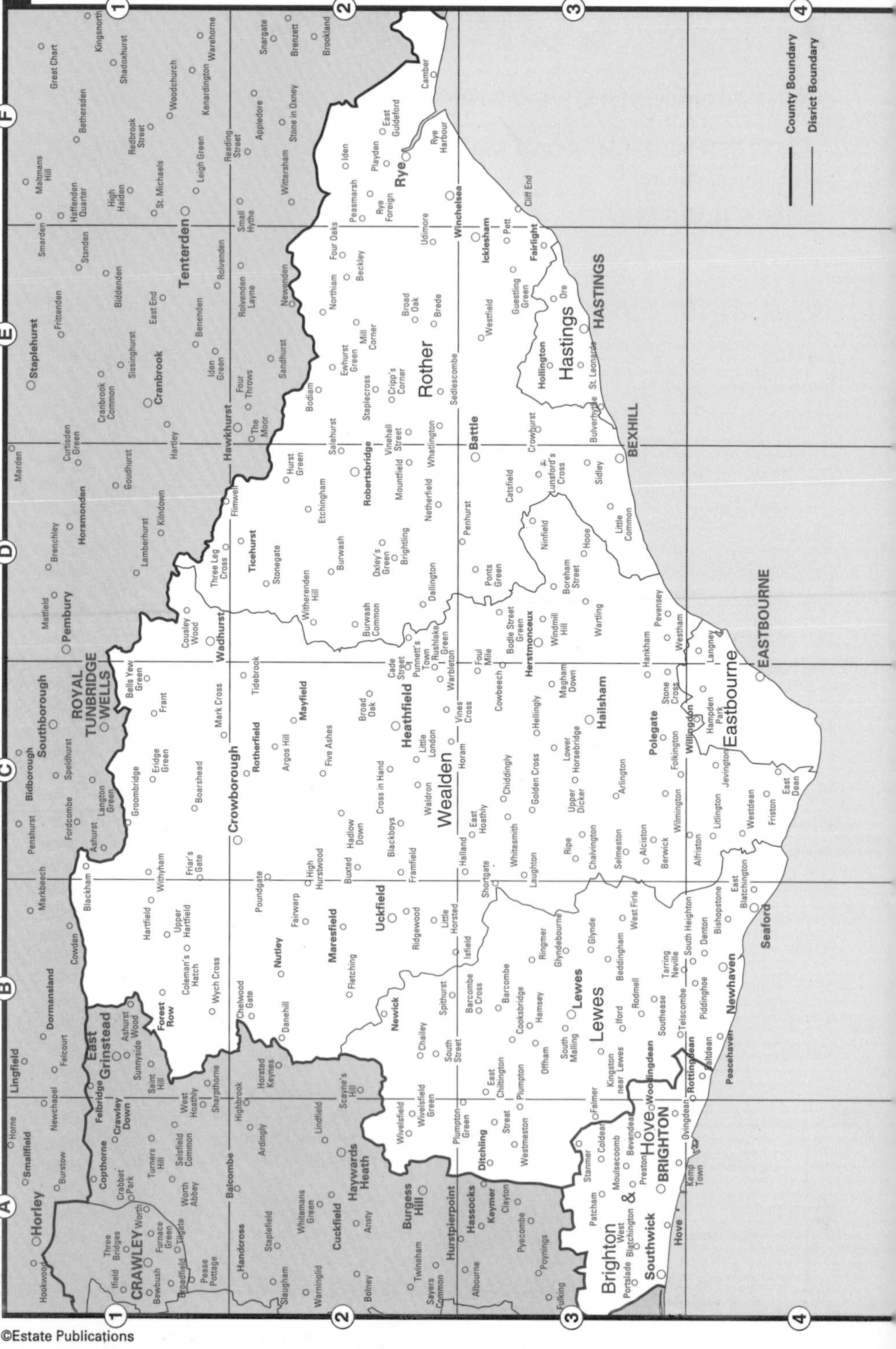

4 ADMINISTRATIVE DISTRICTS — EAST SUSSEX

County Boundary
District Boundary
Rother
Wealden
Lewes
HASTINGS
Hastings
BEXHILL
EASTBOURNE
Eastbourne
Brighton & Hove
BRIGHTON
Hove
ROYAL TUNBRIDGE WELLS
Crowborough
Uckfield
Heathfield
Hailsham
Polegate
Seaford
Newhaven
Peacehaven
Rye
Battle
Winchelsea
Robertsbridge
Wadhurst
Ticehurst
Mayfield
Rotherfield
Forest Row
East Grinstead
Crawley
Horley
Haywards Heath
Burgess Hill
Cuckfield
Hurstpierpoint
Hassocks
Keymer
Ditchling
Newick
Nutley
Maresfield
Herstmonceux
Willingdon
Rottingdean
Woodingdean
Southwick
Portslade
Tenterden
Cranbrook
Hawkhurst
Staplehurst
Pembury
Southborough
Bidborough
Horsmonden
Dormansland
Lingfield
Smallfield
Copthorne
Felbridge
Crawley Down
Balcombe
Handcross
Icklesham
Fairlight
Hollington
St. Leonards
Camber
Pevensey
Westham
Langney
Hampden Park
Alfriston
Berwick
Ringmer
Barcombe
Plumpton
Chailey
Telscombe
Saltdean
Ovingdean
Kemp Town
Stanmer
Falmer
Patcham

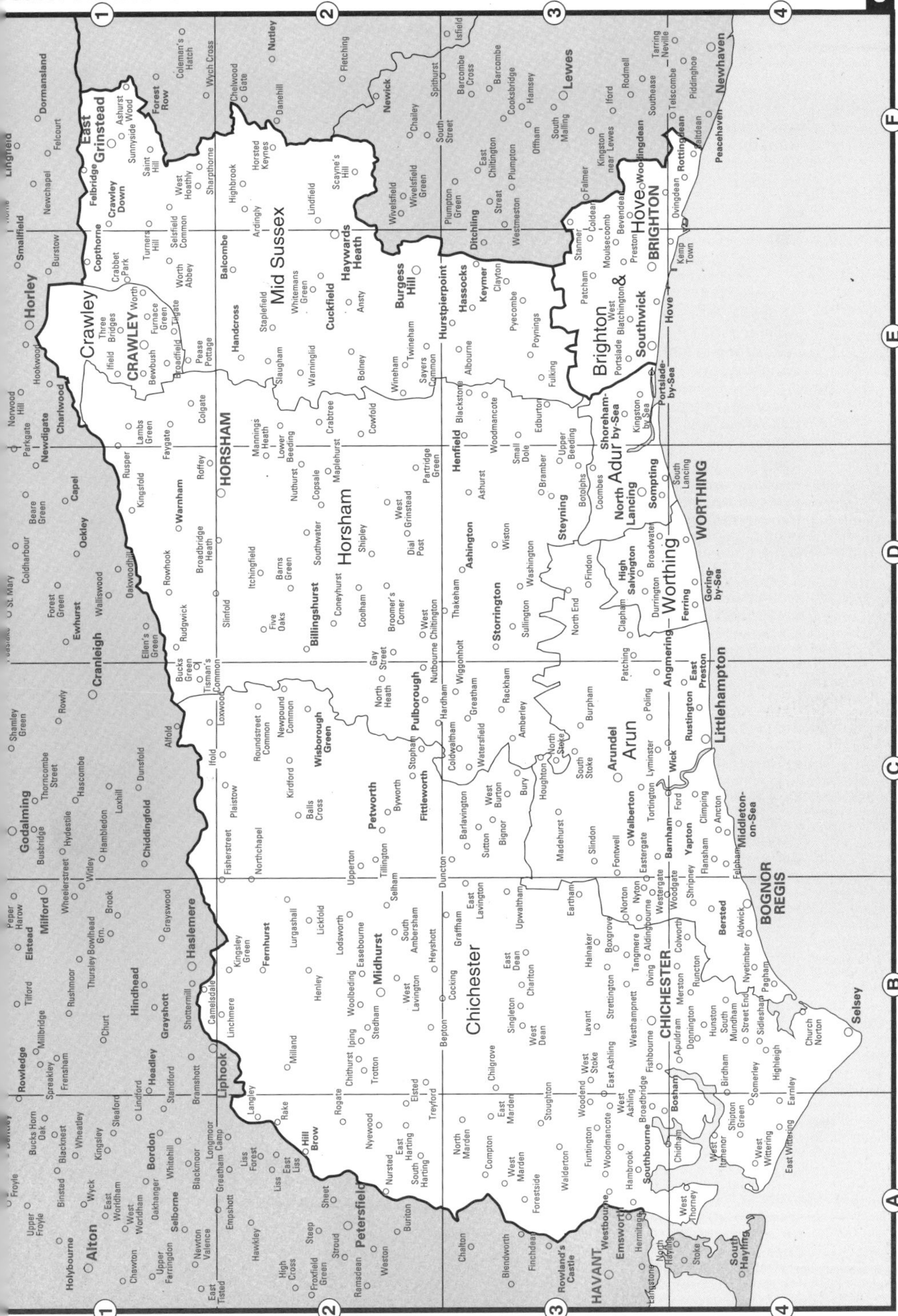
1
2
3
4
A
B
C
D
E
F
Crawley
CRAWLEY
Mid Sussex
Horsham
HORSHAM
Chichester
CHICHESTER
Arun
Adur
Worthing
WORTHING
Brighton & Hove
BRIGHTON
Hove
BOGNOR REGIS
Littlehampton
East Grinstead
Haywards Heath
Burgess Hill
Midhurst
Petworth
Pulborough
Arundel
Shoreham-by-Sea
Selsey
Horley
Haslemere
Petersfield
HAVANT
Lewes
Newhaven

GAZETTEER INDEX TO ROAD MAP
with Populations

County of East Sussex population **690,447**

Districts:

Brighton	143,582	
Eastbourne	81,395	
Hastings	80,820	
Hove	85,364	
Lewes	87,389	
Rother	81,683	
Wealden	130,214	

Alciston **121**	9 E6	
Alfriston **761**	9 E7	
Arlington **533**	9 E6	
Ashburnham **329**	*	
Ashurstwood	8 C2	
Barcombe **1,353**	9 C5	
Barcombe Cross	9 C5	
Battle **5,732**	11 B5	
Beckley **1,025**	10 D4	
Beddingham **230**	9 D6	
Bell's Yew Green	8 F6	
Berwick **232**	9 E6	
Bevendean	9 B6	
Bexhill-on-Sea. **35,222**	11 B6	
Birling Gap	9 E8	
Bishopstone	9 D7	
Blackboys	8 E4	
Blackham	8 E1	
Boarshead	8 E2	
Bodiam **346**	10 C3	
Bodle Street Green	11 A5	
Boreham Street	11 A6	
Brede **1,764**	10 D4	
Brightling **367**	10 A4	
Brighton **88,667**	9 B7	
Broad Oak	10 D4	
Broadoak	8 F4	
Bulverhythe	11 C6	
Burwash **2,506**	10 A4	
Burwash Common	10 A4	
Buxted **3,071**	8 E4	
Cade Street	8 F4	
Camber **1,108**	10 F4	
Catsfield **767**	11 B5	
Chailey **2,548**	8 C4	
Chalvington with Ripe **785**	9 E6	
Chelwood Gate	8 C3	
Chiddingly **866**	9 E5	
Cliff End	11 E5	
Coldean	9 B6	
Coleman's Hatch	8 D2	
Cooden	11 B6	
Cooksbridge	9 C5	
Cousley Wood	10 A2	
Cowbeech	11 A5	
Cripp's Corner	10 C4	
Cross in Hand	8 F4	
Crowborough **19,120**	8 E3	
Crowhurst **896**	11 C5	
Cuckmere Valley **213**	*	

Dallington **319**	10 A4	
Danehill **1,879**	8 C3	
Denton	9 D7	
Ditchling **1,882**	9 B5	
Duddleswell	8 D3	
East Blatchington	9 D7	
East Chiltington **302**	9 C5	
East Dean **1,725**	9 F8	
East Guldeford **60**	10 F4	
East Hoathly **1,206**	9 E5 .	
Eastbourne **60,674**	11 A7	
Eastdean & Friston **1,662**	9 F8	
Eridge Green	8 F2	
Etchingham **738**	10 B3	
Ewhurst **1,004**	10 C4	
Fairlight **1,605**	11 D5	
Fairlight Cove	11 E6	
Fairwarp	8 D3	
Falmer **184**	9 B6	
Firle **303**	9 D6	
Five Ashes	8 E3	
Fletching **977**	8 C4	
Flimwell	10 B3	
Folkington	9 F7	
Forest Row **4,762**	8 C2	
Foul Mile	9 F5	
Four Oaks	10 D4	
Framfield **1,773**	8 E4	
Frant **1,445**	8 F2	
Friar's Gate	8 D2	
Friston & East Dean **1,662**	9 E7	
Glynde **204**	9 D6	
Glyndebourne	9 D6	
Golden Cross	9 E5	
Groombridge	8 E2	
Guestling Green **1,431**	11 D5	
Hadlow Down **648**	8 E4	
Hailsham **17,938**	9 F6	
Halland	9 E5	
Hampden Park **7,954**	9 F7	
Hamsey **534**	9 C5	
Hankham	9 F6	
Hartfield **2,026**	8 D2	
Hastings **63,976**	11 D6	
Heathfield & Waldron **10,676**	8 F4	
Hellingly **1,526**	9 F5	
Herstmonceux **2,334**	11 A5	
High Hurstwood	8 E3	
Hollington **5,977**	11 C5	
Hooe **376**	11 B6	
Horam **2,393**	9 F5	
Horsebridge	9 F5	
Hove **67,602**	9 A6	
Hurst Green **1,417**	10 B3	
Icklesham **2,443**	11 D5	
Iden **499**	10 E4	
Iford **195**	9 C6	
Isfield **535**	*	

Jarvis Brook		8 E3
Jevington & Willingdon	**5,846**	9 F7
Kemp Town		9 B7
Kingston near Lewes	**616**	9 C6
Langney	**12,867**	11 A7
Laughton	**516**	9 E5
Lewes	**15,376**	9 C6
Litlington		9 E7
Little Common		11 B6
Little Horsted	**210**	9 E5
Little London		8 F4
Long Man	**377**	*
Lunsford's Cross		11 B6
Magham Down		9 F5
Maresfield	**3,095**	8 D4
Mark Cross		8 F3
Mayfield	**3,515**	8 F3
Millcorner		10 D4
Moulsecoomb	**9,749**	9 B6
Mountfield	**475**	10 B4
Netherfield		10 B4
Newhaven	**10,210**	9 D7
Newick	**2,445**	8 C4
Ninfield	**1,448**	11 B5
Northiam	**1,810**	10 D3
Nutley		8 D3
Offham		9 C5
Ovingdean		9 B7
Oxley's Grn		10 B4
Patcham	**8,762**	9 B6
Peacehaven	**12,992**	9 C7
Peasmarsh	**911**	10 E4
Penshurst	**36**	11 B5
Pestalozzi		11 C5
Pett	**706**	11 D5
Pevensey	**2,833**	11 A6
Pevensey Bay		11 A7
Piddinghoe	**230**	9 C7
Playden	**323**	10 E4
Plumpton	**1,404**	10 E4
Polegate	**7,606**	9 F6
Ponts Green		11 A5
Portslade		9 A6
Portslade-by-Sea	**17,762**	9 A7
Preston	**9,740**	9 B6
Punnett's Town		10 A4
Ridgewood		8 D4
Ringmer	**4,456**	9 D5
Ripe & Chalvington	**785**	9 E6
Robertsbridge		10 B4
Rodmell	**413**	9 C6
Rotherfield	**3,096**	8 F3
Rottingdean	**8,949**	9 B7
Rushlake Green		10 A4
Rye	**4,207**	10 E4
Rye Foreign	**197**	10 E4
Rye Harbour		10 E4
St Ann (Without)	**278**	*
St John (Without)	**45**	*
St Leonards	**10,867**	11 C6
Salehurst	**2,211**	10 C4
Saltdean		9 C7
Seaford	**20,933**	9 D7
Sedlescombe	**1,299**	10 C4
Sedlescombe Street		10 C4
Selmeston	**171**	9 E6
Shortgate		9 D5
Sidley	**5,330**	11 B6
South Heighton	**998**	9 D7
South Malling		9 C5
South Street		9 C5
Southease	**29**	9 C6
Southwick		9 A6
Spithurst		8 D5
Stanmer	**7,933**	9 B6
Staple Cross		10 C4
Stone Cross		9 F7
Stonegate		10 A3
Streat	**170**	9 B5
Tarring Neville	**22**	9 D6
Telscombe	**6,808**	9 C7
Three Leg Cros		10 B3
Ticehurst	**3,118**	10 B3
Tidebrook		8 F3
Uckfield.	**12,087**	8 D4
Udimore	**336**	10 D4
Upper Dicker		9 E6
Upper Hartfield		8 D2
Vinehall Street		10 C4
Vine's Cross		8 F4
Wadhurst	**4,499**	10 A2
Waldron & Heathfield	**10,676**	8 E4
Warbleton	**1,217**	9 F5
Wartling	**347**	11 A6
West Blatchington		9 A6
Westdean		9 E7
Westfield	**2,461**	11 D5
Westham	**2,980**	11 A7
Westmeston	**333**	9 B5
Whatlington	**332**	9 B5
Whitesmith		9 E5
Willingdon & Jevington	**5,846**	9 F7
Winchelsea	**2,413**	11 E5
Winchelsea Beach		11 E5
Windmill Hill		11 A5
Witherenden Hill		10 A3
Withyham	**2,510**	8 E2
Wivelsfield	**1,896**	8 B4
Wivelsfield Green		8 B4
Woodingdean	**9,782**	9 C6
Wych Cross		8 C3

†Population figures are based upon the 1991 census and relate to the local authority area or parish as constituted at that date. Places with no population figure form part of a larger local authority area or parish. District boundaries are shown on pages 4-5.

Population figures in bold type.

*Parish not shown on map pages 8-11 due to limitation of scale.

ROAD MAP

Scale 3 miles to 1 inch

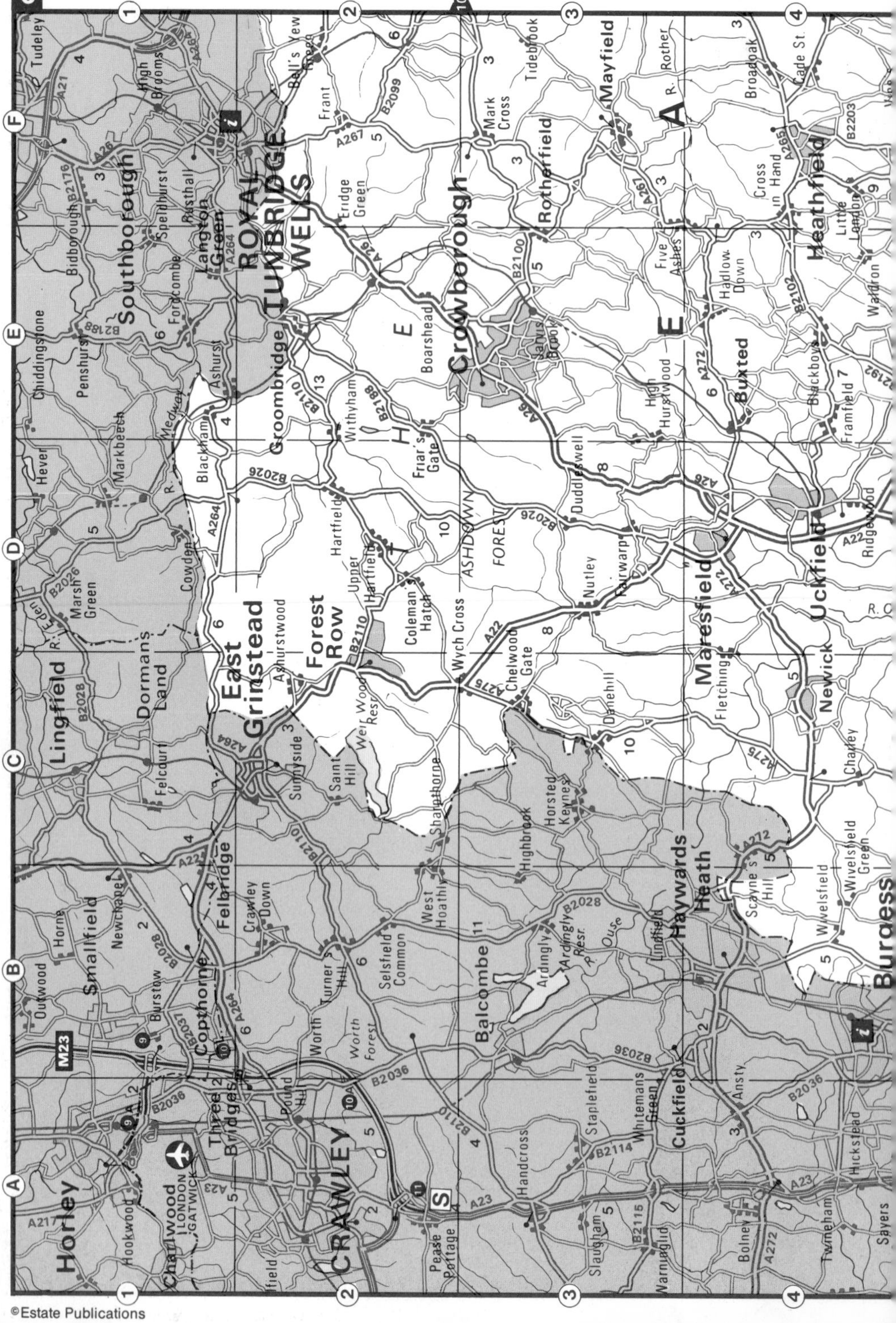
10
ROYAL TUNBRIDGE WELLS
Southborough
Tudeley
High Brooms
Bidborough
Speldhurst
Rusthall
Langton Green
Fordcombe
Penshurst
Chiddingstone
Ashurst
Groombridge
Blackham
Markbeech
Hever
Medway
Bell's Yew Green
Frant
Eridge Green
Mark Cross
Tidebrook
Mayfield
Rotherfield
Crowborough
Boarshead
Jarvis Brook
Withyham
Friar's Gate
Hartfield
Upper Hartfield
Coleman's Hatch
ASHDOWN FOREST
Wych Cross
Chelwood Gate
Forest Row
Ashurstwood
East Grinstead
Weir Wood Resr.
Saint Hill
Sunnyside
Sharpthorne
Horsted Keynes
Highbrook
West Hoathly
Lingfield
Dormans Land
Marsh Green
Cowden
Felcourt
Felbridge
Crawley Down
Smallfield
Horne
Newchapel
Outwood
Burstow
Copthorne
Turner's Hill
Selsfield Common
Worth
Worth Forest
Balcombe
Ardingly
Ardingly Resr.
Ouse
Lindfield
Haywards Heath
Cuckfield
Whitemans Green
Staplefield
Ansty
Handcross
Slaugham
Warninglid
Bolney
Twineham
Sayers
Hickstead
Pease Pottage
CRAWLEY
Pound Hill
Three Bridges
Horley
Hookwood
Charlwood
LONDON GATWICK
Mayfield
Rother
Broadoak
Cade St.
Cross in Hand
Heathfield
Little London
Five Ashes
Hadlow Down
Waldron
Buxted
High Hurstwood
Blackboys
Framfield
Duddleswell
Nutley
Fairwarp
Maresfield
Uckfield
Ridgewood
Danehill
Fletching
Newick
Chailey
Wivelsfield Green
Wivelsfield
Scayne's Hill
Burgess
R. Eden
R. Medway
M23
A21
A26
A264
A267
A22
A275
A272
A23
A217
A26A
A265
A267
B2176
B2188
B2110
B2026
B2028
B2099
B2100
B2102
B2037
B2036
B2114
B2115
B2203
A
E
H
S

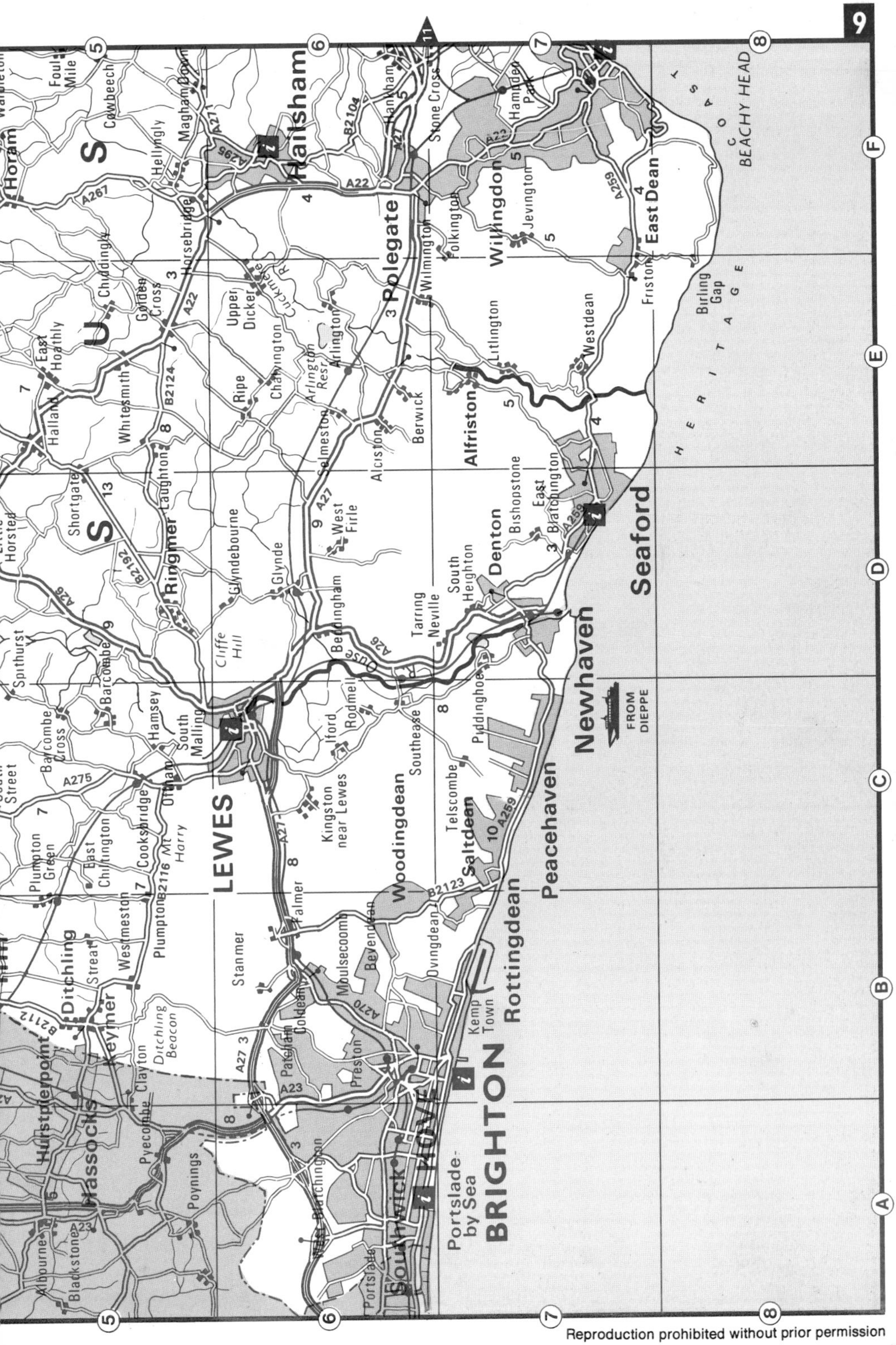
Horam
Foul Mile
Cowbeech
Hellingly
Magham Down
Hailsham
Hankham
Stone Cross
Hampden Park
Polegate
Wilmington
Folkington
Willingdon
Jevington
East Dean
Friston
BEACHY HEAD
Birling Gap
HERITAGE COAST
Westdean
Litlington
Alfriston
Berwick
Alciston
Selmeston
Arlington
Arlington Resr
Chalvington
Upper Dicker
Cuckmere R
Horsebridge
Chiddingly
Golden Cross
East Hoathly
Whitesmith
Halland
Ripe
Laughton
Shortgate
Ringmer
Glyndebourne
Glynde
West Firle
Beddingham
Tarring Neville
South Heighton
Denton
Bishopstone
East Blatchington
Seaford
Newhaven
FROM DIEPPE
Piddinghoe
Southease
Rodmell
Iford
Kingston near Lewes
Telscombe
Saltdean
Peacehaven
Woodingdean
Ovingdean
Rottingdean
Kemp Town
BRIGHTON
HOVE
Portslade-by-Sea
Portslade
Southwick
Patcham
Preston
Coldean
Moulsecoomb
Bevendean
Falmer
Stanmer
LEWES
South Malling
Hamsey
Offham
Mt Harry
Cliffe Hill
Barcombe
Barcombe Cross
Spithurst
Little Horsted
Cooksbridge
East Chiltington
Plumpton Green
Plumpton
Westmeston
Ditchling
Ditchling Beacon
Streat
Keymer
Hassocks
Hurstpierpoint
Clayton
Pyecombe
Poynings
Albourne
Blackstone
Ouse
A22
A23
A26
A27
A259
A267
A270
A271
A275
A295
B2104
B2112
B2116
B2123
B2124
B2192
A
B
C
D
E
F
5
6
7
8
11

ROAD MAP Scale 3 miles to 1 inch

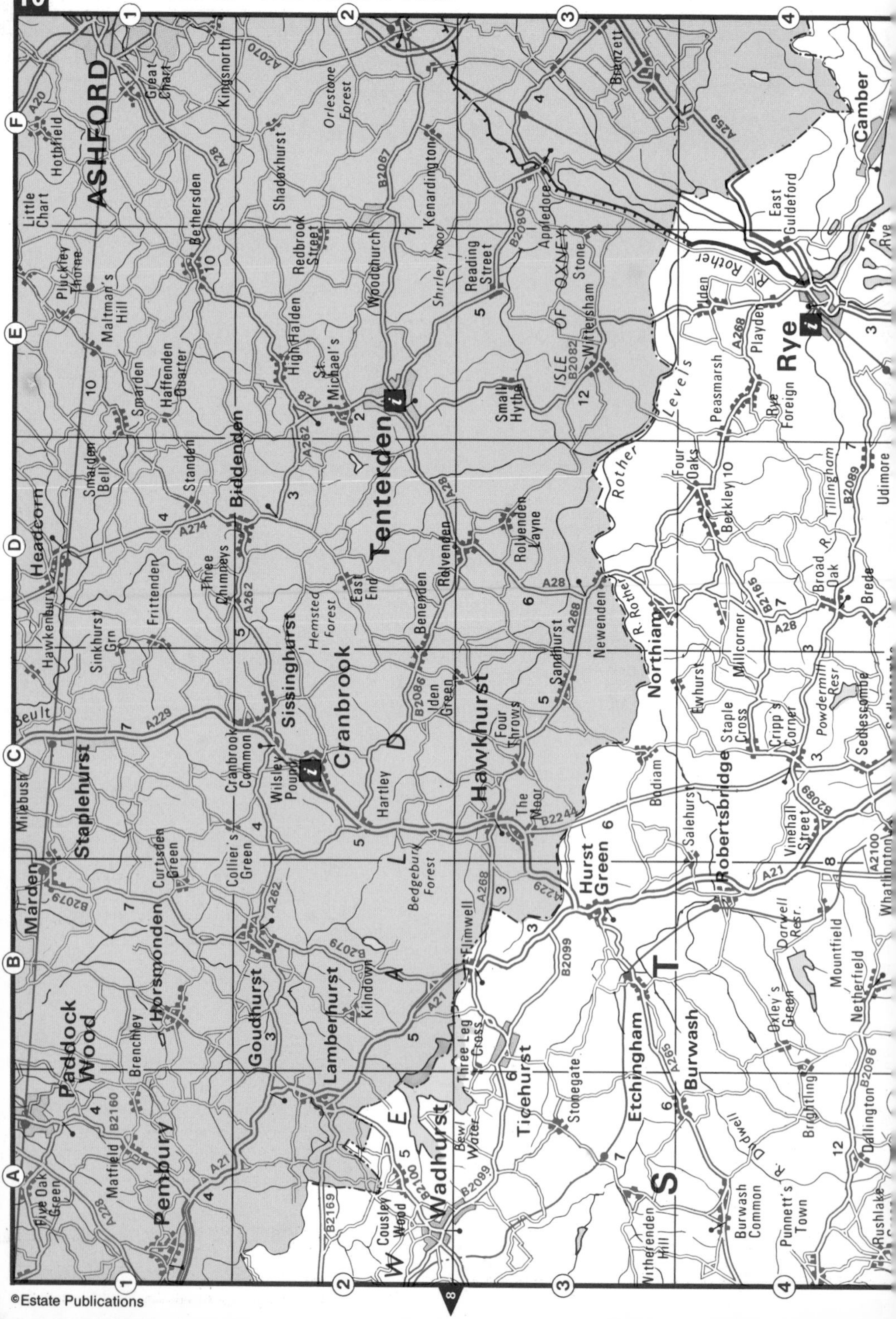
ASHFORD
Great Chart
Kingsnorth
Hothfield
Little Chart
Pluckley Thorne
Maltman's Hill
Smarden
Haffenden Quarter
Bethersden
Shadoxhurst
Orlestone Forest
Kenardington
Brenzett
Camber
East Guldeford
Rye
Appledore
Stone
Reading Street
Shirley Moor
Woodchurch
Redbrook Street
High Halden
St. Michael's
Tenterden
Small Hythe
Wittersham
ISLE OF OXNEY
Peasmarsh
Playden
Iden
Rye Foreign
Smarden Bell
Standen
Biddenden
Headcorn
Three Chimneys
Frittenden
Hawkenbury
Sinkhurst Grn
Sissinghurst
Hemsted Forest
East End
Rolvenden
Rolvenden Layne
Benenden
Sandhurst
Newenden
Four Oaks
Beckley
Broad Oak
Udimore
Brede
Northiam
Millcorner
Ewhurst
Staple Cross
Cripp's Corner
Powdermill Resr
Sedlescombe
Staplehurst
Milebush
Cranbrook Common
Cranbrook
Wilsley Pound
Hartley
Iden Green
Hawkhurst
Four Throws
The Moor
Bodiam
Salehurst
Robertsbridge
Vinehall Street
Marden
Curtisden Green
Collier's Green
Bedgebury Forest
Flimwell
Hurst Green
Etchingham
Burwash
Darwell Resr.
Mountfield
Netherfield
Oxley's Green
Horsmonden
Brenchley
Paddock Wood
Goudhurst
Lamberhurst
Kilndown
Three Leg Cross
Ticehurst
Stonegate
Brightling
Dallington
Pembury
Matfield
Five Oak Green
Wadhurst
Bewl Water
Cousley Wood
Witherenden Hill
Burwash Common
Punnett's Town
Rushlake
R. Rother
Rother Levels
R. Tillingham
R. Dudwell
Beult
WEALD
EAST SUSSEX
A20
A28
A2070
A259
A268
A274
A262
A229
A21
A265
A2100
A228
B2067
B2080
B2082
B2086
B2079
B2160
B2169
B2099
B2089
B2165
B2244
B2096
B2100

8

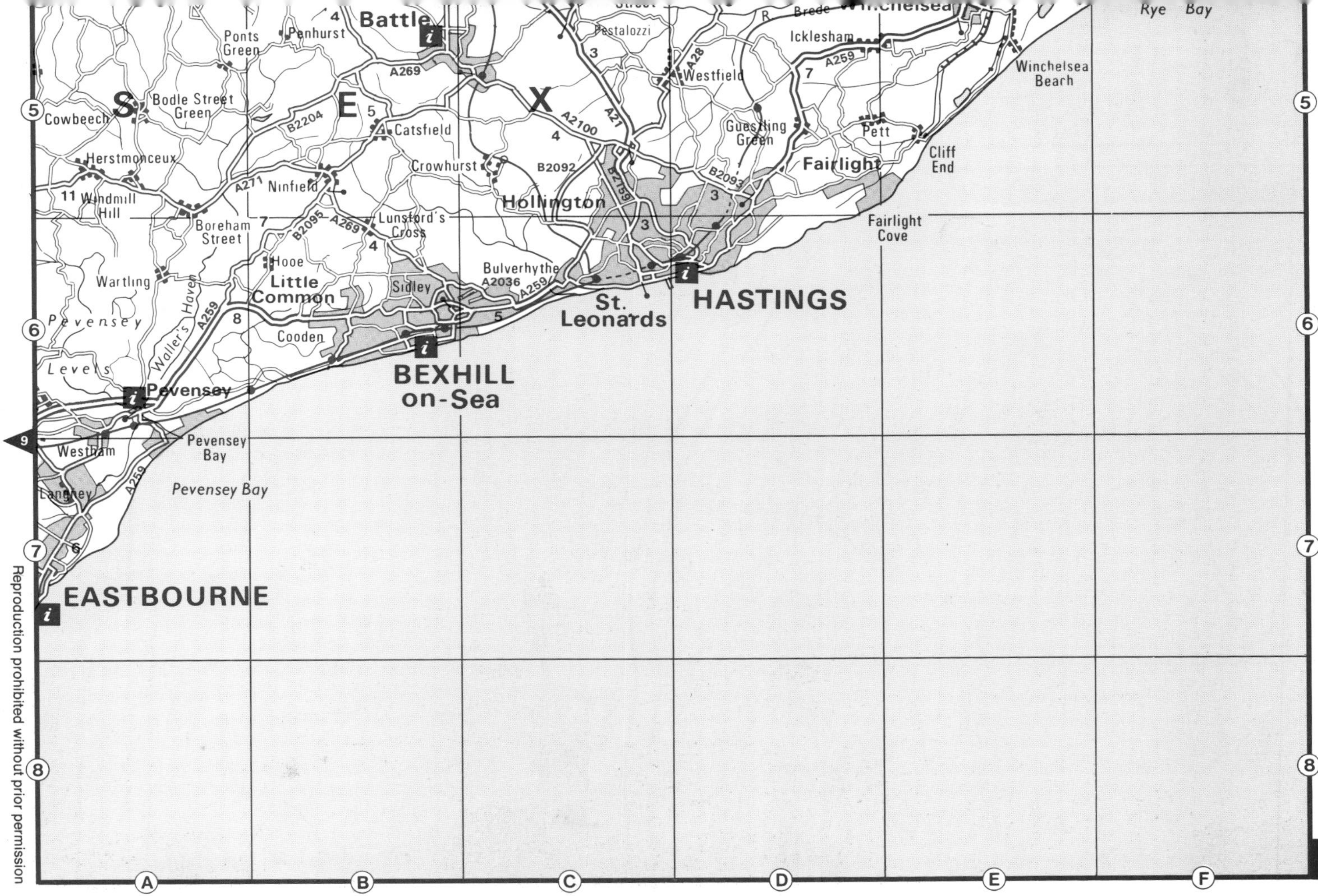
HASTINGS
St. Leonards
BEXHILL on-Sea
EASTBOURNE
Battle
Hollington
Fairlight
Fairlight Cove
Cliff End
Pett
Winchelsea Beach
Rye Bay
Icklesham
Brede
R.
Westfield
Guestling Green
Pestalozzi
Catsfield
Crowhurst
Lunsford's Cross
Bulverhythe
Sidley
Little Common
Cooden
Hooe
Ninfield
Boreham Street
Penhurst
Ponts Green
Bodle Street Green
Cowbeech
Herstmonceux
Windmill Hill
Wartling
Pevensey Levels
Waller's Haven
Pevensey
Pevensey Bay
Westham
Langney
S
E
X
A21
A28
A259
A269
A271
A2100
A2036
B2092
B2093
B2095
B2159
B2204
A
B
C
D
E
F
5
6
7
8
9

12 BATTLE

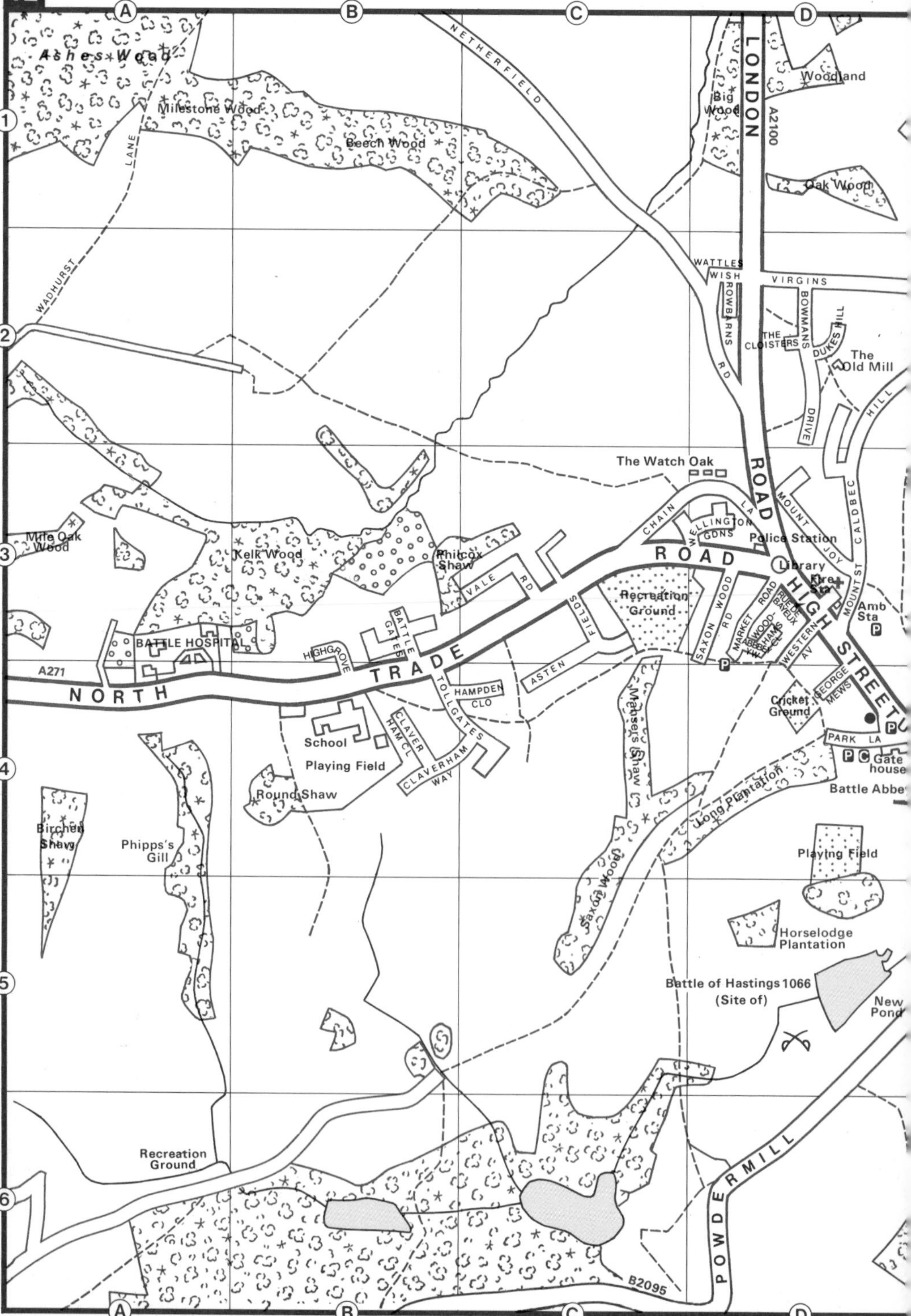
A
B
C
D
1
2
3
4
5
6
Ashes Wood
Milestone Wood
Beech Wood
NETHERFIELD
LONDON
A2100
Big Wood
Woodland
Oak Wood
LANE
WADHURST
WATTLES WISH
ROWBARNS RD
VIRGINS
BOWMANS DRIVE
THE CLOISTERS
DUKES HILL
The Old Mill
HILL
The Watch Oak
ROAD
MOUNT JOY
CALDBEC
CHAIN LA
WELLINGTON GDNS
Police Station
Library
Fire Sta
MOUNT ST
Amb Sta
Mile Oak Wood
Kelk Wood
Philcox Shaw
VALE RD
ROAD
Recreation Ground
SAXON WOOD RD
MARKET ROAD
WOODHAMS CL
BAYEUX
WESTERN AV
HIGH STREET
BATTLE HOSPITAL
A271
NORTH
TRADE
BATTLE GATES
HIGHGROVE
TOLLGATES
HAMPDEN CLO
FIELDS
ASTEN
Cricket Ground
GEORGE MEWS
PARK LA
Gate house
Battle Abbey
School
Playing Field
CLAVERHAM CL
CLAVERHAM WAY
Round Shaw
Long Plantation
Mansers Shaw
Birchen Shaw
Phipps's Gill
Playing Field
Saxon Wood
Horselodge Plantation
Battle of Hastings 1066 (Site of)
New Pond
Recreation Ground
POWDERMILL
B2095

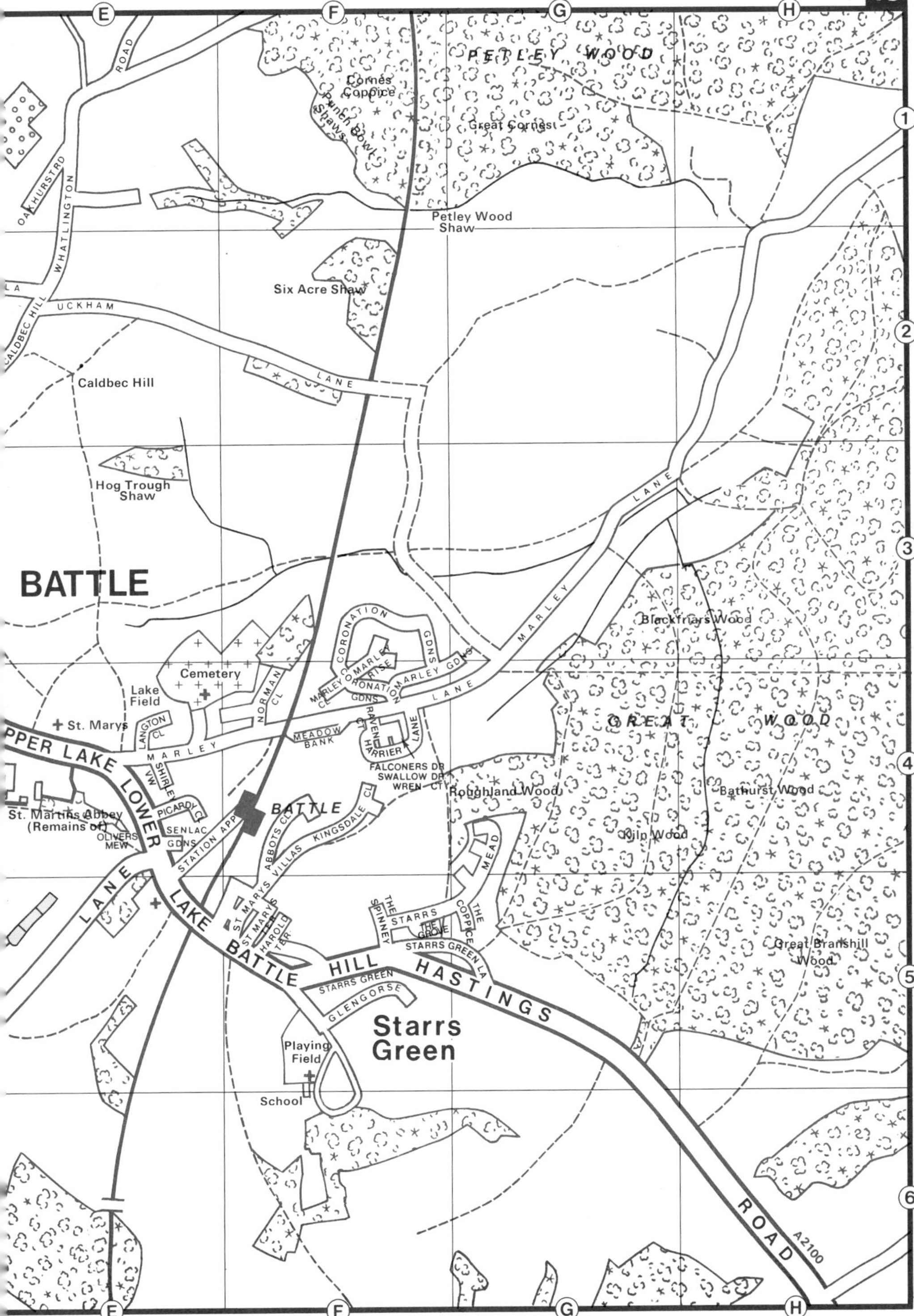
E
F
G
H
1
2
3
4
5
6
PETLEY WOOD
Cornes Coppice
Punch Bowl Shaws
Great Cornes
Petley Wood Shaw
Six Acre Shaw
ROAD
OAKHURST RD
WHATLINGTON
CALDBEC HILL
UCKHAM
LANE
Caldbec Hill
Hog Trough Shaw
BATTLE
Cemetery
Lake Field
St. Marys
NORMAN CL
CORONATION GDNS
MARLEY RISE
MARLEY CL
MARLEY GDNS
LANE
MARLEY
LANE
Blackfriars Wood
GREAT WOOD
LANGTON CL
MARLEY
MEADOW BANK
RAVEN CT
HARRIER
LANE
FALCONERS DR
SWALLOW DR
WREN CT
UPPER LAKE
LOWER
SHIRLEY VW
PICARDY CL
SENLAC GDNS
St. Martins Abbey (Remains of)
OLIVERS MEW
STATION APP
BATTLE
ABBOTS CL
VILLAS
KINGSDALE CL
Roughland Wood
Bathurst Wood
Kiln Wood
MEAD
LANE
LAKE
ST MARYS
ST MARYS
HAROLD TER
THE SPINNEY
STARRS
THE GROVE
THE COPPICE
STARRS GREEN LA
BATTLE HILL
HASTINGS
STARRS GREEN
GLENGORSE
Starrs Green
Great Branshill Wood
Playing Field
School
ROAD
A2100

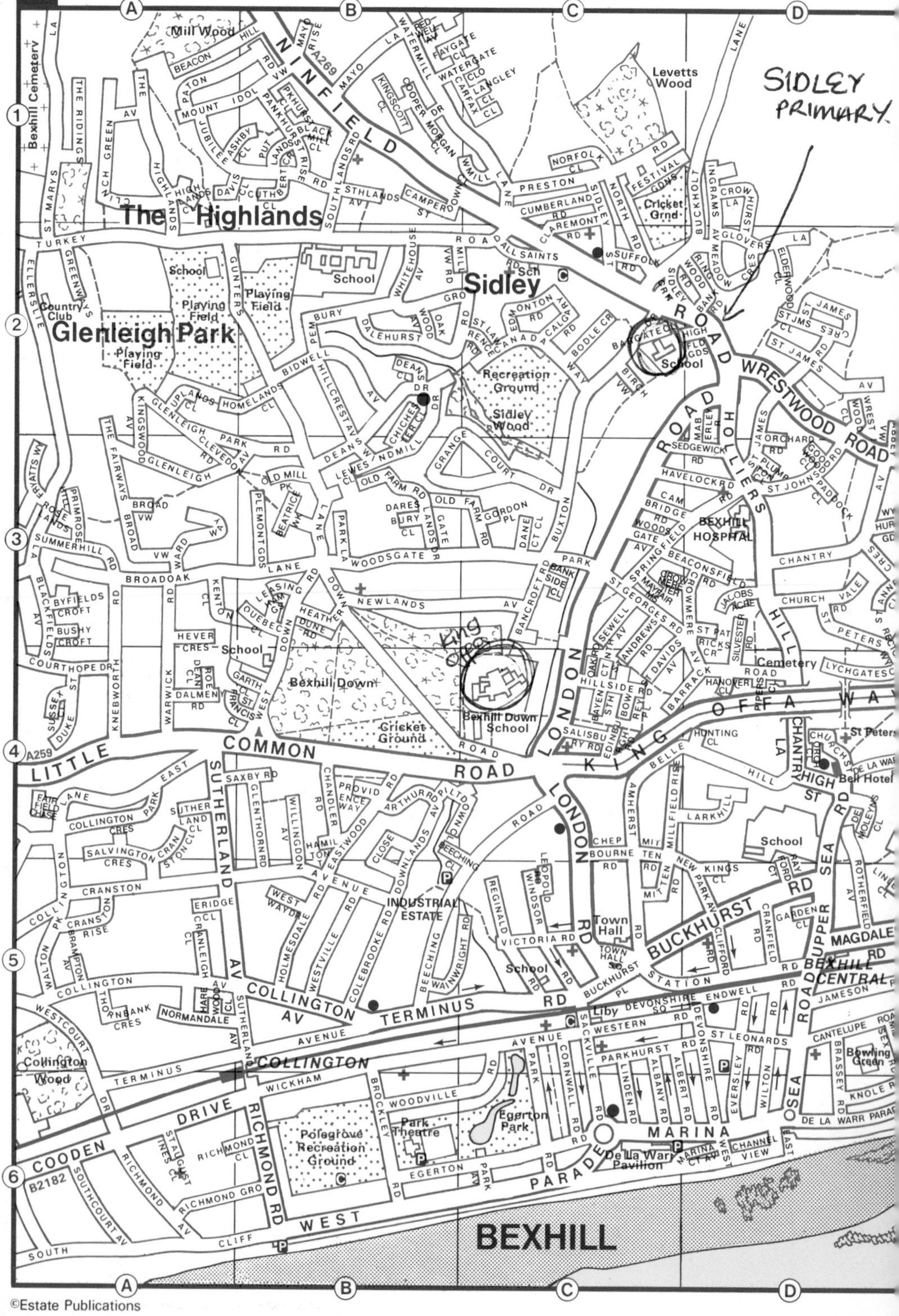

SIDLEY PRIMARY
Mill Wood
Levetts Wood
Bexhill Cemetery
The Highlands
Sidley
Glenleigh Park
Country Club
School
Playing Field
Recreation Ground
Sidley Wood
Cricket Grnd
BEXHILL HOSPITAL
Cemetery
Bexhill Down
Cricket Ground
Bexhill Down School
St Peters
Bell Hotel
INDUSTRIAL ESTATE
Town Hall
Liby
BEXHILL CENTRAL
COLLINGTON
Collington Wood
Polegrove Recreation Ground
Park Theatre
Egerton Park
Bowling Green
De La Warr Pavilion
BEXHILL
NINFIELD RD
A269
TURKEY RD
LONDON RD
WRESTWOOD ROAD
KING OFFA WAY
LITTLE COMMON ROAD
A259
SUTHERLAND AV
COLLINGTON AV
TERMINUS RD
COODEN DRIVE
B2182
RICHMOND RD
WEST PARADE
MARINA
DE LA WARR PARADE
BUCKHURST RD
SEA RD
WEST CLIFF
SOUTH CLIFF

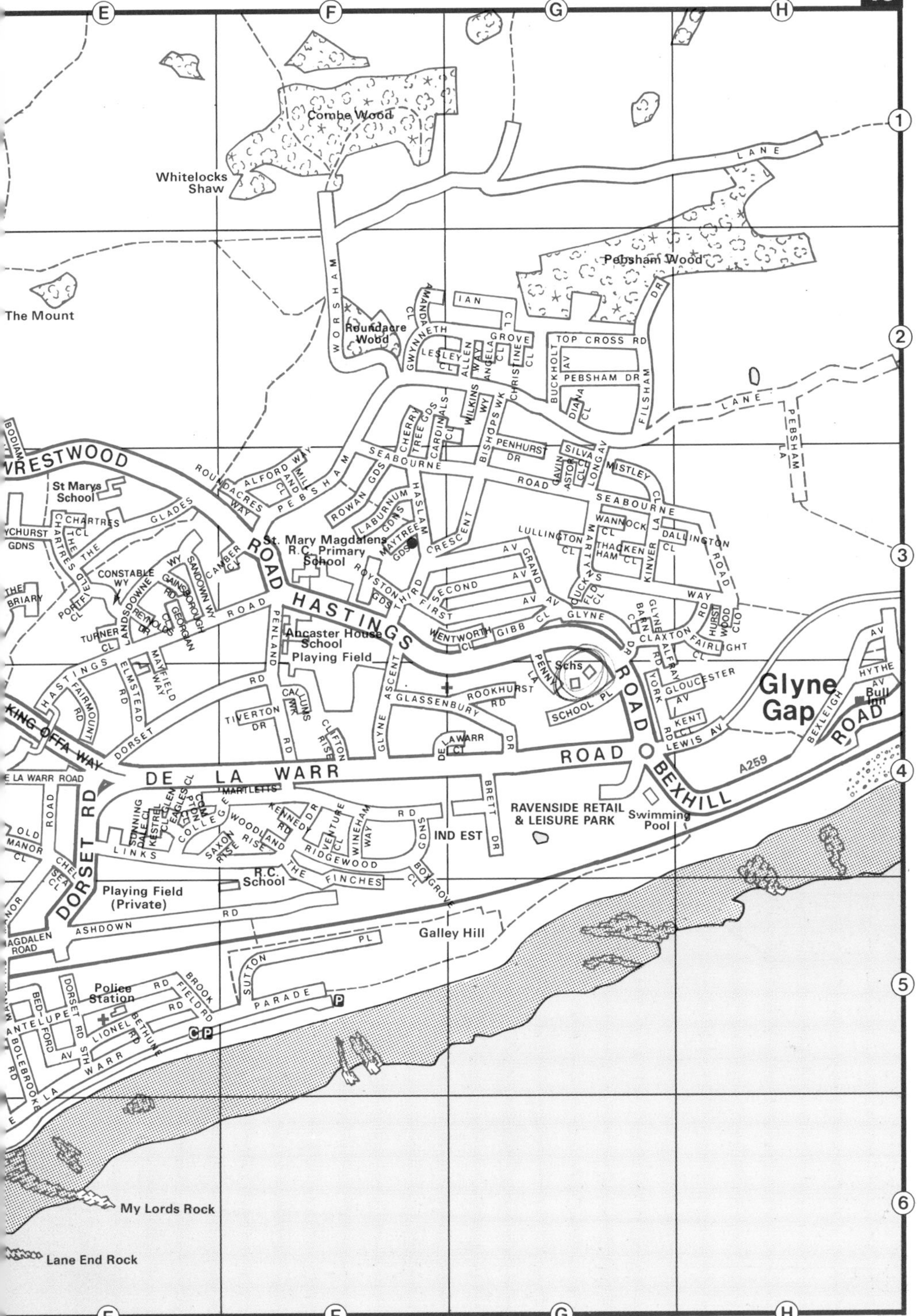
E
F
G
H
1
2
3
4
5
6
Combe Wood
Whitelocks Shaw
LANE
Pebsham Wood
The Mount
WORSHAM
Roundacre Wood
AMANDA CL
IAN CL
GWYNNETH
GROVE
TOP CROSS RD
LESLEY CL
ALLEN WAY
ANGELA CL
CHRISTINE CL
BUCKHOLT AV
PEBSHAM DR
DIANA CL
FILSHAM DR
LANE
PEBSHAM LA
WILKINS WY
BISHOPS WK
CHERRY TREE GDS
CARDINALS CL
PENHURST DR
SILVA CL
LONG AV
MISTLEY CL
GAVIN
ASTOR CL
SEABOURNE ROAD
SEABOURNE
BODIAM
WRESTWOOD
ROUNDACRES WAY
ALFORD WAY
MILLAND CL
PEBSHAM
St Marys School
CHARTRES CL
GLADES
CHARTRES
THE
ROWAN GDS
LABURNUM GDS
HASLAM
CRESCENT
WANNOCK CL
THACKENHAM CL
KINVER LA
DALLINGTON CL
DALLINGTON ROAD
LULLINGTON CL
MARTYNS
GRAND AV
St. Mary Magdalens R.C. Primary School
MAYTREE GDS
ROYSTON GDS
THIRD
FIRST
SECOND AV
AV
WAY
HURST WOOD CLO
BARN CL
GLYNE
GLYNE DR
CLAXTON
FAIRLIGHT
HOLLYCHURST GDNS
THE BRIARY
CONSTABLE WY
PORTFIELD CL
GAINSBOROUGH RD
SANDOWN WY
CAMBER CL
ROAD
HASTINGS
LANSDOWNE
REYNOLDS DR
GEORGIAN
TURNER CL
PENLAND RD
Ancaster House School
Playing Field
WENTWORTH CL
GIBB CL
GLYNE
AV
PENNY LA
Schs
SCHOOL PL
ROAD
YORK RD
ALFRAY RD
GLOUCESTER AV
KENT CL
LEWIS AV
Glyne Gap
HYTHE AV
BEXLEIGH AV
Bull Inn
ROAD
HASTINGS
FAIRMOUNT RD
ELMSTEAD RD
MAYFIELD WAY
DORSET RD
CALLUMS WK
TIVERTON DR
CLIFTON RISE
GLYNE ASCENT
GLASSENBURY
ROOKHURST RD
DE LA WARR CL
KING OFFA WAY
DORSET
ROAD
BEXHILL
A259
DE LA WARR ROAD
DE LA WARR
OLD MANOR CL
ROAD
DORSET RD
MARTLETTS
SUNNINGDALE CL
KESTREL CL
GLENEAGLES
COLLEGE
SAXON RISE
WOODLAND RISE
KENNEDY RD
VENTURE CL
WINEHAM WAY
RD
GDNS
IND EST
BRETT DR
RAVENSIDE RETAIL & LEISURE PARK
Swimming Pool
LINKS
RIDGEWOOD
THE FINCHES
BOXGROVE CL
CHELSEA CL
R.C. School
Playing Field (Private)
ASHDOWN RD
MAGDALEN ROAD
Galley Hill
PL
SUTTON
PARADE
P
BROOK FIELD RD
Police Station
RD
RD
BEDFORD AV
DORSET RD
ANTELUPE
LIONEL RD
BETHUNE
STH
CP
WARR
BOLEBROOKE RD
LA
My Lords Rock
Lane End Rock

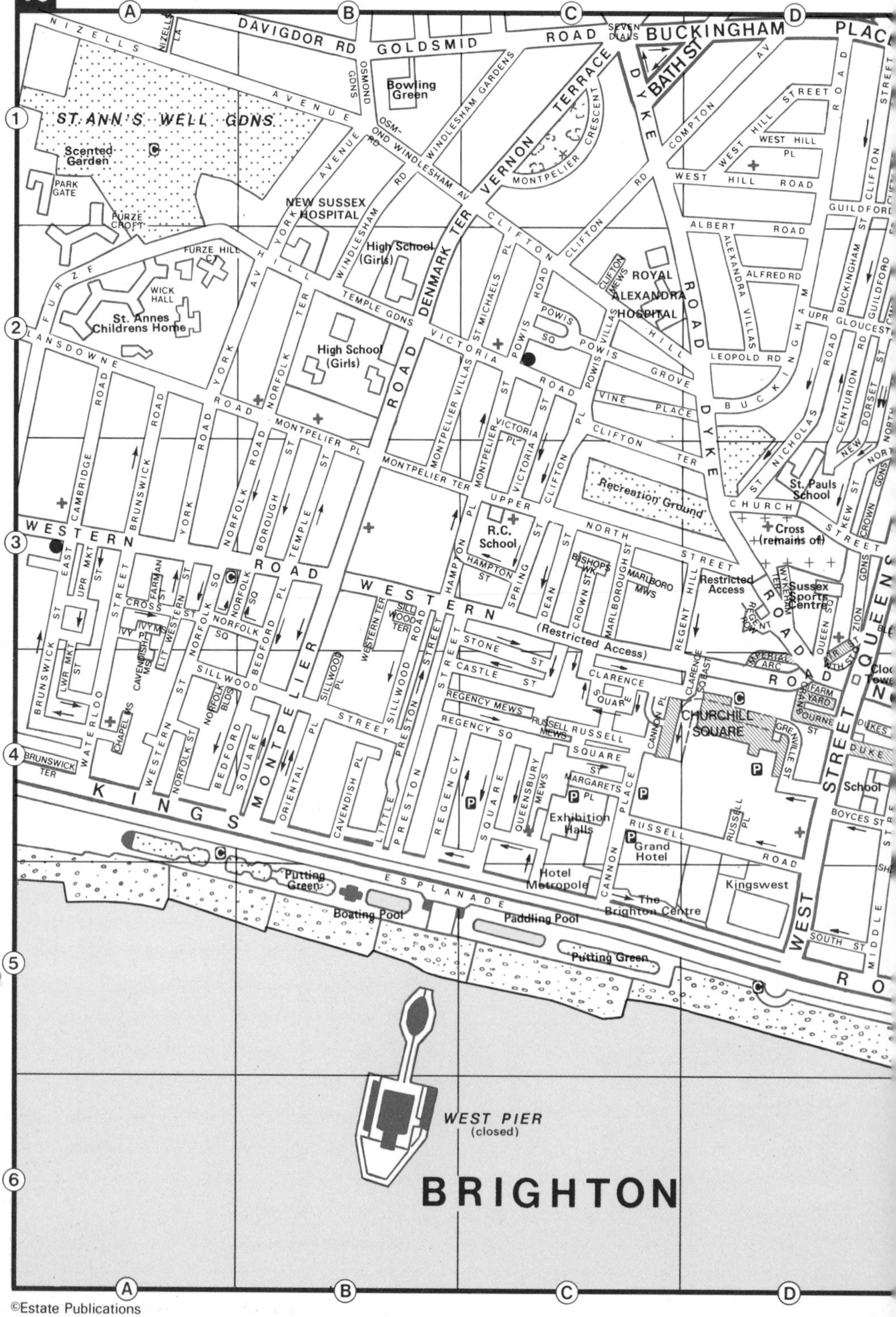
A
B
C
D
1
2
3
4
5
6
NIZELLS AVENUE
NIZELLS LA
DAVIGDOR RD
GOLDSMID ROAD
SEVEN DIALS
BUCKINGHAM PLACE
BATH ST
DYKE ROAD
OSMOND GDNS
OSMOND RD
Bowling Green
WINDLESHAM GARDENS
WINDLESHAM AV
WINDLESHAM RD
VERNON TERRACE
MONTPELIER CRESCENT
DENMARK TER
CLIFTON RD
CLIFTON HILL
CLIFTON TER
COMPTON AV
WEST HILL STREET
WEST HILL PL
WEST HILL ROAD
ALBERT ROAD
ALEXANDRA VILLAS
ALFRED RD
CLIFTON ROAD
GUILDFORD ST
GUILDFORD RD
BUCKINGHAM ST
BUCKINGHAM ROAD
UPR GLOUCESTER
ST. ANN'S WELL GDNS
Scented Garden
PARK GATE
FURZE CROFT
FURZE HILL
FURZE HILL CT
WICK HALL
St. Annes Childrens Home
NEW SUSSEX HOSPITAL
High School (Girls)
YORK AVENUE
YORK AV
YORK ROAD
YORK RD
TEMPLE GDNS
VICTORIA ROAD
ST MICHAELS PL
POWIS SQ
POWIS ROAD
POWIS GROVE
POWIS VILLAS
CLIFTON MEWS
ROYAL ALEXANDRA HOSPITAL
LEOPOLD RD
VINE PLACE
ST NICHOLAS ROAD
CENTURION RD
NEW DORSET ST
LANSDOWNE ROAD
NORFOLK TER
NORFOLK ROAD
NORFOLK SQ
NORFOLK ST
NORFOLK BLDS
MONTPELIER PL
MONTPELIER ROAD
MONTPELIER TER
MONTPELIER VILLAS
MONTPELIER ST
VICTORIA PL
VICTORIA ST
CLIFTON PL
CLIFTON ST
Recreation Ground
CHURCH STREET
St. Pauls School
KEW ST
CROWN GDNS
CAMBRIDGE ROAD
BRUNSWICK ROAD
BOROUGH ST
TEMPLE ST
WESTERN ROAD
UPPER NORTH STREET
R.C. School
HAMPTON PL
HAMPTON ST
SPRING ST
DEAN ST
CROWN ST
BISHOPS WK
MARLBOROUGH ST
MARLBORO MWS
REGENT HILL
Cross (remains of)
Restricted Access
WYKEHAM TER
REGENT ROW
Sussex Sports Centre
QUEEN SQ
ZION GDNS
QUEENS ROAD
EAST ST
UPR MKT ST
FARMAN ST
CROSS ST
IVY PL
IVY MS
CAVENDISH MS
LIT WESTERN ST
BEDFORD PL
SILLWOOD TER
WESTERN TER
SILLWOOD ROAD
PRESTON STREET
(Restricted Access)
STONE ST
CASTLE ST
CLARENCE SQUARE
CLARENCE SQ
CANNON PL
IMPERIAL ARC
FARM YARD
CRANBOURNE ST
CHURCHILL SQUARE
GRENVILLE ST
WEST STREET
DUKES
DUKE
BRUNSWICK ST
LWR MKT ST
WATERLOO ST
CHAPEL MS
SILLWOOD STREET
SILLWOOD PL
REGENCY MEWS
REGENCY SQ
RUSSELL MEWS
RUSSELL SQUARE
MARGARETS ST
ST MARGARETS PL
BRUNSWICK TER
WESTERN ST
BEDFORD SQUARE
MONTPELIER
ORIENTAL PL
CAVENDISH PL
LITTLE PRESTON
PRESTON ST
REGENCY SQUARE
QUEENSBURY MEWS
CANNON PLACE
RUSSELL PL
RUSSELL ROAD
School
BOYCES ST
MIDDLE ST
SOUTH ST
KINGS ROAD
Exhibition Halls
Grand Hotel
Hotel Metropole
Kingswest
ESPLANADE
Putting Green
Boating Pool
Paddling Pool
The Brighton Centre
WEST PIER (closed)
BRIGHTON

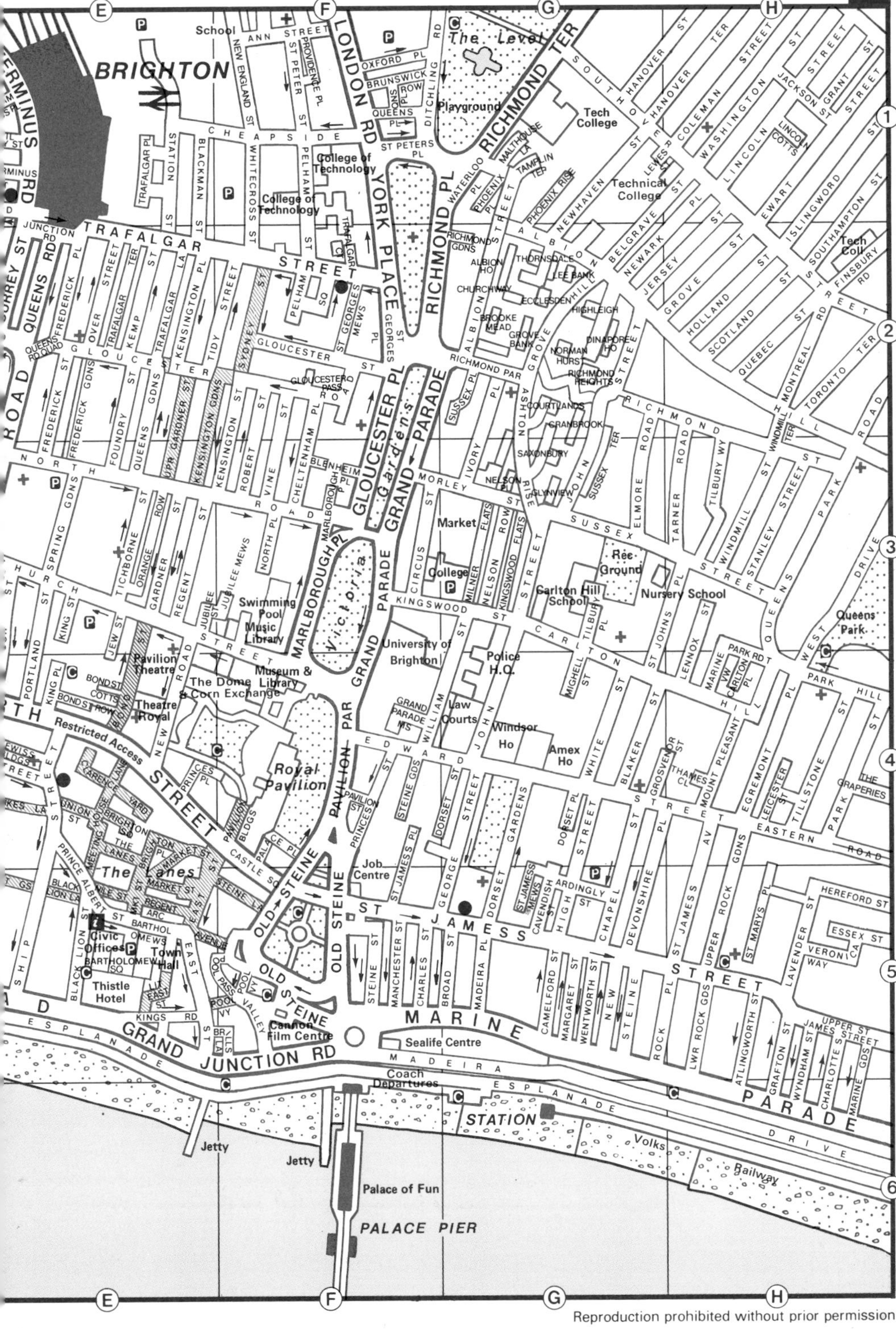
E
F
G
H
1
2
3
4
5
6
BRIGHTON
School
ANN STREET
LONDON RD
NEW ENGLAND ST
ST PETER ST
PROVIDENCE PL
OXFORD PL
BRUNSWICK ROW
QUEENS PL
DITCHLING RD
The Level
Playground
RICHMOND TER
SOUTH ST
HANOVER ST
HANOVER TER
COLEMAN ST
WASHINGTON ST
JACKSON ST
GRANT ST
Tech College
TERMINUS RD
TRAFALGAR PL
STATION ST
BLACKMAN ST
WHITECROSS ST
PELHAM ST
CHEAPSIDE
College of Technology
YORK PLACE
ST PETERS PL
RICHMOND PL
WATERLOO PL
PHOENIX PL
MALTHOUSE LA
TAMPLIN TER
PHOENIX RISE
NEWHAVEN ST
LEWES ST
Technical College
LINCOLN ST
LINCOLN COTTS
EWART ST
ISLINGWORD ST
SOUTHAMPTON ST
JUNCTION RD
TRAFALGAR STREET
QUEENS RD
SURREY ST
FREDERICK PL
OVER ST
TRAFALGAR TER
KEMP ST
TRAFALGAR LA
KENSINGTON PL
TIDY ST
SYDNEY ST
PELHAM SQ
TRAFALGAR CT
ST GEORGES MEWS
ST GEORGES PL
RICHMOND GDNS
ALBION HO
CHURCHWAY
THORNSDALE
LEE BANK
ECCLESDEN
BROOKE MEAD
GROVE BANK
HIGHLEIGH
DINAPORE HO
NORMAN HURST
RICHMOND HEIGHTS
ALBION HILL
BELGRAVE ST
NEWARK PL
JERSEY ST
GROVE ST
HOLLAND ST
SCOTLAND ST
QUEBEC ST
MONTREAL RD
TORONTO TER
Tech Coll
FINSBURY RD
QUEENS RD QUAD
GLOUCESTER ST
GLOUCESTER RD
GLOUCESTER PASS
GLOUCESTER PL
Gardens
GRAND PARADE
RICHMOND PAR
SUSSEX PL
IVORY PL
ASHTON RISE
COURTLANDS
CRANBROOK
SAXONBURY
NELSON PL
GLYNVIEW
JOHN ST
SUSSEX TER
RICHMOND ST
ELMORE RD
TARNER RD
TILBURY WY
WINDMILL TER
FREDERICK GDNS
FOUNDRY ST
QUEENS GDNS
UPR GARDNER ST
KENSINGTON GDNS
KENSINGTON ST
ROBERT ST
VINE ST
CHELTENHAM PL
BLENHEIM PL
MARLBOROUGH PL
NORTH ROAD
MORLEY ST
Market
CIRCUS ST
MILNER FLATS
NELSON ROW
KINGSWOOD FLATS
College
SUSSEX ST
Rec Ground
Carlton Hill School
Nursery School
WINDMILL ST
STANLEY ST
QUEENS PARK RD
WEST DRIVE
Queens Park
SPRING GDNS
TICHBORNE ST
ORANGE ROW
GARDNER ST
REGENT ST
JUBILEE ST
JUBILEE MEWS
NORTH PL
Swimming Pool
Music Library
Victoria
KINGSWOOD ST
CHURCH ST
KING ST
JEW ST
PORTLAND ST
Pavilion Theatre
NEW ROAD
Museum & Library
The Dome & Corn Exchange
University of Brighton
Police H.Q.
CARLTON HILL
MIGHELL ST
TILBURY PL
ST JOHNS PL
LENNOX ST
MARINE VW
CARLTON PL
PARK RD T
PARK HILL
KING PL
BOND ST
BOND ST COTTS
BOND ST ROW
Theatre Royal
Restricted Access
NORTH STREET
GRAND PARADE MS
WILLIAM ST
Law Courts
JOHN ST
Windsor Ho
Amex Ho
WHITE ST
BLAKER ST
GROSVENOR ST
THAMES CL
MOUNT PLEASANT
EGREMONT PL
LEICESTER ST
TILLSTONE ST
PARK ST
THE GRAPERIES
EDWARD STREET
PRINCES PL
Royal Pavilion
PAVILION PAR
PAVILION BLDGS
PAVILION ST
PRINCES ST
STEINE GDS
ST JAMES PL
DORSET ST
GEORGE STREET
DORSET GARDENS
DORSET PL
EASTERN ROAD
CLARENCE YARD
UNION ST
MEETING HOUSE LA
BRIGHTON SQ
THE LANES
MARKET ST
The Lanes
PRINCE ALBERT ST
BLACK LION LA
DUKE ST
MKT ST
REGENT ARC
EAST ST
CASTLE SQ
STEINE LA
PALACE PL
OLD STEINE
Job Centre
ST JAMES MEWS
CAVENDISH ST
ARDINGLY ST
HIGH ST
CHAPEL ST
DEVONSHIRE PL
ST JAMES AV
UPPER ROCK GDNS
ST MARYS PL
HEREFORD ST
ESSEX ST
VERONICA WAY
LAVENDER ST
ST BARTHOLOMEWS
Civic Offices
BARTHOLOMEW SQ
Town Hall
Thistle Hotel
AVENUE
POOL VY
POOL PASS
POOL VALLEY
ST JAMES'S STREET
STEINE ST
MANCHESTER ST
CHARLES ST
BROAD ST
MADEIRA PL
CAMELFORD ST
MARGARET ST
WENTWORTH ST
NEW STEINE
ROCK PL
LWR ROCK GDS
ATLINGWORTH ST
GRAFTON ST
WYNDHAM ST
CHARLOTTE ST
UPPER JAMES ST
MARINE GDS
SHIP ST
BLACK LION ST
KINGS RD
BRILLS LA
Cannon Film Centre
Sealife Centre
MARINE PARADE
GRAND JUNCTION RD
ESPLANADE
MADEIRA DRIVE
Coach Departures
STATION
Volks Railway
Jetty
Palace of Fun
PALACE PIER

CROWBOROUGH

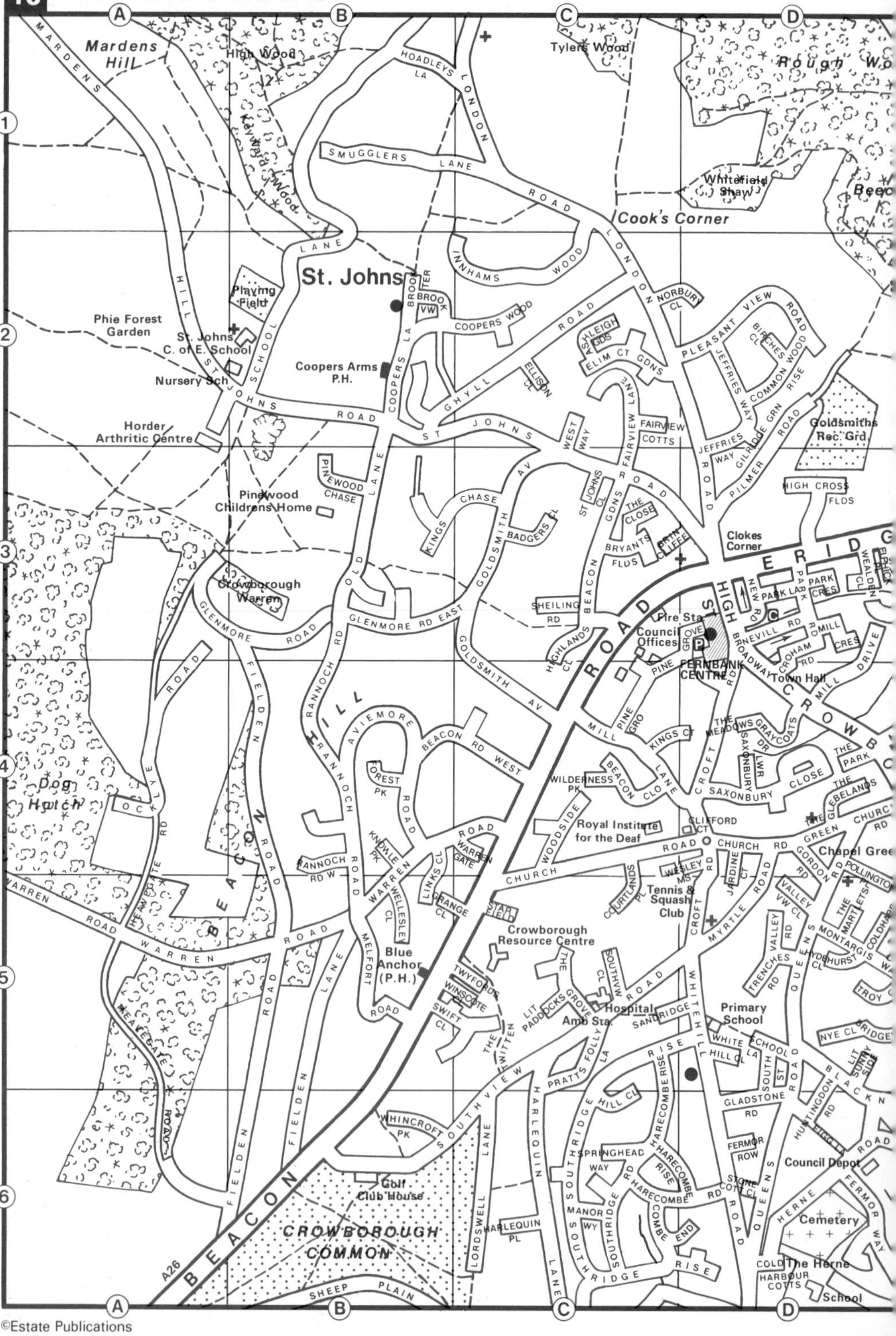
A
B
C
D
1
2
3
4
5
6
Mardens Hill
MARDENS HILL
High Wood
Kevin Wood
Tylers Wood
Rough Wood
HOADLEYS LA
LONDON ROAD
SMUGGLERS LANE
Whitefield Shaw
Cook's Corner
LANE
St. Johns
Playing Field
Phie Forest Garden
St. Johns C. of E. School
Nursery Sch
SCHOOL
BROOK TER
BROOK VW
COOPERS LA
COOPERS WOOD
Coopers Arms P.H.
INNHAMS WOOD
NORBURY CL
PLEASANT VIEW ROAD
BIRCHES CL
COMMON WOOD RISE
JEFFRIES WAY
GILRIDGE GRN
PILMER ROAD
ASHLEIGH GDS
ELIM CT GDNS
ELLISON CL
GHYLL ROAD
ST JOHNS ROAD
Horder Arthritic Centre
WEST WAY
FAIRVIEW LANE
FAIRVIEW COTTS
Goldsmiths Rec. Grd.
HIGH CROSS FLDS
PINEWOOD CHASE
Pinewood Childrens Home
KINGS CHASE
GOLDSMITH AV
BADGERS CL
ST JOHNS CL
THE CLOSE
BRYANTS FLDS
BRIN CLIFFE
Clokes Corner
ERIDGE ROAD
Crowborough Warren
GLENMORE ROAD
OLD RD
GLENMORE RD EAST
SHEILING RD
BEACON GDNS
HIGHLANDS CL
Fire Sta.
Council Offices
GROVE
PINE GROVE
FERNBANK CENTRE
NEW RD
PARK LA
PARK CRES
WEALDEN CL
NEVILL RD
MILL CRES
CROHAM RD
BROADWAY
Town Hall
MILL DRIVE
CROWBOROUGH
FIELDEN ROAD
RANNOCH RD
BEACON HILL
AVIEMORE
BEACON RD WEST
MILL LANE
PINE GRO
KINGS CT
THE MEADOWS
GRAYCOATS DR
SAXONBURY CLOSE
LWR SAXONBURY
THE PARK
THE GLEBELANDS
CROFT RD
FOREST PK
FOREST ROAD
WILDERNESS PK
BEACON CLOSE
Dog Hutch
OCKLEY RD
RANNOCH RD W
KNOWLE PK
WARREN GATE
LINKS CL
WELLESLEY CL
Royal Institute for the Deaf
WOODSIDE
CLIFFORD CT
CHURCH ROAD
CHURCH RD
GREEN
Chapel Green
WESLEY MS
JARDINE CT
COURTLANDS PL
Tennis & Squash Club
MYRTLE ROAD
GORDON RD
POLLINGTON
VALLEY VW CL
THE MARTLETS
COLDHARBOUR
WARREN ROAD
HEAVEGATE RD
GRANGE CL
STAR FIELD
Crowborough Resource Centre
MELFORT ROAD
TRENCHES ROAD
VALLEY RD
QUEENS RD
MONTARGIS WAY
HYDEHURST CL
Blue Anchor (P.H.)
TWYFORDS
WINSCOTE
SWIFT CL
THE TWITTEN
LIT PADDOCKS
THE GROVE
SOUTHVIEW RD
Hospital
Amb Sta.
SANDRIDGE
Primary School
WHITEHILL RD
WHITE HILL LA
WHITEHILL CL
SCHOOL LA
SOUTH ST
TROY
NYE CL
BRIDGE
LIT SUNNY SIDE
BLACKNESS ROAD
SOUTHVIEW
PRATTS FOLLY LA
RISE
HARECOMBE RISE
SOUTHRIDGE HILL CL
GLADSTONE RD
HUNTINGDON RD
FERMOR ROW
Council Depot
WHINCROFT PK
SPRINGHEAD WAY
HARECOMBE RD
STONE CROSS
FIELDEN LANE
HARLEQUIN LANE
LORDSWELL LANE
Golf Club House
CROWBOROUGH COMMON
HARLEQUIN PL
MANOR WY
SOUTHRIDGE RD
HARECOMBE END
HERNE
FERMOR WAY
Cemetery
The Herne
COLDHARBOUR COTTS
School
SOUTHRIDGE RISE
BEACON ROAD
A26
SHEEP PLAIN

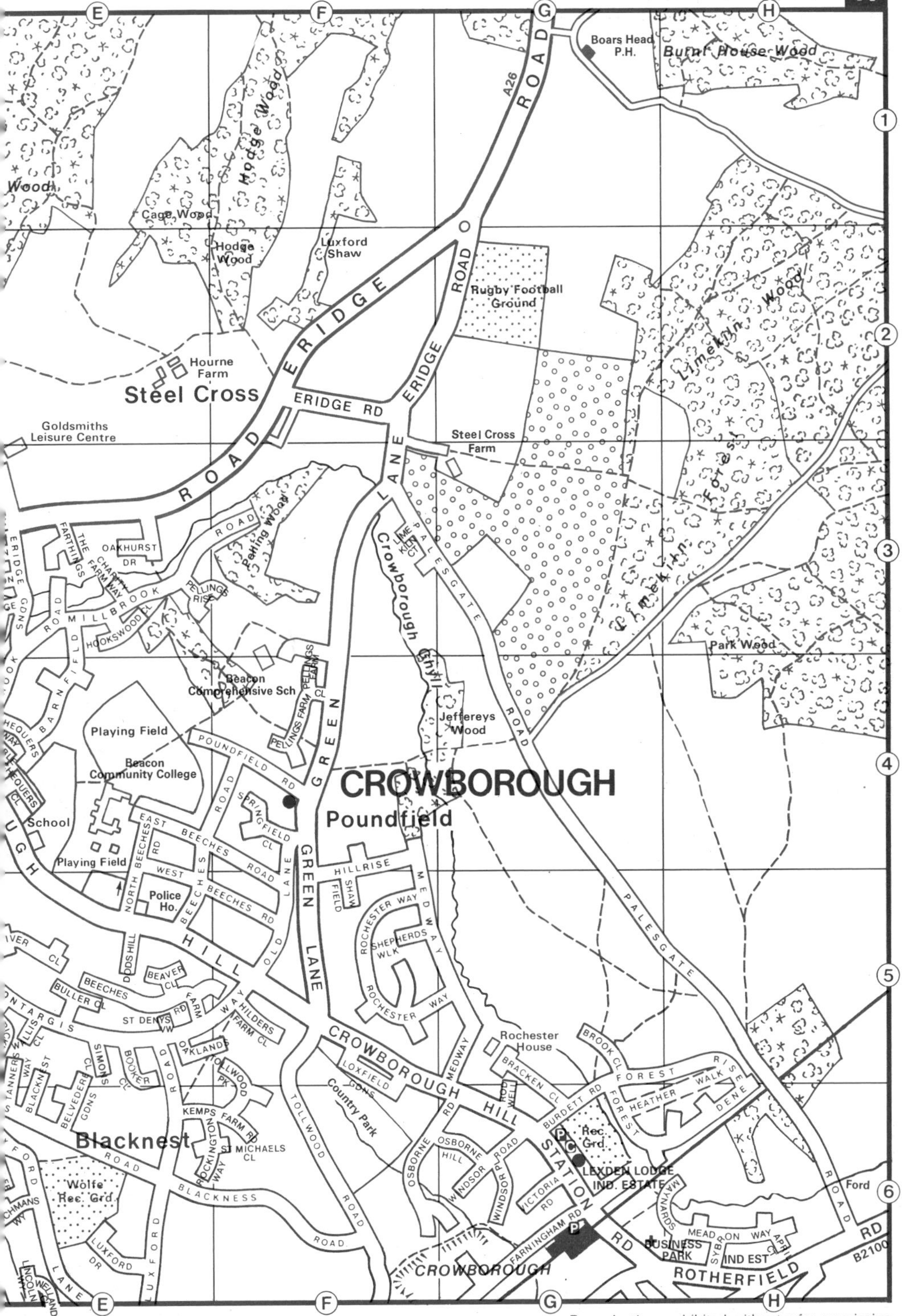
E
F
G
H
1
2
3
4
5
6
Boars Head P.H.
Burnt House Wood
A26
ROAD
Wood
Hodge Wood
Cage Wood
Hodge Wood
Luxford Shaw
ERIDGE
ROAD
Rugby Football Ground
ERIDGE
Hourne Farm
Steel Cross
ERIDGE RD
Limekiln Wood
Goldsmiths Leisure Centre
Steel Cross Farm
ROAD
LANE
Limekiln Forest
Pelling Wood
OAKHURST DR
FARTHINGS
THE FARM WAY
CHARITY
MILLBROOK
PELLINGS RISE
HOOKSWOOD CL
LIME KILN CT
Crowborough Ghyll
PALESGATE
Park Wood
BARNFIELD
Beacon Comprehensive Sch
PELLINGS FARM CL
Playing Field
Jeffereys Wood
Beacon Community College
POUNDFIELD RD
GREEN
ROAD
CROWBOROUGH
Poundfield
School
SPRINGFIELD CL
EAST BEECHES ROAD
Playing Field
NORTH BEECHES RD
WEST BEECHES RD
HILLRISE
SHAW FIELD
MEDWAY
PALESGATE
Police Ho.
GREEN LANE
ROCHESTER WAY
SHEPHERDS WLK
DODDS HILL
HILL
OLD LANE
BEAVER CL
BEECHES
BULLER CL
FARM RD
HILDERS FARM CL
ROCHESTER WAY
ST DENYS VW
Rochester House
BROOK CL
OAKLANDS
CROWBOROUGH HILL
LOXFIELD GDNS
MEDWAY
BRACKEN CL
FOREST
RISE
WALK
HEATHER
DENE
FOREST
TOLLWOOD PK
KEMPS FARM RD
Country Park
BURDETT RD
Rec. Grd.
BLACKNEST
BELVEDERE GDNS
SIMONS CL
BOOKER CL
ROAD
Blacknest
ROCKINGTON WAY
ST MICHAELS CL
TOLLWOOD
OSBORNE RD
OSBORNE HILL
WINDSOR PL
WINDSOR ROAD
STATION
LEXDEN LODGE IND. ESTATE
ROAD
Ford
Wolfe Rec. Grd
BLACKNESS
ROAD
VICTORIA RD
MAYNARDS
MEAD ON WAY
FARNINGHAM RD
RD
BUSINESS PARK
SYBRON WAY
IND EST
RD
B2100
LUXFORD DR
LUXFORD
LANE
ROAD
CROWBOROUGH
ROTHERFIELD
LINCOLN WY
WELLAND
E
F
G
H

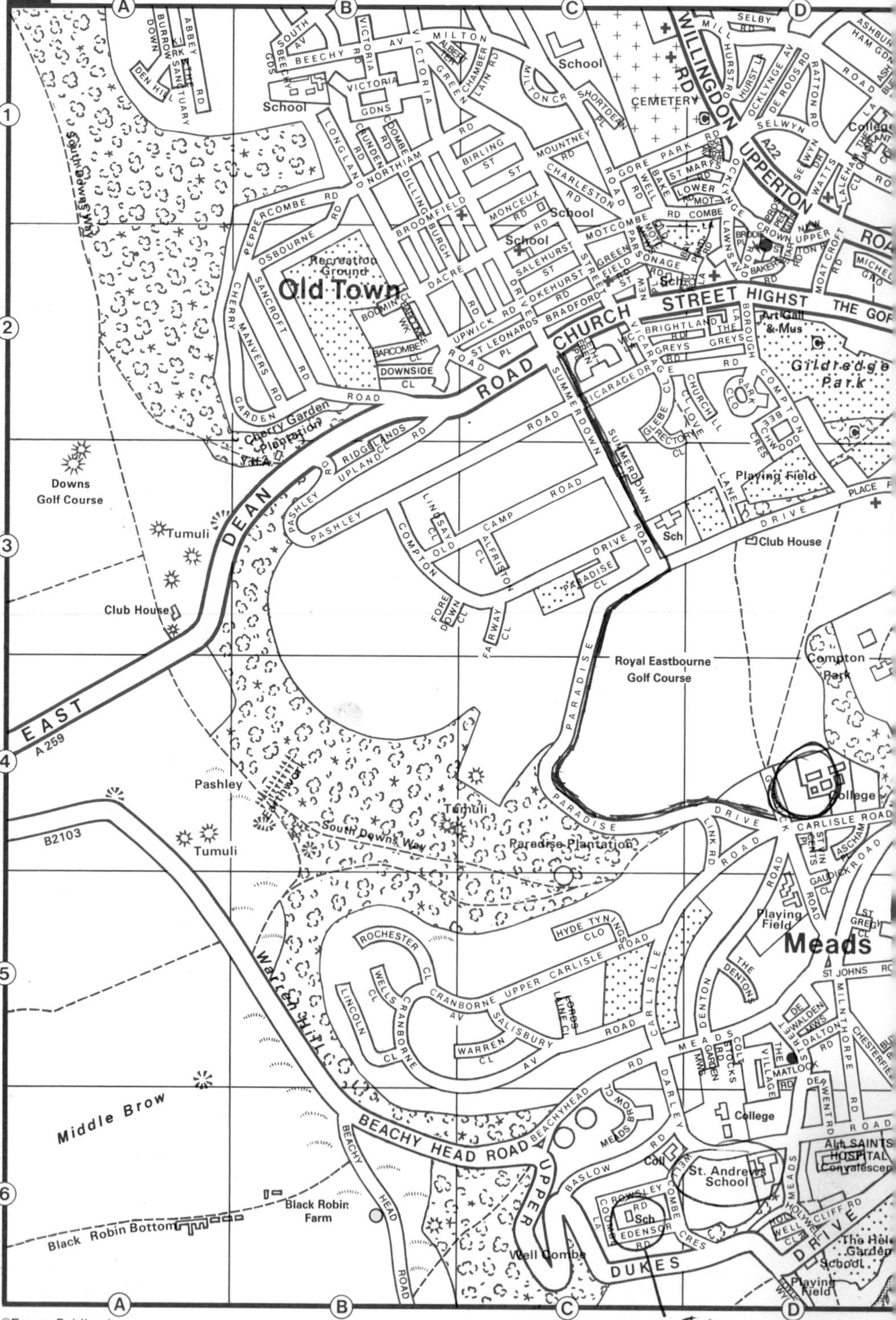
Old Town
Meads
Recreation Ground
Cherry Garden Plantation
Y.H.A.
Downs Golf Course
Tumuli
Club House
Pashley
Earthwork
South Downs Way
Paradise Plantation
Royal Eastbourne Golf Course
Compton Park
Gildredge Park
Art Gall & Mus
Playing Field
College
St. Andrews School
All Saints Hospital
Middle Brow
Black Robin Farm
Black Robin Bottom
Well Combe
Cemetery
School
Sch
EAST DEAN ROAD
A 259
B2103
CHURCH STREET
HIGH ST
THE GOFFS
WILLINGDON RD
UPPERTON ROAD
A22
PARADISE DRIVE
CARLISLE ROAD
BEACHY HEAD ROAD
UPPER DUKES DRIVE
MEADS RD
DARLEY RD
BASLOW RD
DUKES DRIVE
WARREN HILL
BEACHY HEAD ROAD
SUMMERDOWN ROAD
COMPTON DRIVE
CAMP ROAD
PASHLEY RD
UPPER CARLISLE ROAD
CRANBORNE AV
SALISBURY RD
WARREN CL
ROCHESTER CL
LINCOLN CL
WELLS CL
HYDE TYNINGS CLO
DENTON RD
THE DENTONS
LINK RD
ST JOHNS RD
MILNTHORPE RD
DERWENT RD
CHESTERFIELD
HOLYWELL DRIVE
CLIFF RD
MEADS ST
GAUDICK RD
ASCHAM
VICARAGE DR
GLEBE CL
CHURCH LA
GREYS RD
BOROUGH LA
MOTCOMBE LA
OCKLYNGE AV
RATTON RD
SELWYN RD
GORE PARK RD
CHARLESTON RD
MOUNTNEY RD
BIRLING ST
MONCEUX RD
SALEHURST RD
OKEHURST RD
BRADFORD ST
ST LEONARDS PL
UPWICK RD
DACRE RD
BROOMFIELD ST
DILLINGBURGH RD
NORTHIAM RD
LONGLAND RD
CRUNDEN RD
VICTORIA DR
VICTORIA GDNS
BEECHY AV
MILTON RD
MILTON CR
SHORTDEAN PL
OSBOURNE RD
PEPPERCOMBE RD
SANCROFT RD
MANVERS RD
CHERRY GARDEN ROAD
BODMIN CL
BARCOMBE CL
DOWNSIDE CL
RIDGELANDS CL
UPLAND RD
LINDSAY CL
ALFRISTON CL
FOREDOWN CL
FARWAY CL
PARADISE CL
DEN HILL
ABBEY RD
SANCTUARY
SOUTH AV
A B C D
1 2 3 4 5 6

St. John's Mead

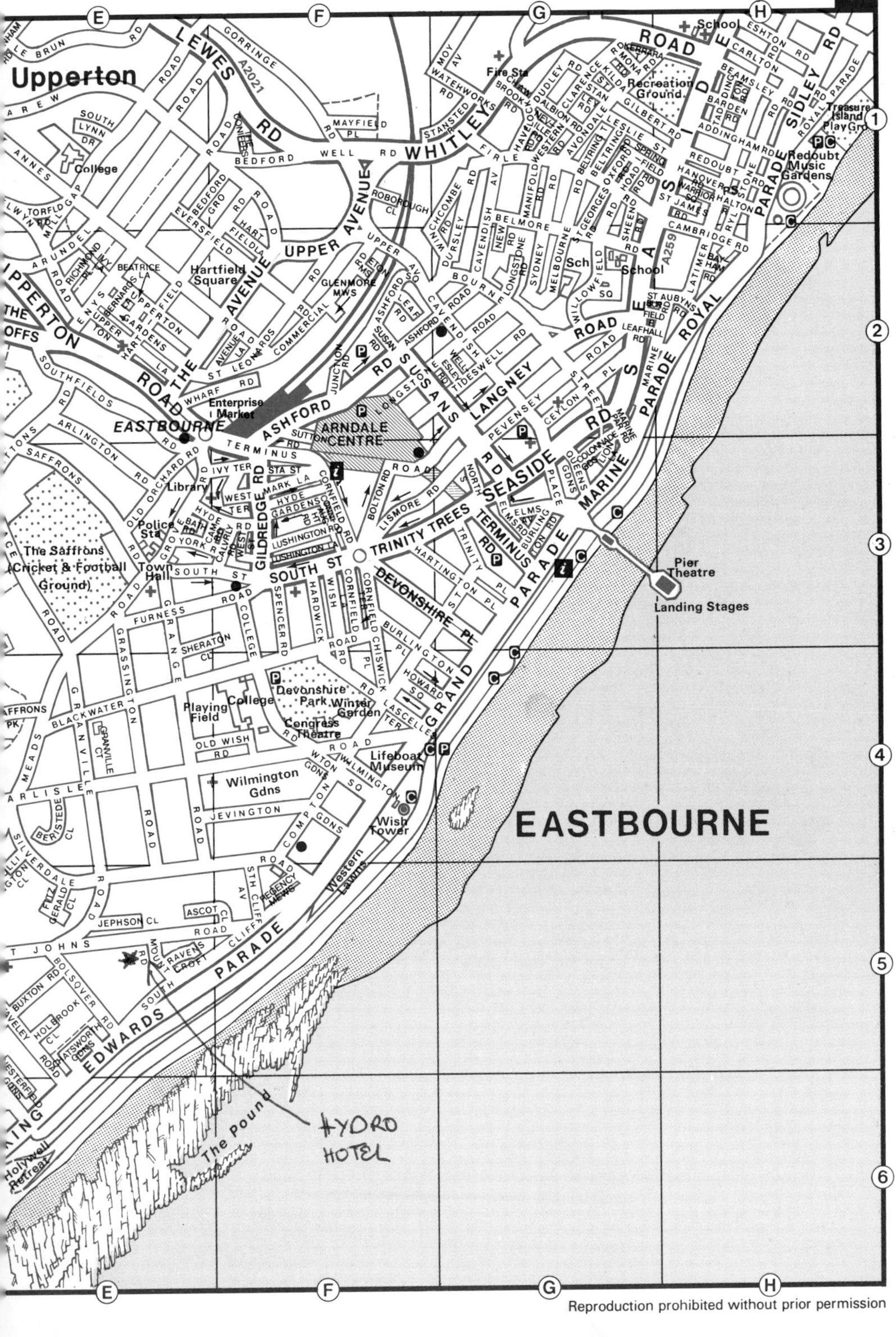
Upperton
College
Hartfield Square
UPPER AVENUE
THE AVENUE
WHITLEY RD
LEWES RD
GORRINGE
A2021
BEDFORD WELL RD
MAYFIELD PL
Fire Sta
Recreation Ground
School
Treasure Island PlayGrd
Redoubt Music Gardens
ROYAL PARADE
SIDLEY RD
SEASIDE
A259
Sch
School
LANGNEY RD
ASHFORD RD
TERMINUS RD
Enterprise Market
EASTBOURNE
ARNDALE CENTRE
Library
Police Sta
Town Hall
The Saffrons (Cricket & Football Ground)
SOUTH ST
TRINITY TREES
GILDREDGE RD
DEVONSHIRE PL
GRAND PARADE
MARINE PARADE
Pier Theatre
Landing Stages
Devonshire Park
Winter Garden
Congress Theatre
Playing Field
College
Lifeboat Museum
Wilmington Gdns
Wish Tower
Western Lawns
EASTBOURNE
KING EDWARDS PARADE
The Pound
Holywell Retreat
HYDRO HOTEL
Reproduction prohibited without prior permission

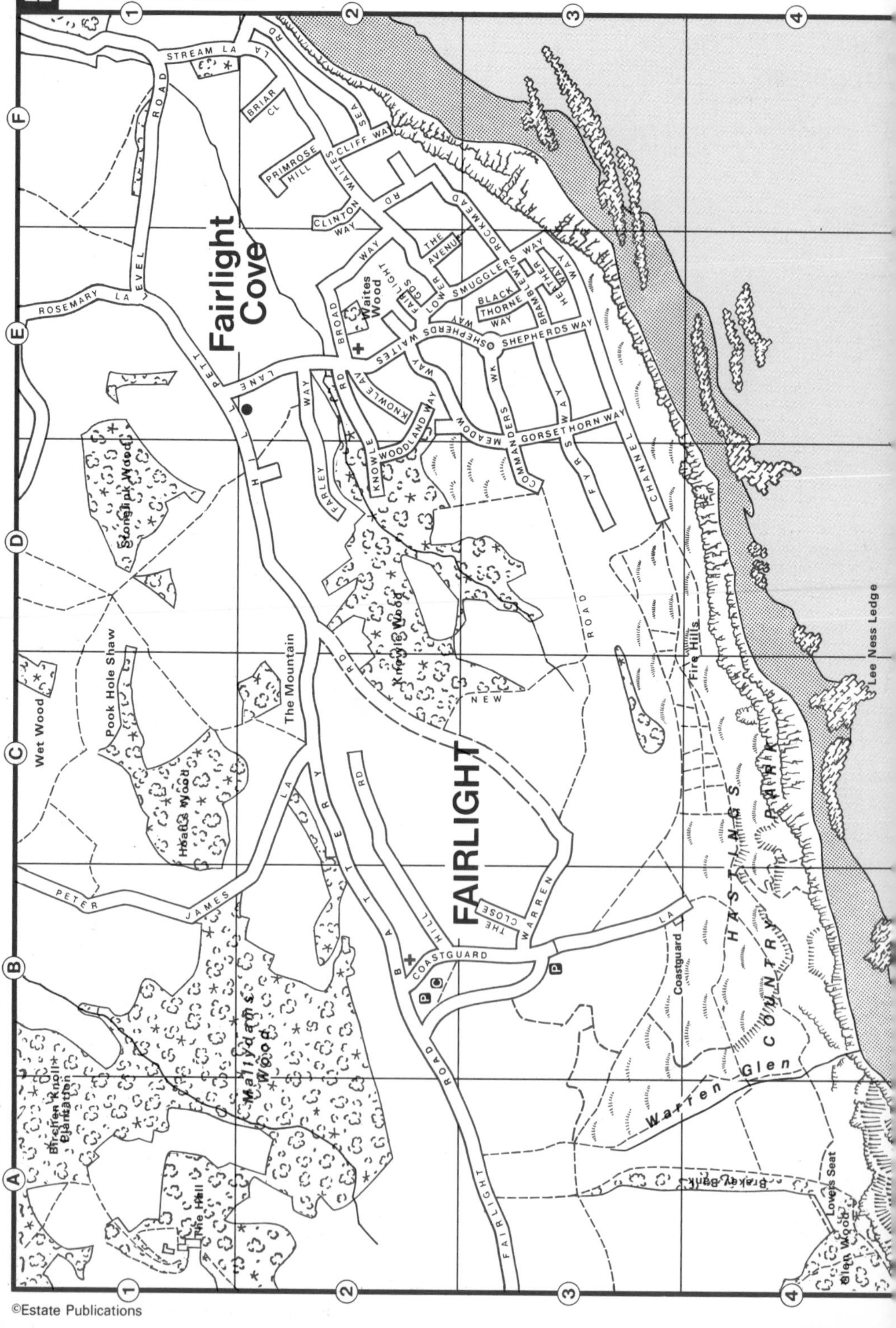
Fairlight Cove
FAIRLIGHT
STREAM LA
SEA RD
BRIAR CL
PRIMROSE HILL
CLIFF WAY
WAITES LA
CLINTON WAY
ROCKMEAD RD
THE AVENUE
BROAD WAY
SMUGGLERS WAY
LOWER WAITES LA
FAIRLIGHT GDNS
Waites Wood
BLACKTHORNE WAY
BRAMBLE WAY
HEATHER WAY
SHEPHERDS WAY
KNOWLE AV
KNOWLE RD
WOODLAND WAY
MEADOW WAY
GORSETHORN WAY
COMMANDERS WK
FYRS WAY
CHANNEL WAY
FARLEY WAY
LEVEL ROAD
ROSEMARY LA
PETT LEVEL ROAD
LANE
PETT HILL
Stonelink Wood
Pook Hole Shaw
Wet Wood
Hoath's Wood
The Mountain
Knowle Wood
NEW ROAD
Fire Hills
Lee Ness Ledge
HASTINGS COUNTRY PARK
PETER JAMES LA
BATTERY HILL
HILL RD
THE CLOSE
WARREN RD
COASTGUARD LA
Coastguard
Mallydams Wood
Warren Glen
Birchen Knoll Plantation
The Hall
FAIRLIGHT ROAD
Brakey Bank
Lovers Seat
Glen Wood

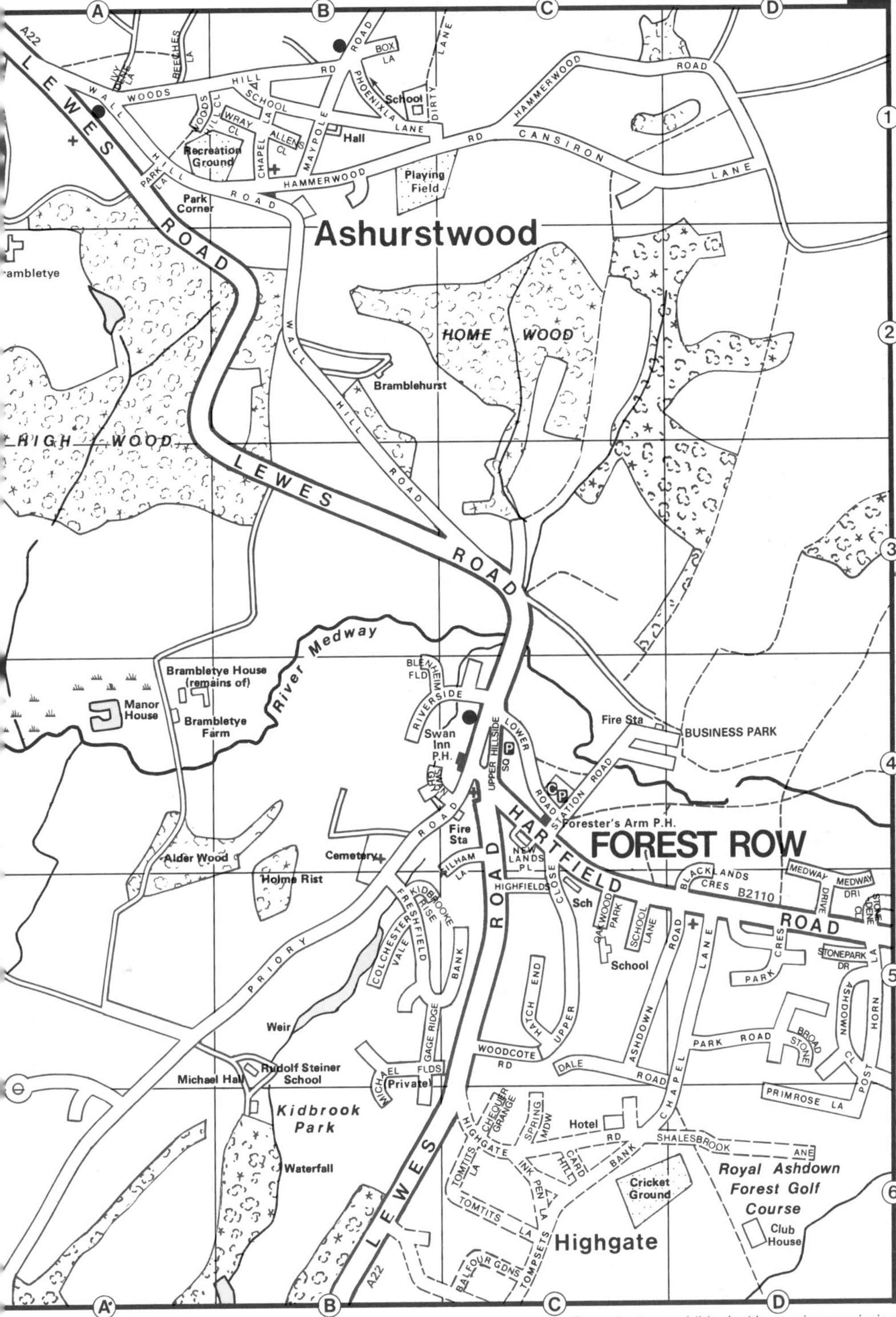
A
B
C
D
1
2
3
4
5
6
A22
LEWES
ROAD
IVY DENE LA
BEECHES LA
WALL
WOODS
HILL
RD
ROAD
BOX LA
PHOENIX LA
School
DIRTY LANE
ROAD
HAMMERWOOD
WOODS HILL CL
SCHOOL
WRAY CL
ALLENS CL
CHAPEL LA
MAYPOLE
Hall
LANE
RD
CANSIRON
LANE
Recreation Ground
PARK HILL LA
HAMMERWOOD
ROAD
Playing Field
Park Corner
Ashurstwood
Brambletye
WALL HILL ROAD
HOME WOOD
Bramblehurst
HIGH WOOD
LEWES
ROAD
River Medway
BLENHEIM FLD
Brambletye House (remains of)
Manor House
Brambletye Farm
RIVERSIDE
Swan Inn P.H.
UPPER HILLSIDE SQ
LOWER ROAD
STATION ROAD
Fire Sta
BUSINESS PARK
Forester's Arm P.H.
FOREST ROW
HARTFIELD
ROAD
Fire Sta
Alder Wood
Cemetery
Holme Rist
NEW LANDS PL
SILHAM LA
HIGHFIELDS
CLOSE
Sch
BLACKLANDS CRES
B2110
MEDWAY
MEDWAY DRIVE
MEDWAY DRI
STONE DENE CL
ROAD
OAKWOOD PARK
SCHOOL LANE
ROAD
LANE
KIDBROOKE RISE
FRESHFIELD
COLCHESTER VALE
BANK
PRIORY
HATCH END
UPPER
School
ASHDOWN
PARK CRES
STONEPARK DR
ASHDOWN CL
HORN LA
GAGE RIDGE
Weir
WOODCOTE RD
DALE
ROAD
CHAPEL
PARK ROAD
BROAD STONE
Rudolf Steiner School
Michael Hall
MICHAEL FLDS
(Private)
CHEQUER GRANGE
SPRING MDW
Hotel
POST
PRIMROSE LA
Kidbrook Park
HIGHGATE
RD
SHALESBROOK LANE
CARD HILL
BANK
Waterfall
TOMTITS LA
INK PEN LA
Cricket Ground
Royal Ashdown Forest Golf Course
LEWES
TOMTITS LA
Highgate
Club House
A22
BALFOUR GDNS
TOMPSETS

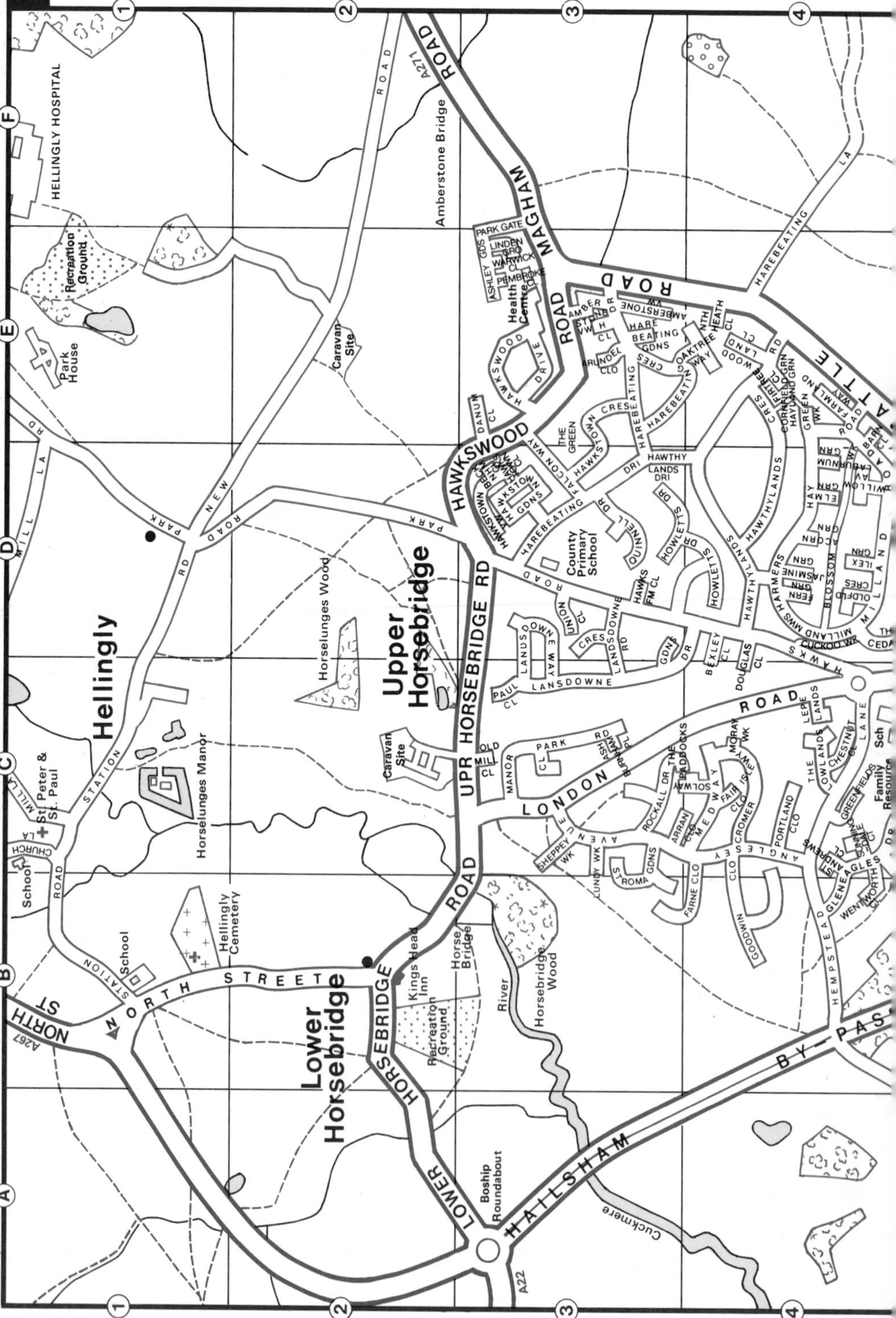
1
2
3
4
A
B
C
D
E
F
HELLINGLY HOSPITAL
Recreation Ground
Park House
MILL LA
RD
Hellingly
St. Peter & St. Paul
CHURCH LA
School
ROAD
STATION
Horselunges Manor
Hellingly Cemetery
NORTH ST
A267
NORTH STREET
Lower Horsebridge
HORSEBRIDGE
Kings Head Inn
Horse Bridge
Recreation Ground
River
Horsebridge Wood
LOWER ROAD
Boship Roundabout
HAILSHAM BY-PASS
A22
Cuckmere
NEW ROAD
PARK RD
PARK ROAD
Caravan Site
Amberstone Bridge
A271
ROAD
MAGHAM ROAD
Horselunges Wood
Upper Horsebridge
UPR HORSEBRIDGE RD
OLD MILL CL
MANOR
PARK CL
ASH RD
BURNHAM PL
LONDON ROAD
HAWKSWOOD
HAWKSWOOD DRIVE
DANUM CL
PARK GATE
ASHLEY GDS
LINDEN GRO
WARWICK CL
PEMBROKE CL
Health Centre
AMBERSTONE VW
AMBERSTONE
ROAD
HAREBEATING GDNS
ARUNDEL CLO
HAREBEATING CRES
HAREBEATING DRI
OAKTREE WAY
HEATH CL
WOOD LAND CL
HAWKSTOWN CRES
THE GREEN
FALCON WAY
HAWKSTOWN GDNS
HAWTHY LANDS DRI
County Primary School
QUINNELL DR
HOWLETTS DR
HOWLETTS
HAWKS FM CL
UNION CL
LANSDOWNE WAY
LANSDOWNE CRES
LANSDOWNE RD
LANSDOWNE
PAUL CL
GDNS
BEXLEY CL
DOUGLAS CL
HAWKS RD
HAWTHYLANDS
HAWTHYLANDS RD
HAREBEATING LA
HARMERS
CORNFIELD GRN
HAYLAND GRN
FARMLAND WAY
LABURNUM GRN
WILLOW GRN
ELM GRN
ACORN GRN
JASMINE GRN
FERN GRN
BLOSSOM WK
ILEX GRN
OLDFIELD CRES
MILLAND MWS
MILLAND RD
CUCKOO WK
CEDA
THE PADDOCKS
MORAY WK
SOLWAY
MEDWAY
FAIR ISLE CLO
ROCKALL DR
ARRAN CLO
CROMER
SHEPPEY WK
AVENUE
LUNDY WK
ST ROMA GDNS
FARNE CLO
ANGLESEY
GOODWIN CLO
PORTLAND CLO
THE LOWLANDS
CHESTNUT CL
LANE
GREENFIELDS
Family Resource
Sch
SUNNINGDALE CT
ST ANDREWS
GLENEAGLES
WENTWORTH CL
HEMPSTEAD

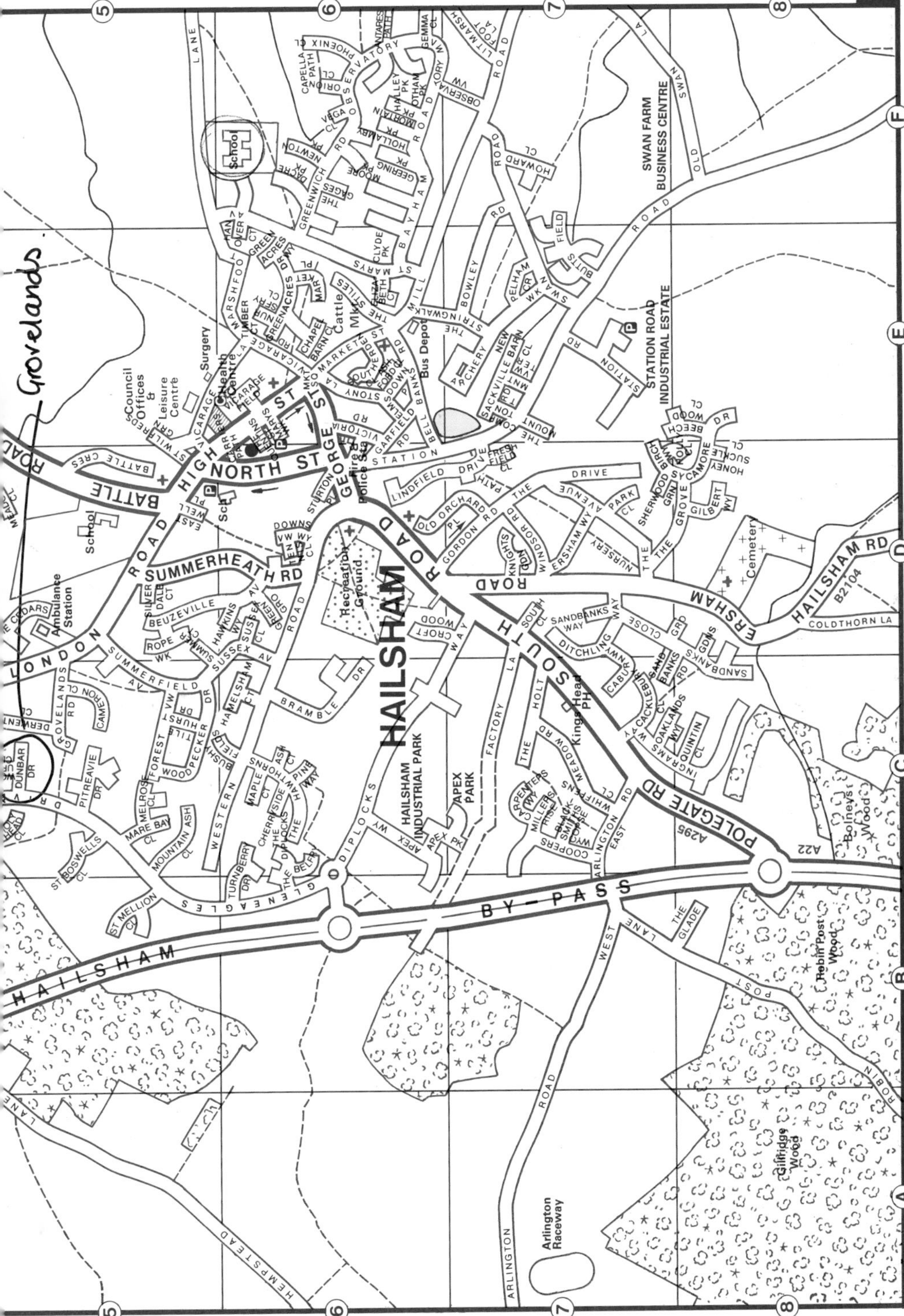

HAILSHAM
Grovelands
SWAN FARM BUSINESS CENTRE
STATION ROAD INDUSTRIAL ESTATE
HAILSHAM INDUSTRIAL PARK
APEX PARK
Recreation Ground
Cemetery
Council Offices & Leisure Centre
Health Centre
Surgery
School
Ambulance Station
Bus Depot
Cattle Mkt
Fire & Police Sta
Kings Head PH
Bolneys Wood
Robin Post Wood
Gilfridge Wood
Arlington Raceway
HAILSHAM BY-PASS
A22
A295
B2104
NORTH ST
HIGH ST
GEORGE ST
BATTLE ROAD
LONDON ROAD
SOUTH ROAD
POLEGATE RD
ERSHAM ROAD
HAILSHAM RD
COLDTHORN LA
STATION ROAD
SWAN ROAD
MILL ROAD
BAYHAM ROAD
OBSERVATORY ROAD
SUMMERHEATH RD
WESTERN ROAD
DIPLOCKS WY
ARLINGTON ROAD
WEST ROAD
POST LANE
ROBIN POST LANE
HEMPSTEAD LANE
FACTORY LA
GLENEAGLES
BATTLE CRES
SUMMERFIELD AV
BRAMBLE DR
LINDFIELD DRIVE
THE DRIVE

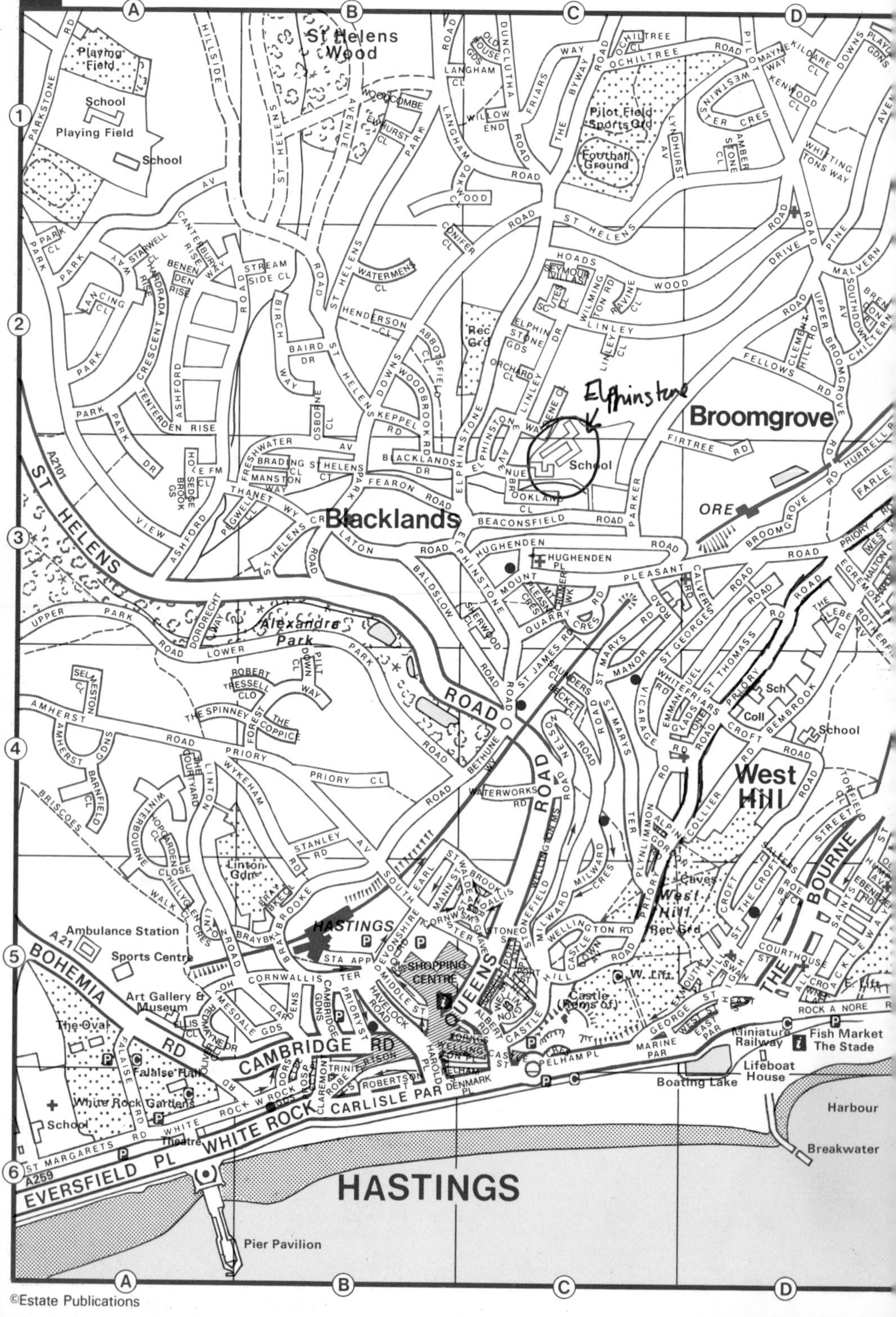
A
B
C
D
1
2
3
4
5
6
St Helens Wood
Playing Field
School
Playing Field
School
Pilot Field Sports Grd
Football Ground
Rec Grd
Elphinstone
School
Broomgrove
Blacklands
ORE
Alexandra Park
West Hill
Linton Gdn
Caves
West Hill Rec Grd
HASTINGS
SHOPPING CENTRE
Castle (Rems of)
W. Lift
E. Lift
Fish Market
The Stade
Miniature Railway
Lifeboat House
Boating Lake
Harbour
Breakwater
Ambulance Station
Sports Centre
Art Gallery & Museum
The Oval
Falaise Hall
White Rock Gardens
School
Theatre
Pier Pavilion
HASTINGS
ST HELENS ROAD
A2101
BOHEMIA RD
A21
CAMBRIDGE RD
WHITE ROCK
EVERSFIELD PL
A259
CARLISLE PAR
QUEENS ROAD
PELHAM PL
ROCK A NORE
UPPER PARK ROAD
LOWER PARK ROAD
AMHERST ROAD
PRIORY ROAD
BETHUNE WY
ELPHINSTONE ROAD
FEARON ROAD
BEACONSFIELD ROAD
HUGHENDEN ROAD
LATON ROAD
PLEASANT ROAD
ST HELENS PARK ROAD
ST HELENS AV
PARK VIEW
ASHFORD ROAD
ST HELENS WOOD ROAD
ST HELENS DOWN
BROOMGROVE RD
FELLOWS RD
LINLEY DR
FIRTREE RD
THE BOURNE
SCHOOL

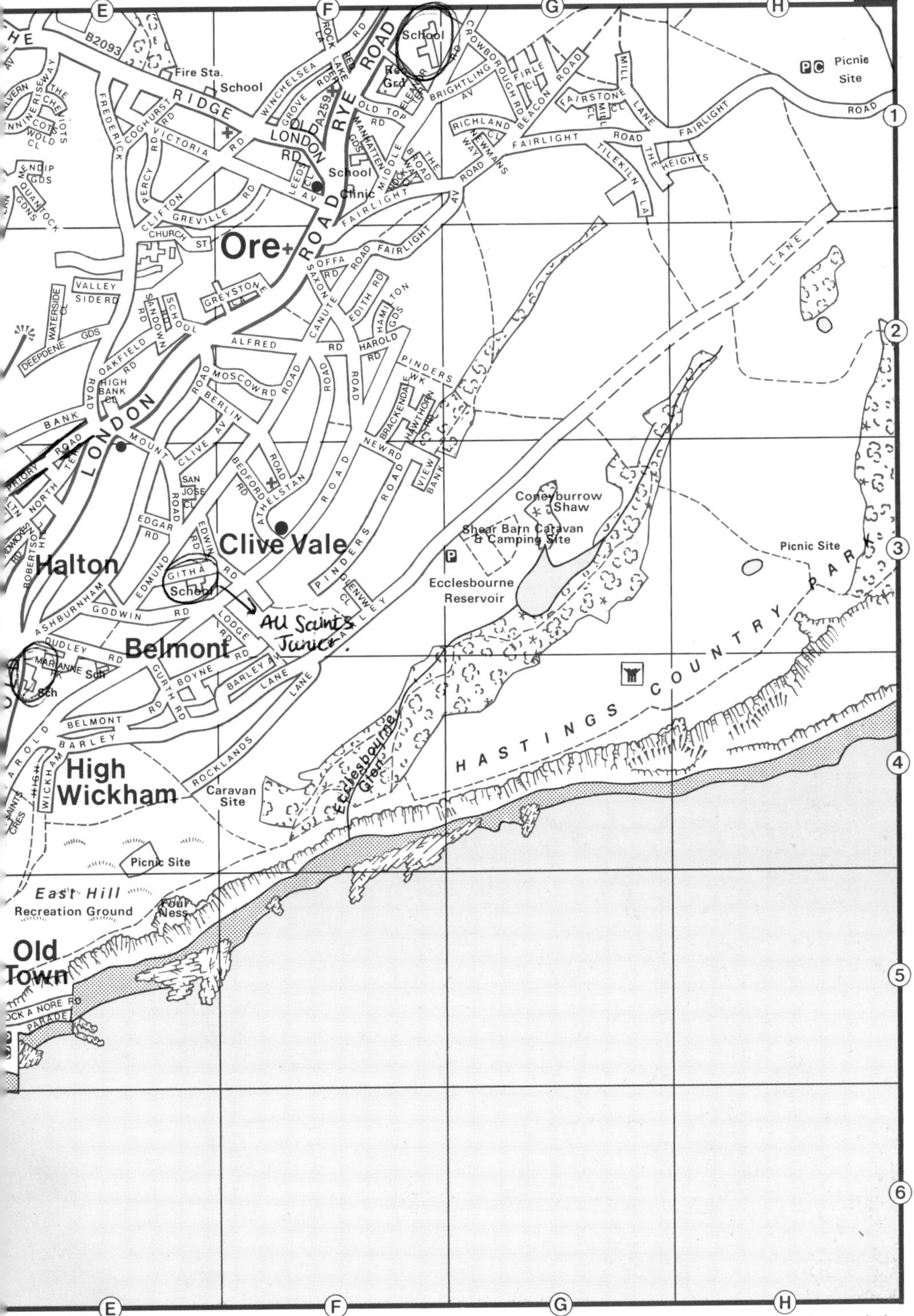

← Red Lake

School

E B2093 F RYE ROAD G H

Fire Sta.
School

RIDGE
OLD LONDON ROAD

School
Clinic

Ore+

FAIRLIGHT ROAD

Richland
Crowborough Road

Fairlight

Picnic Site

HASTINGS COUNTRY PARK

Halton

Clive Vale

Coneyburrow Shaw

Shear Barn Caravan & Camping Site

Ecclesbourne Reservoir

Picnic Site

Belmont

All Saints Junior

High Wickham

Caravan Site

Picnic Site

East Hill Recreation Ground

Four Ness

Old Town

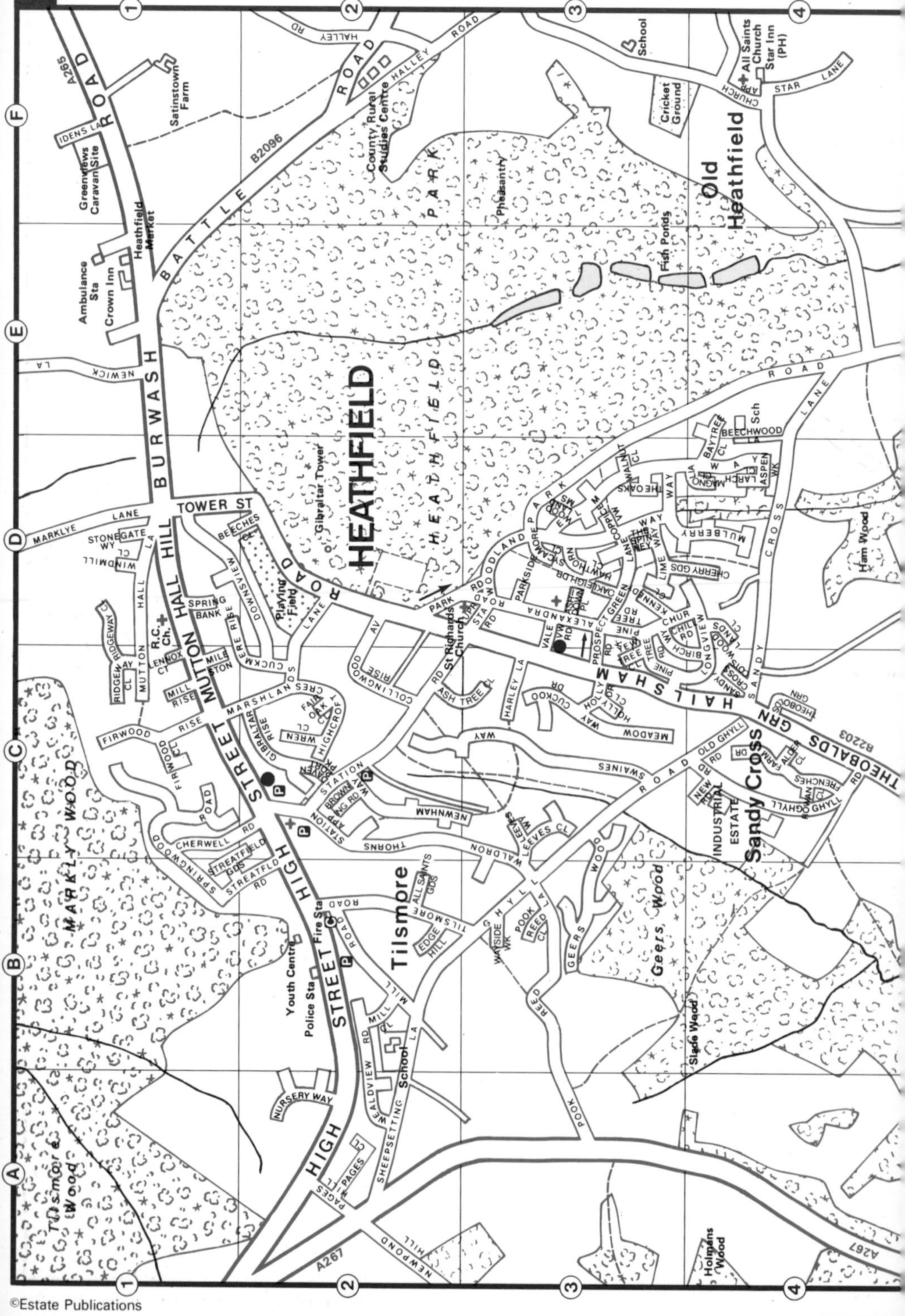
HEATHFIELD
Old Heathfield
Tilsmore
Sandy Cross
HEATHFIELD PARK
BURWASH ROAD
A265
BATTLE ROAD
B2096
HALLEY ROAD
HALLEY RD
School
All Saints Church
Star Inn (PH)
STAR LANE
CHURCH APP
Cricket Ground
Satinstown Farm
IDENS LA
Greenviews Caravan Site
Heathfield Market
Ambulance Sta
Crown Inn
County Rural Studies Centre
Pheasantry
Fish Ponds
NEWICK LA
MARKLYE LANE
TOWER ST
STONEGATE WY
WINDMILL CL
HALL LA
MUTTON HALL HILL
MUTTON HALL LA
R.C. Ch.
RIDGEWAY CL
RIDGEWAY
LENNOX CT
MILL RISE
MILESTONE
SPRING BANK
DOWNSVIEW
CUCKMERE RISE
BEECHES CL
Playing Field
Gibraltar Tower
STATION RD
MARSHLANDS LANE
MARSHLANDS CRES
FAIR OAK CT
HIGHCROFT
WREN CL
GIBRALTAR RISE
FIRWOOD RISE
FIRWOOD CL
CHERWELL RD
SPRINGWOOD RD
STREATFIELD GDS
STREATFIELD RD
HIGH STREET
STATION RD
STATION APP
STATION WAY
BROWNING RD
NEWNHAM WAY
THORNS
WALDRON
LEEVES WAY
LEEVES CL
COLLINGWOOD AV
COLLINGWOOD RISE
St Richards Church
ASH TREE CL
PARK RD
WOODLAND WAY
PARKSIDE
STATION RD
HARLEY LA
VALE RD
ALEXANDRA RD
PROSPECT
GREEN LANE
HAWTHORN
SYCAMORE
COPPICE
THE OAKS
WALNUT CL
MULBERRY
CHERRY GDS
LIME WAY
KENNEDY CL
OAKLEIGH DR
PINE TREE
PINE TREE CL
CHURCHILL
BIRCH WAY
LONGVIEW
WOODLANDS CL
SANDY CROSS
BAYTREE CL
BEECHWOOD LA
MAGNOLIA CL
LARCH WAY
ASPEN WK
Sch
Ham Wood
CROSS LANE
ROAD
HAILSHAM RD
CUCKOO DR
HOLLY DR
HOLLY CL
MEADOW WAY
SWAINES WAY
OLD GHYLL RD
NEW RD
INDUSTRIAL ESTATE
GHYLL RD
ROWAN CL
FRENCHES FARM DR
ALDER CL
THEOBALDS GRN
THEOBALDS RD
B2203
MARKLY WOOD
Geers Wood
Slade Wood
WOOD
GEERS
POOK REED CL
REED LA
POOK REED LA
WAYSIDE WK
GHYLL
TILSMORE RD
ALL SAINTS GDS
EDGE HILL
Fire Sta
Youth Centre
Police Sta
MILL RD
MILL LA
MILL CL
WEALDVIEW RD
School
SHEEPSETTING
NURSERY WAY
PAGES LA
PAGES
HIGH STREET
NEWPOND HILL
A267
Tilsmore Wood
Holmans Wood
1
2
3
4
A
B
C
D
E
F

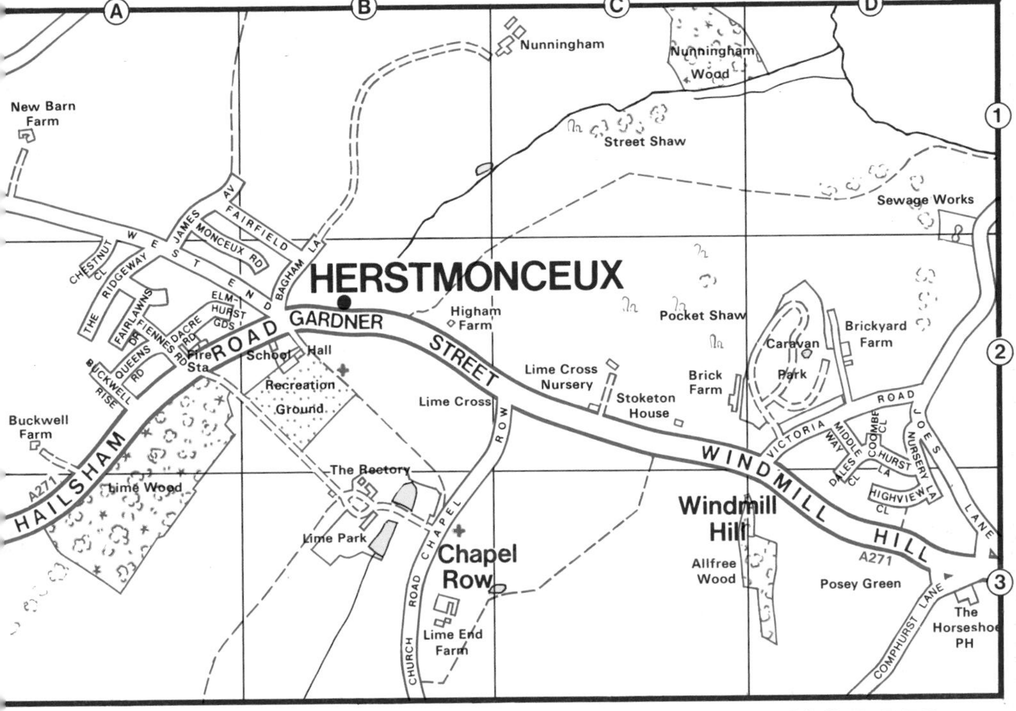
A
B
C
D
1
2
3
Nunningham
Nunningham Wood
New Barn Farm
Street Shaw
Sewage Works
HERSTMONCEUX
GARDNER
STREET
ROAD
HAILSHAM
A271
WEST END
JAMES AV
FAIRFIELD
MONCEUX RD
BAGHAM LA
CHESTNUT CL
THE RIDGEWAY
FAIRLAWNS DR
ELM-HURST GDS
DACRE RD
FIENNES RD
QUEENS RD
BUCKWELL RISE
Fire Sta
School
Hall
Recreation Ground
Higham Farm
Pocket Shaw
Brickyard Farm
Caravan Park
Lime Cross Nursery
Brick Farm
Stoketon House
Lime Cross
Buckwell Farm
VICTORIA ROAD
WAY
MIDDLE
COOMBE CL
HURST LA
NURSERY LA
DALES CL
HIGHVIEW CL
JOES LANE
WINDMILL HILL
Windmill Hill
The Rectory
Lime Wood
Lime Park
CHAPEL ROW
Chapel Row
Allfree Wood
A271
Posey Green
The Horseshoe PH
COMPHURST LANE
CHURCH ROAD
Lime End Farm

HORAM

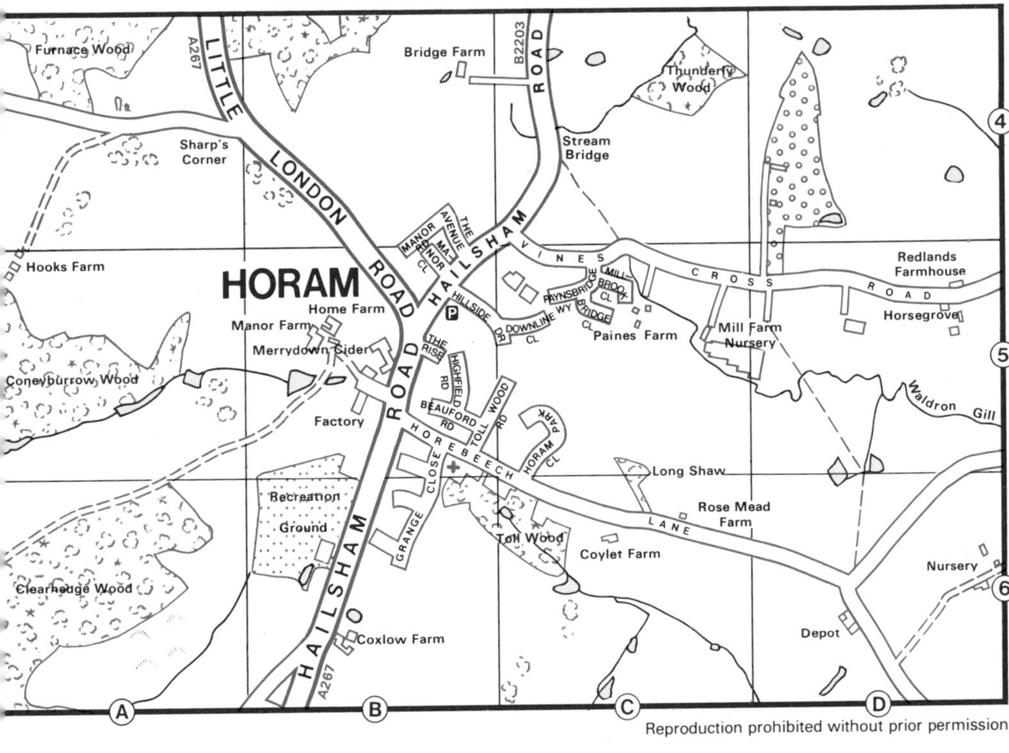
Furnace Wood
A267
LITTLE LONDON ROAD
B2203 ROAD
Bridge Farm
Thunderly Wood
4
5
6
Sharp's Corner
Stream Bridge
HAILSHAM ROAD
MANOR RD
THE AVENUE
MANOR CL
Hooks Farm
HORAM
VINES CROSS ROAD
Redlands Farmhouse
MILL BROOK CL
PAYNSBRIDGE WY
BRIDGE CL
HILLSIDE DR
DOWNLINE CL
Home Farm
Manor Farm
Merrydown Cider
THE RISE
HIGHFIELD RD
Paines Farm
Mill Farm Nursery
Horsegrove
Coneyburrow Wood
Waldron Gill
BEAUFORD RD
TOLL WOOD RD
HORAM PARK CL
Factory
HOREBEECH LANE
Long Shaw
Rose Mead Farm
CLOSE
GRANGE
Recreation Ground
Toll Wood
Coylet Farm
Nursery
Clearhedge Wood
HAILSHAM
A267
Coxlow Farm
Depot
A
B
C
D

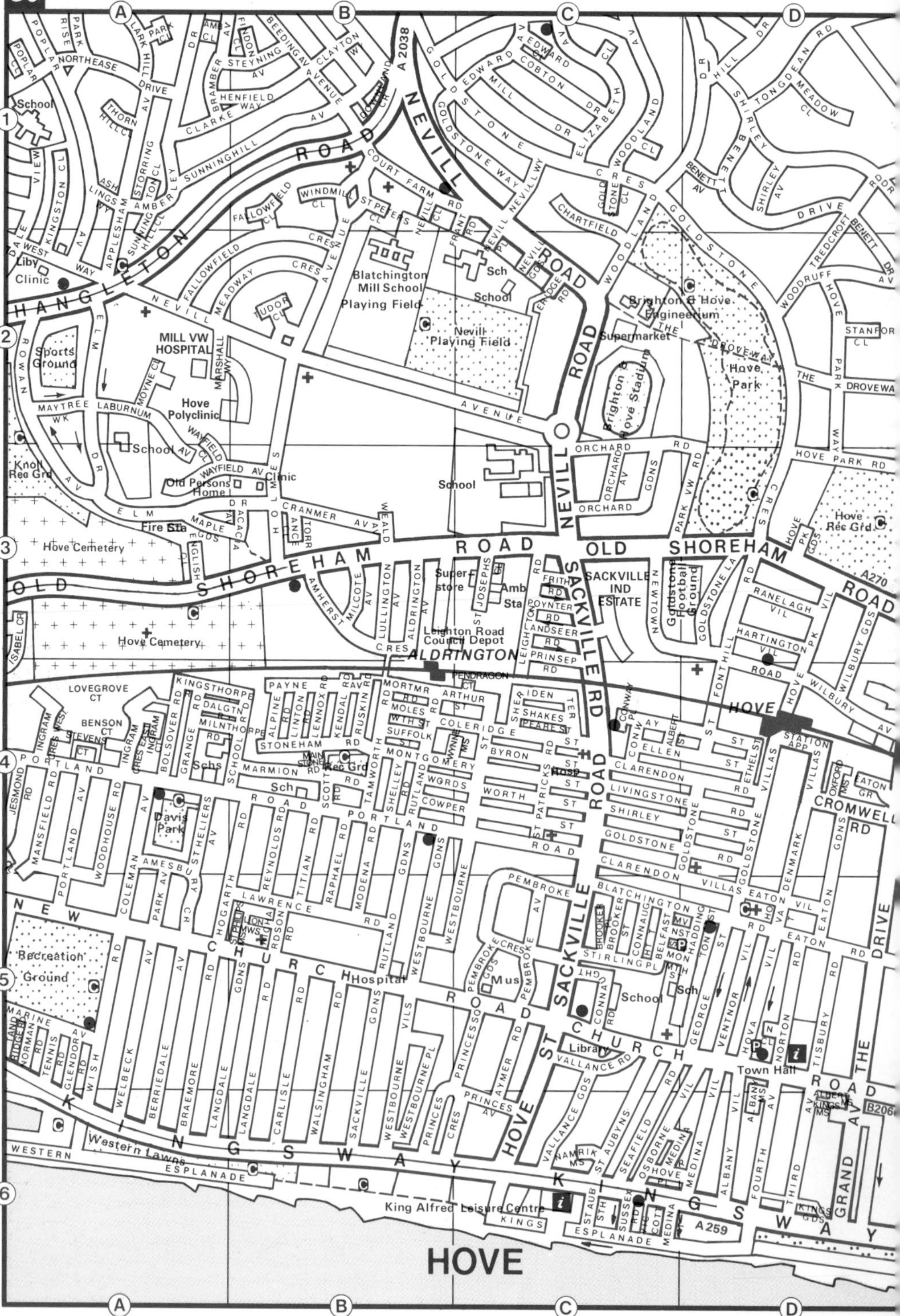
A
B
C
D
1
2
3
4
5
6
POPLAR CL
PARK RISE
NORTHEASE
LARK HILL
PARK CL
School
THORN HILL CL
DRIVE
STEYNING AV
FINDON CL
BEEDING AV
CLAYTON WY
BRAMBER
HENFIELD WAY
CLARKE AV
AVENUE
SUNNINGHILL AV
A 2038
NEVILL
COURT FARM RD
GOLDSTONE WAY
EDWARD AV
EDWARD CL
COBTON DR
MILL DR
ELIZABETH
WOODLAND
SHIRLEY DR
TONGDEAN RD
MEADOW CL
BENETT AV
SHIRLEY AV
DRIVE
TREDCROFT
BENETT
VIEW
KINGSTON CL
ASHLINGS WY
STORRING TON CL
AMBERLEY
APPLESHAM
SUNNING HILL CL
ROAD
WINDMILL CL
FALLOWFIELD
ST PETERS CL
FRANT RD
NEVILL PL
NEVILL GDNS
CRES
CHARTFIELD
GOLDSTONE CRES
GOLDSTONE CL
WEST WAY
Liby
Clinic
HANGLETON
FALLOWFIELD
MEADWAY
CRES
TUDOR CL
Blatchington Mill School
Playing Field
Sch
School
Nevill Playing Field
ROAD
ERRIDGE RD
Brighton & Hove Engineerium
THE DROVEWAY
Hove Park
WOODRUFF AV
STANFORD CL
ROWAN
Sports Ground
ELM
MILL VW HOSPITAL
MARSHALL WY
Supermarket
Brighton & Hove Stadium
THE DROVEWAY
PARK
MAYTREE WK
LABURNUM
MOYNE CL
Hove Polyclinic
AVENUE
WAYFIELD
WAYFIELD AV
School
Knoll Rec Grd
DR
AV
Old Persons Home
Clinic
HOLMES
School
ORCHARD RD
ORCHARD AV
GDNS
PARK VW RD
ORCHARD
HOVE PARK RD
WAY
CRES
Hove Rec Grd
ELM
MAPLE GDNS
ACACIA AV
CRANMER AV
TORRANCE
WEALD AV
Fire Sta
Hove Cemetery
ENGLISH CL
ROAD
OLD SHOREHAM
HOVE PK GDS
A270
OLD
SHOREHAM
AMHERST
MILCOTE AV
LULLINGTON AV
ALDRINGTON AV
Super store
JOSEPHS
Amb Sta
FRITH RD
SACKVILLE
SACKVILLE IND ESTATE
NEWTOWN
Goldstone Football Ground
GOLDSTONE LA
RANELAGH VIL
WILBURY GDS
POYNTER RD
LANDSEER RD
PRINSEP RD
LEIGHTON
Leighton Road Council Depot
CRES
ISABEL CR
Hove Cemetery
ALDRINGTON
PENDRAGON CT
HARTINGTON VIL
ROAD
HOVE
WILBURY
LOVEGROVE CT
BENSON CT
STEVENS CT
INGRAM CRES WEST
INGRAM CRES EAST
KINGSTHORPE
DALGTN
MILNTHORPE
BOLSOVER RD
GRANGE
SCHOOL RD
PAYNE
ALPINE
LINTON
LENNOX RD
KENDAL RD
RUSKIN
MORTMR RD
MOLES WTH ST
ARTHUR ST
SUFFOLK ST
STONEHAM RD
COLERIDGE
WYNNE MS
SHERIDEN
SHAKESPEARE ST
TER
CONWAY PL
CONWAY
ELLEN
ALBERT
FONTHILL
ETHEL ST
VILLAS
STATION APP
OXFORD MS
EATON GR
CROMWELL RD
PORTLAND
Schs
MARMION
MAIN STONES RD
Rec Grd
TAMWORTH
MONTGOMERY
BYRON
Hosp
CLARENDON
JESMOND RD
MANSFIELD RD
PORTLAND AV
WOODHOUSE RD
Davis Park
ST HELIERS AV
Sch
ROAD
SCOTT RD
SHELLEY RD
RUTLAND RD
WORDS WORTH
COWPER
ST PATRICKS
LIVINGSTONE
SHIRLEY
GOLDSTONE
PORTLAND
GDNS
ROAD
RD
ST
COLEMAN AV
AMESBURY CR
PARK AV
HOGARTH RD
REYNOLDS RD
TITIAN RD
RAPHAEL RD
MODENA RD
WESTBOURNE
PEMBROKE
CLARENDON
VILLAS
EATON
DENMARK VIL
NEW
LAWRENCE
RICHARDSON RD
RUTLAND
BLATCHINGTON
BROOKER PL
BROOKER ST
CONNAUGHT TER
BELFAST ST
HADDINGTON ST
MV
Recreation Ground
CHURCH
PEMBROKE CRES
STIRLING PL
MONMOUTH ST
Hospital
Mus
Sch
School
ROAD
PEMBROKE GDS
PRINCESSO
AYMER RD
ST
CHURCH
Library
VALLANCE RD
GEORGE
VENTNOR VIL
HOVE
NORTON
TISBURY
Town Hall
ROAD
MARINE
NORMAN RD
TENNIS RD
GLENDOR RD
WISH RD
AV
WELBECK AV
BERRIEDALE AV
BRAEMORE RD
LANGDALE RD
LANGDALE GDNS
CARLISLE RD
WALSINGHAM RD
SACKVILLE GDNS
WESTBOURNE GDNS
WESTBOURNE PL
PRINCES CRES
PRINCES AV
HOVE
VALLANCE GDS
ST AUBYNS
SEAFIELD RD
OSBORNE VIL
MEDINA VIL
ALBANY VIL
FOURTH AV
THIRD AV
ALBERT MS
KINGS MS
THE DRIVE
GRAND AV
B2066
KINGSWAY
Western Lawns
WESTERN
ESPLANADE
NAMRIK MS
HOVE PL
MEDINA PL
King Alfred Leisure Centre
KINGS
ST AUBYNS STH
SUSSEX RD
MEDINA COTT
A259
KINGS GDNS
KINGSWAY
ESPLANADE
HOVE

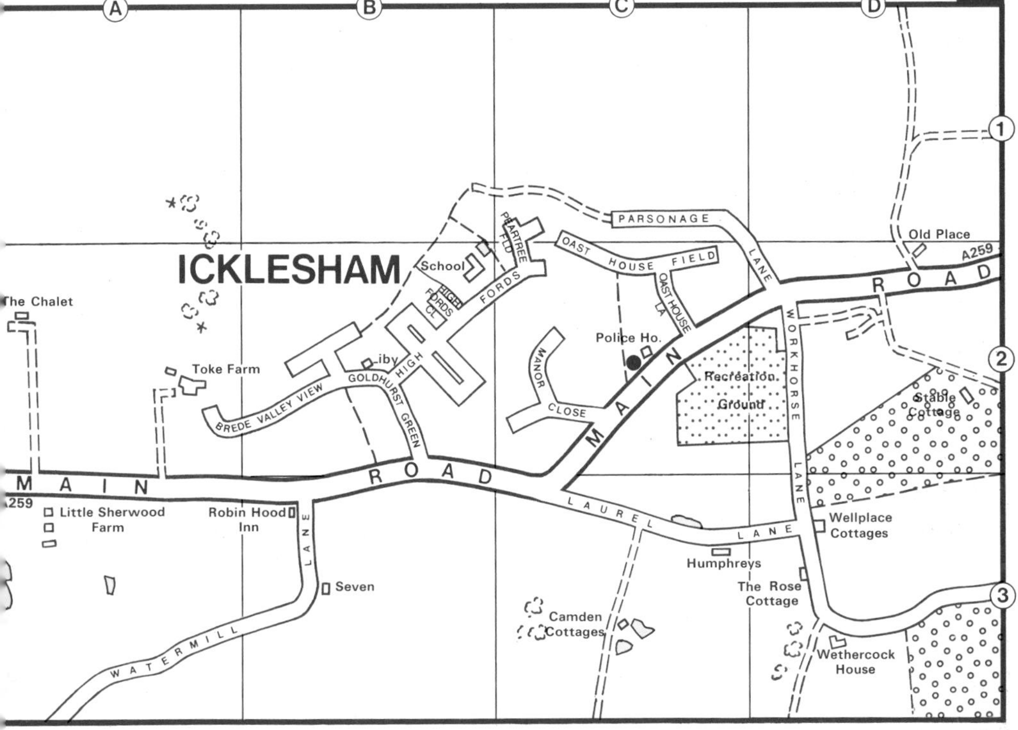

ICKLESHAM

The Chalet

Toke Farm

iby

School

PEARTREE PO

FORDS CL

HIGH ST

GOLDHURST GREEN

BREDE VALLEY VIEW

OAST HOUSE FIELD

OAST HOUSE LA

PARSONAGE

MANOR CLOSE

Police Ho.

Recreation Ground

Old Place

A259

ROAD

WORKHORSE LANE

Stable Cottage

MAIN ROAD

A259

Little Sherwood Farm

Robin Hood Inn

WATERMILL LANE

Seven

LAUREL LANE

Humphreys

Camden Cottages

The Rose Cottage

Wellplace Cottages

Wethercock House

CAMBER

Pound Field Farm

FARM LANE

DRAFFIN LA

NEW LYDD ROAD

Golf Course

LINKS

SCOTTS ACRE

OLD LYDD ROAD

Pontins Holiday Village

Camber

TANDRIDGE WY

DENHAM WY

PETER WD

DUNES AV

SEA RD

OLD LYDD RD

Royal Miniature Golf

Royal William P.H.

DANIEL AV

FIRST AV

SECOND AV

Maddiesons Camber Caravan Park

Broomhill Creek

Camber Sands

YATES CL

PELWOOD RD

SAUNDERS WY

THE SUTTONS

Silver Sands Caravan Park

CP

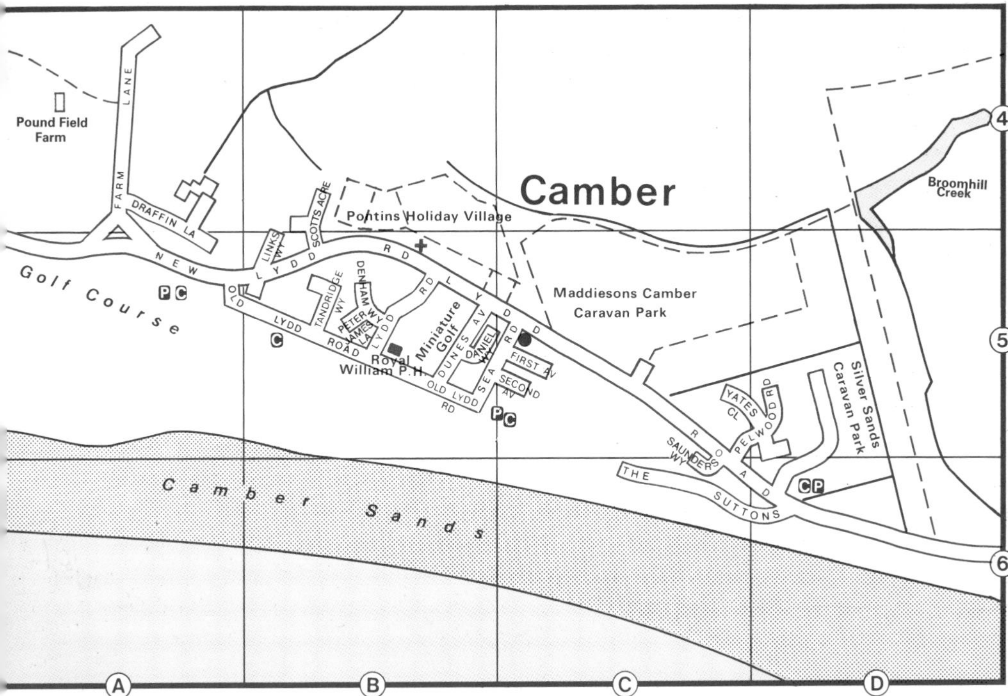

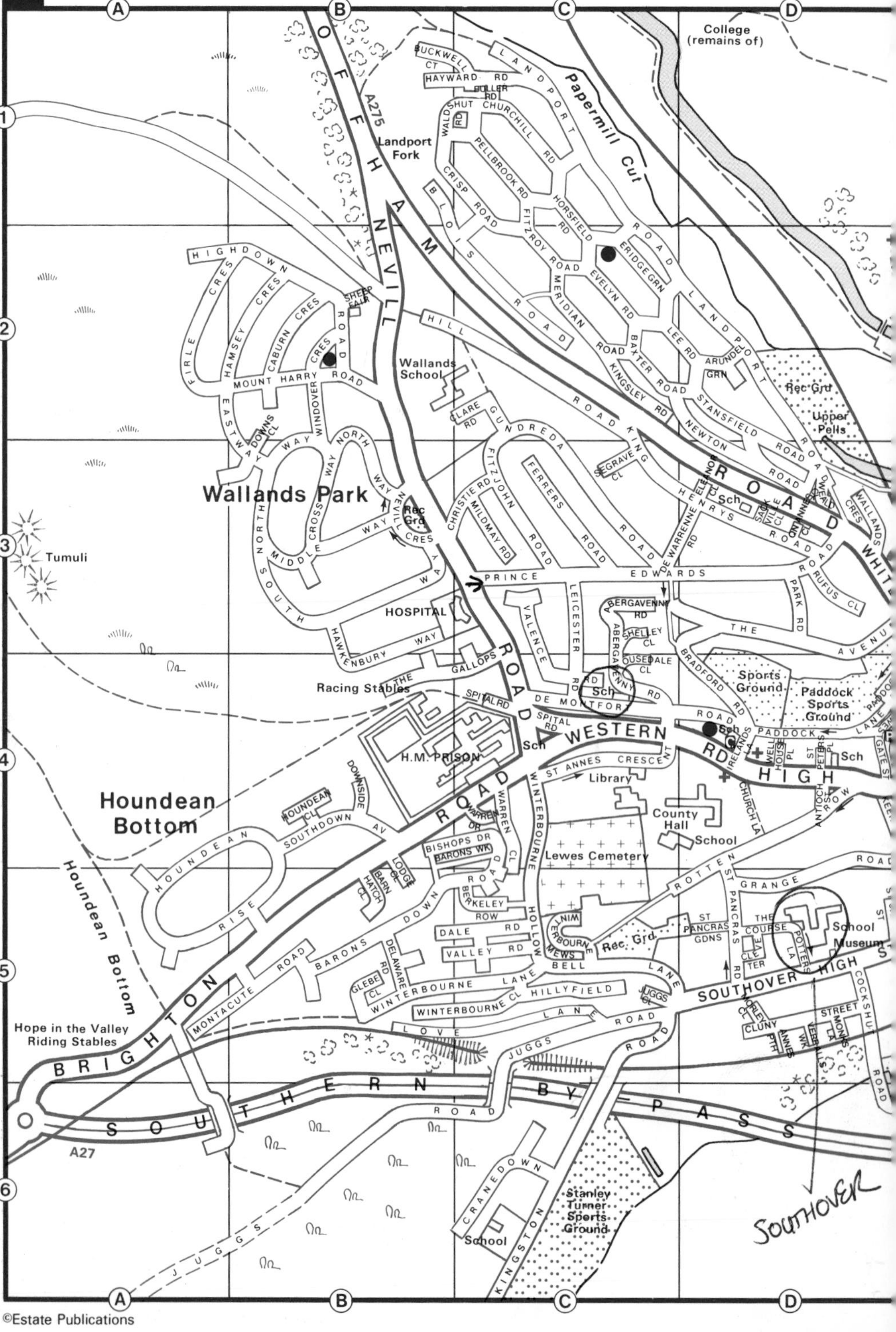
A
B
C
D
1
2
3
4
5
6
College (remains of)
Papermill Cut
Landport Fork
A275
OFFHAM
NEVILL
BUCKWELL CT
HAYWARD RD
BULLER RD
LANDPORT ROAD
WALDSHUT RD
CHURCHILL RD
PELLBROOK RD
CRISP ROAD
BLOIS ROAD
HORSFIELD RD
FITZROY ROAD
ERIDGE GRN
EVELYN RD
MERIDIAN ROAD
LEE RD
BAXTER ROAD
ARUNDEL GRN
KINGSLEY RD
STANSFIELD ROAD
NEWTON ROAD
KING ROAD
Rec Grd
Upper Pells
HIGHDOWN
FIRLE CRES
HAMSEY CRES
CABURN CRES
SHEEP FAIR
MOUNT HARRY ROAD
WINDOVER CRES
EASTWAY
DOWNS CL
NORTH WAY
CROSS WAY
MIDDLE WAY
SOUTH WAY
NEVILL CRES
Rec Grd
HILL ROAD
Wallands School
CLARE RD
GUNDREDA ROAD
FITZJOHN RD
CHRISTIE RD
MILDMAY RD
FERRERS ROAD
SEGRAVE CL
ELEANOR CL
HENRYS
DE WARRENNE RD
SACKVILLE CL
ST ANNES CL
Sch
ROAD
WALLANDS CRES
WHIT
Wallands Park
Tumuli
PRINCE EDWARDS ROAD
HOSPITAL
HAWKENBURY WAY
VALENCE RD
LEICESTER RD
ABERGAVENNY RD
SHELLEY CL
OUSEDALE CL
PARK RD
RUFUS CL
THE AVENUE
BRADFORD RD
Sports Ground
Paddock Sports Ground
THE GALLOPS
Racing Stables
SPITAL RD
DE MONTFORT RD
Sch
WESTERN RD
IRELANDS LA
WELLHOUSE PL
ST PETERS PL
PADDOCK LANE
Sch
H.M. PRISON
ST ANNES CRESCENT
Library
HIGH ST
CHURCH LA
ANTIOCH ST
County Hall
School
Houndean Bottom
DOWNSIDE
HOUNDEAN CL
SOUTHDOWN AV
WARREN DR
WARREN CL
WINTERBOURNE HOLLOW
Lewes Cemetery
BISHOPS DR
BARONS WK
HOUNDEAN RISE
LODGE CL
BARN HATCH CL
BERKELEY ROW
ROTTEN ROW
GRANGE ROAD
ST PANCRAS RD
ST PANCRAS GDNS
THE COURSE
POTTERS LA
School
Museum
DALE RD
VALLEY RD
DOWN ROAD
BARONS ROAD
DELAWARE RD
GLEBE CL
WINTERBOURNE MEWS
Rec. Grd
BELL LANE
CLEVE TER
SOUTHOVER HIGH ST
MONTACUTE ROAD
WINTERBOURNE LANE
WINTERBOURNE CL
HILLYFIELD
JUGGS CL
MORLEY CL
CLUNY ST
ANNES PTH
VERRALLS WK
MONKS LA
COCKSHUT
Hope in the Valley Riding Stables
BRIGHTON ROAD
LOVE LANE
JUGGS ROAD
SOUTHERN BY-PASS
A27
CRANEDOWN
KINGSTON ROAD
School
Stanley Turner Sports Ground
JUGGS
SOUTHOVER

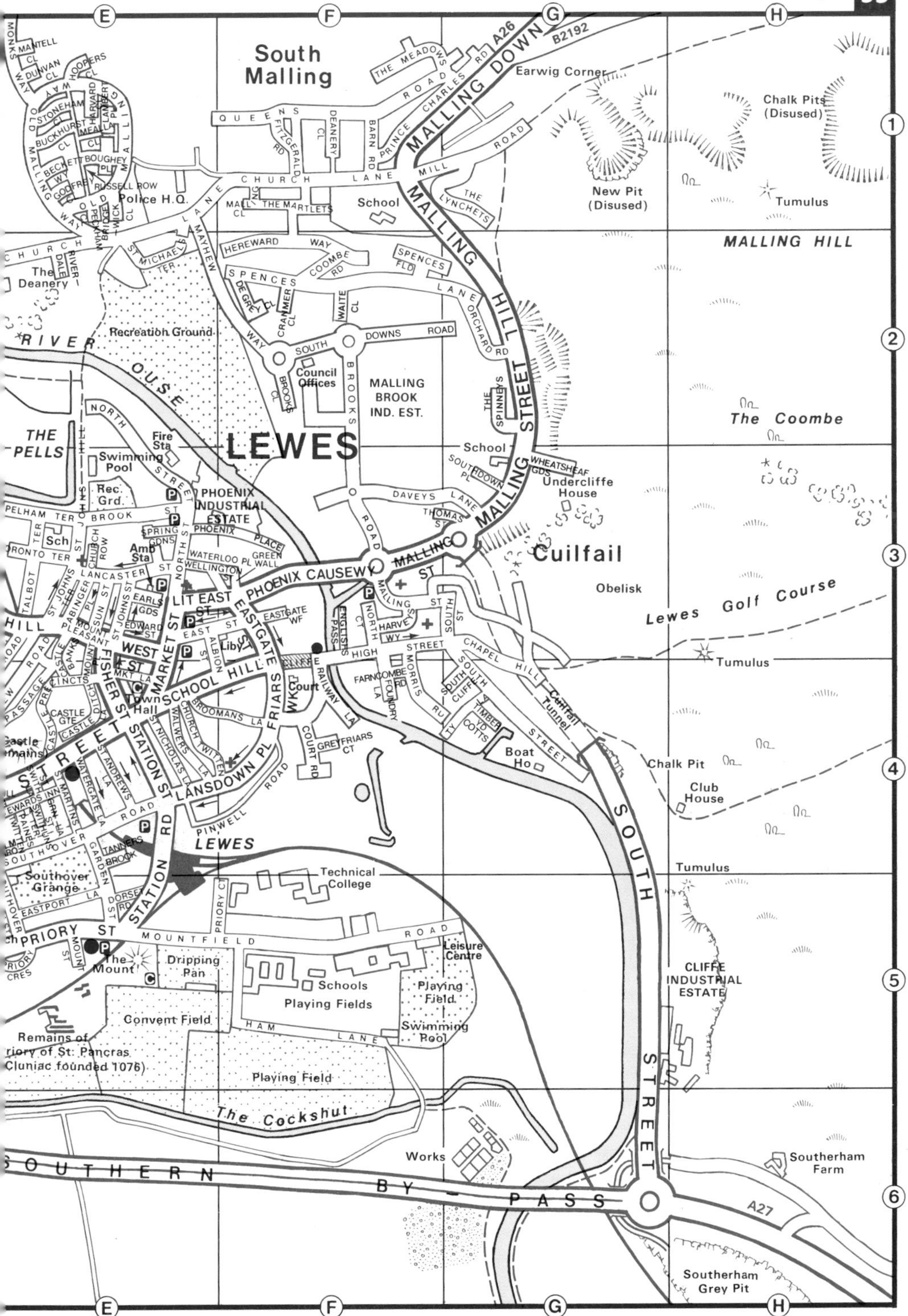
E
F
G
H
1
2
3
4
5
6
South Malling
LEWES
Cuilfail
Earwig Corner
B2192
A26
MALLING DOWN
MALLING HILL
MALLING STREET
MALLING ST
Chalk Pits (Disused)
New Pit (Disused)
Tumulus
Malling Hill
The Coombe
Obelisk
Lewes Golf Course
Chalk Pit
Club House
CLIFFE INDUSTRIAL ESTATE
Southerham Farm
Southerham Grey Pit
A27
SOUTH STREET
SOUTHERN BY - PASS
Works
The Cockshut
Playing Field
Convent Field
Remains of Priory of St. Pancras Cluniac founded 1076
Playing Fields
Schools
Swimming Pool
Playing Field
Leisure Centre
Dripping Pan
The Mount
Technical College
Southover Grange
THE PELLS
RIVER OUSE
Recreation Ground
Police H.Q.
The Deanery
School
Council Offices
MALLING BROOK IND. EST.
Fire Sta
Swimming Pool
Rec. Grd.
PHOENIX INDUSTRIAL ESTATE
PHOENIX CAUSEWY
Amb Sta
Sch
Liby
Court
Town Hall
Castle Remains
Undercliffe House
Boat Ho
Cuilfail Tunnel
CHURCH LANE
QUEENS ROAD
SPENCES LANE
SOUTH DOWNS ROAD
DAVEYS LANE
HIGH STREET
SCHOOL HILL
EASTGATE
FRIARS WK
LANSDOWN PL
STATION RD
STATION ST
FISHER ST
MARKET ST
WEST ST
PRIORY ST
MOUNTFIELD ROAD
HAM LANE
PINWELL ROAD
SOUTHOVER
CHAPEL HILL
SOUTH ST
LEWES

MARESFIELD

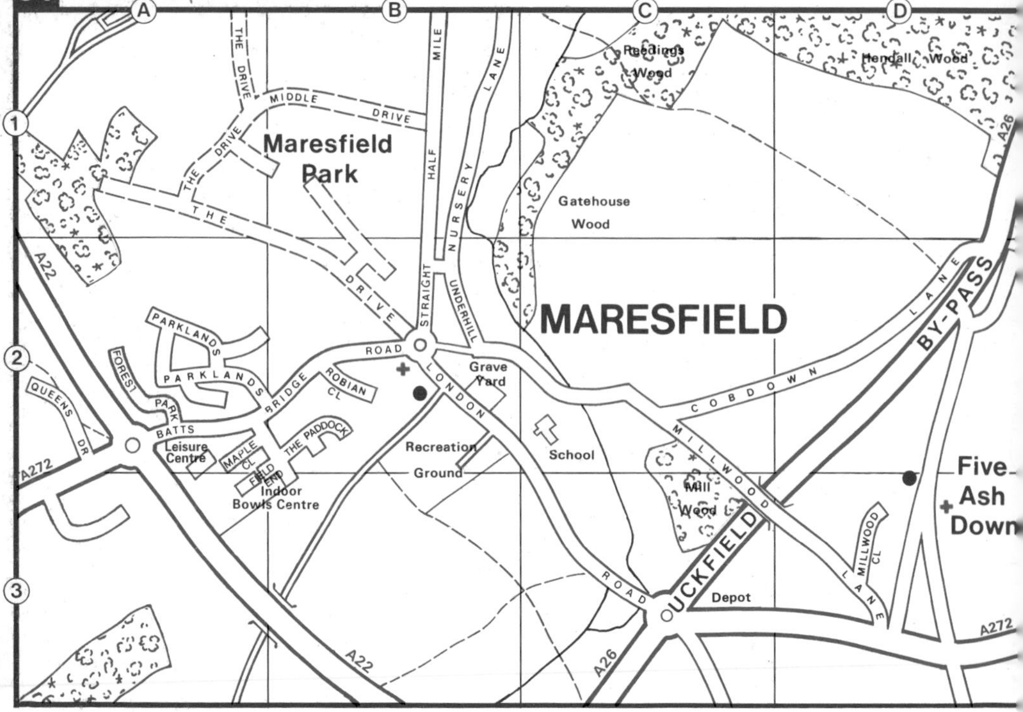
A
B
C
D
1
2
3
THE DRIVE
MIDDLE DRIVE
Maresfield Park
THE DRIVE
HALF MILE
STRAIGHT
NURSERY LANE
UNDERHILL
Readings Wood
Hendall Wood
Gatehouse Wood
A26
A22
MARESFIELD
LANE
BY-PASS
PARKLANDS
PARKLANDS
FOREST
PARK
BRIDGE
ROAD
ROBIAN CL
LONDON
Grave Yard
COBDOWN
QUEENS DR
BATTS
Leisure Centre
MAPLE CL
FIELD END
THE PADDOCK
Recreation Ground
School
MILLWOOD
Mill Wood
Five Ash Down
Indoor Bowls Centre
A272
UCKFIELD
ROAD
MILLWOOD CL
LANE
Depot
A22
A26
A272

BUXTED

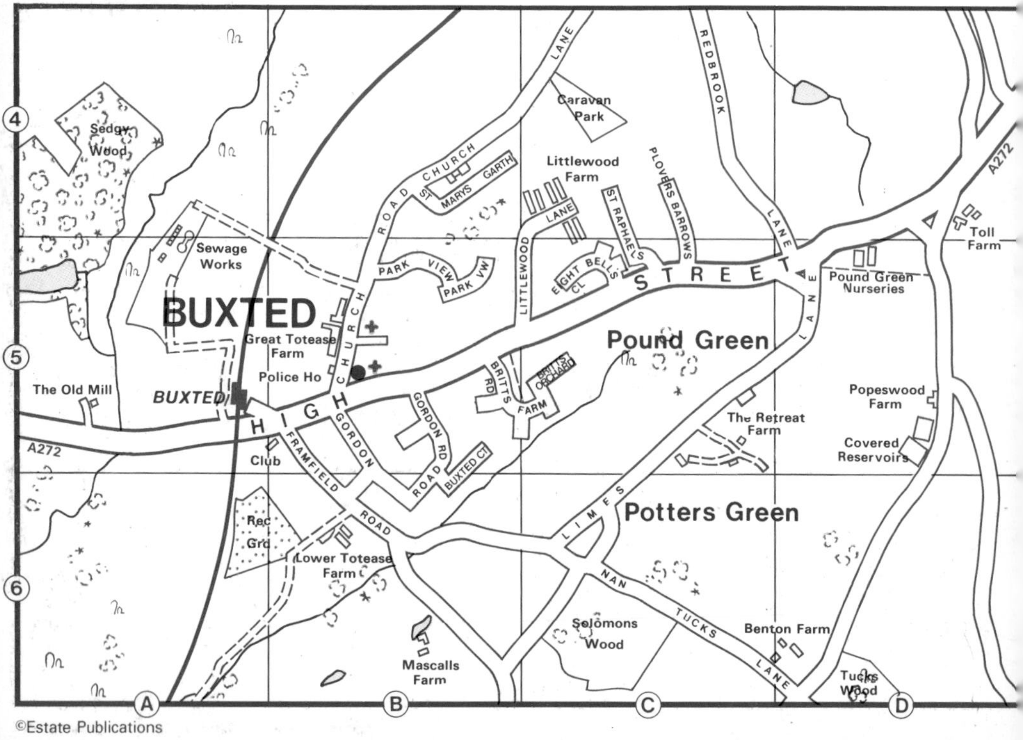
LANE
REDBROOK
Caravan Park
4
Sedgy Wood
Littlewood Farm
PLOVERS BARROWS
CHURCH
ST MARYS GARTH
ROAD
LANE
ST RAPHAELS
A272
LANE
Toll Farm
Sewage Works
PARK VIEW
PARK VW
LITTLEWOOD
EIGHT BELLS CL
STREET
Pound Green Nurseries
BUXTED
CHURCH
Great Totease Farm
Pound Green
LANE
5
Police Ho
BRITTS RD
BRITTS ORCHARD
FARM
The Old Mill
BUXTED
HIGH
GORDON
GORDON RD
Popeswood Farm
The Retreat Farm
A272
Club
FRAMFIELD
ROAD
BUXTED CT
Covered Reservoirs
Rec Grd
ROAD
LIMES
Potters Green
Lower Totease Farm
NAN
TUCKS
6
Selomons Wood
Benton Farm
Mascalls Farm
LANE
Tucks Wood
A
B
C
D

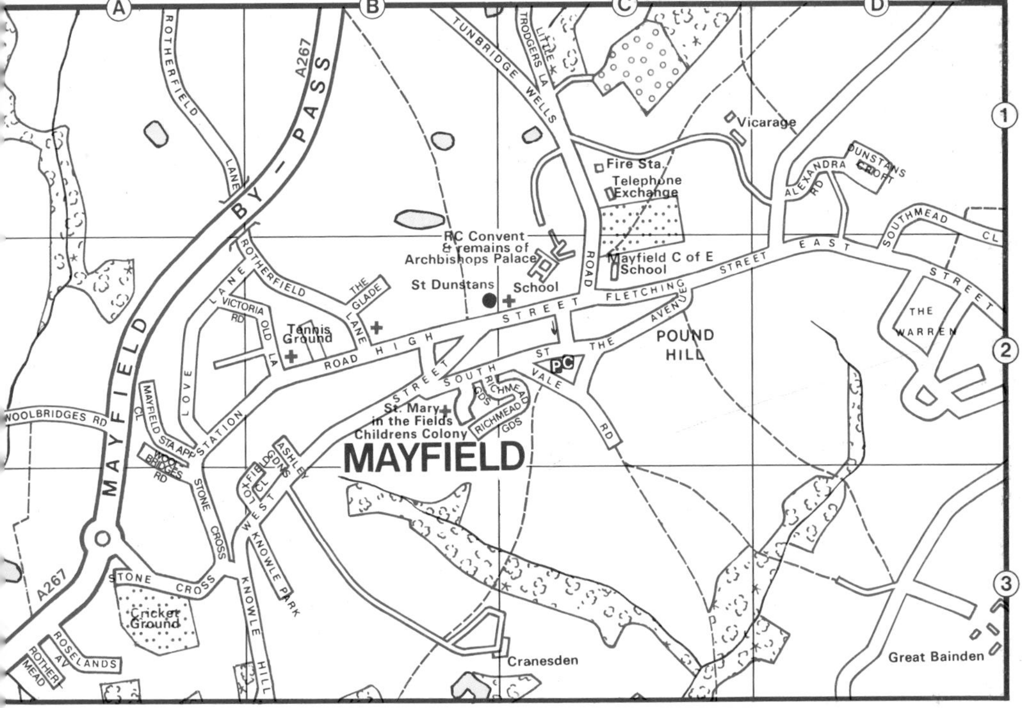
MAYFIELD
A267
BY-PASS
MAYFIELD
ROTHERFIELD LANE
TUNBRIDGE WELLS ROAD
LITTLE TRODGERS LA
Vicarage
Fire Sta.
Telephone Exchange
ALEXANDRA RD
DUNSTANS CROFT
SOUTHMEAD CL
EAST STREET
RC Convent & remains of Archbishops Palace
St Dunstans
School
Mayfield C of E School
FLETCHING STREET
THE AVENUE
POUND HILL
THE WARREN
ROTHERFIELD LANE
THE GLADE
VICTORIA RD
OLD LA
Tennis Ground
HIGH STREET
ROAD
LOVE LANE
SOUTH ST
VALE RD
RICHMEAD GDS
St. Mary in the Fields Childrens Colony
WOOLBRIDGES RD
MAYFIELD CL
STA APP
STATION RD
WOOLBRIDGES RD
ASHLEY GDNS
FOXFIELD CL
WEST ST
STONE CROSS
KNOWLE PARK
KNOWLE HILL
STONE CROSS
Cricket Ground
ROSELANDS AV
ROTHER MEAD
Cranesden
Great Bainden
A
B
C
D
1
2
3

DITCHLING

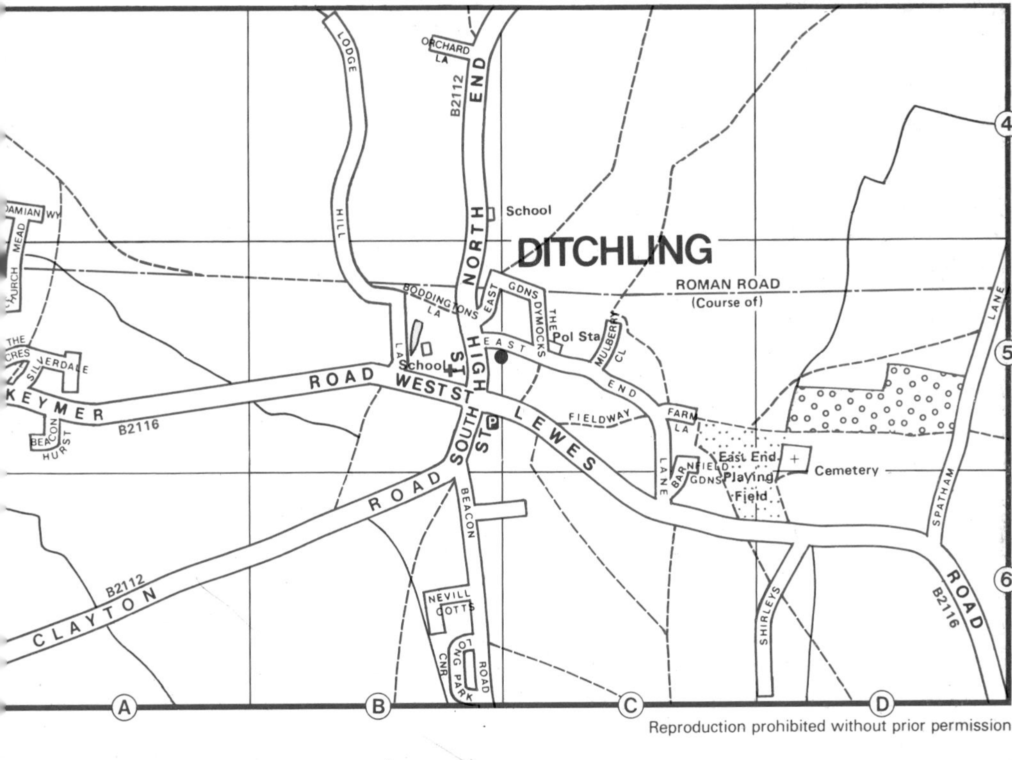
ORCHARD LA
LODGE HILL
B2112
NORTH END
School
DITCHLING
DAMIAN WY
CHURCH MEAD
ROMAN ROAD (Course of)
BODDINGTONS LA
EAST GDNS
DYMOCKS THE
Pol Sta
MULBERRY CL
THE CRES
SILVERDALE
LA
School
HIGH ST
EAST END
KEYMER ROAD
WEST ST
B2116
BEACON HURST
LEWES
FIELDWAY
FARM LA
LANE
BARNFIELD GDNS
East End Playing Field
Cemetery
SOUTH ST
BEACON
ROAD
CLAYTON
B2112
NEVILL COTTS
LONG PARK CNR
ROAD
SHIRLEYS
SPATHAM LANE
B2116
ROAD
A
B
C
D
4
5
6

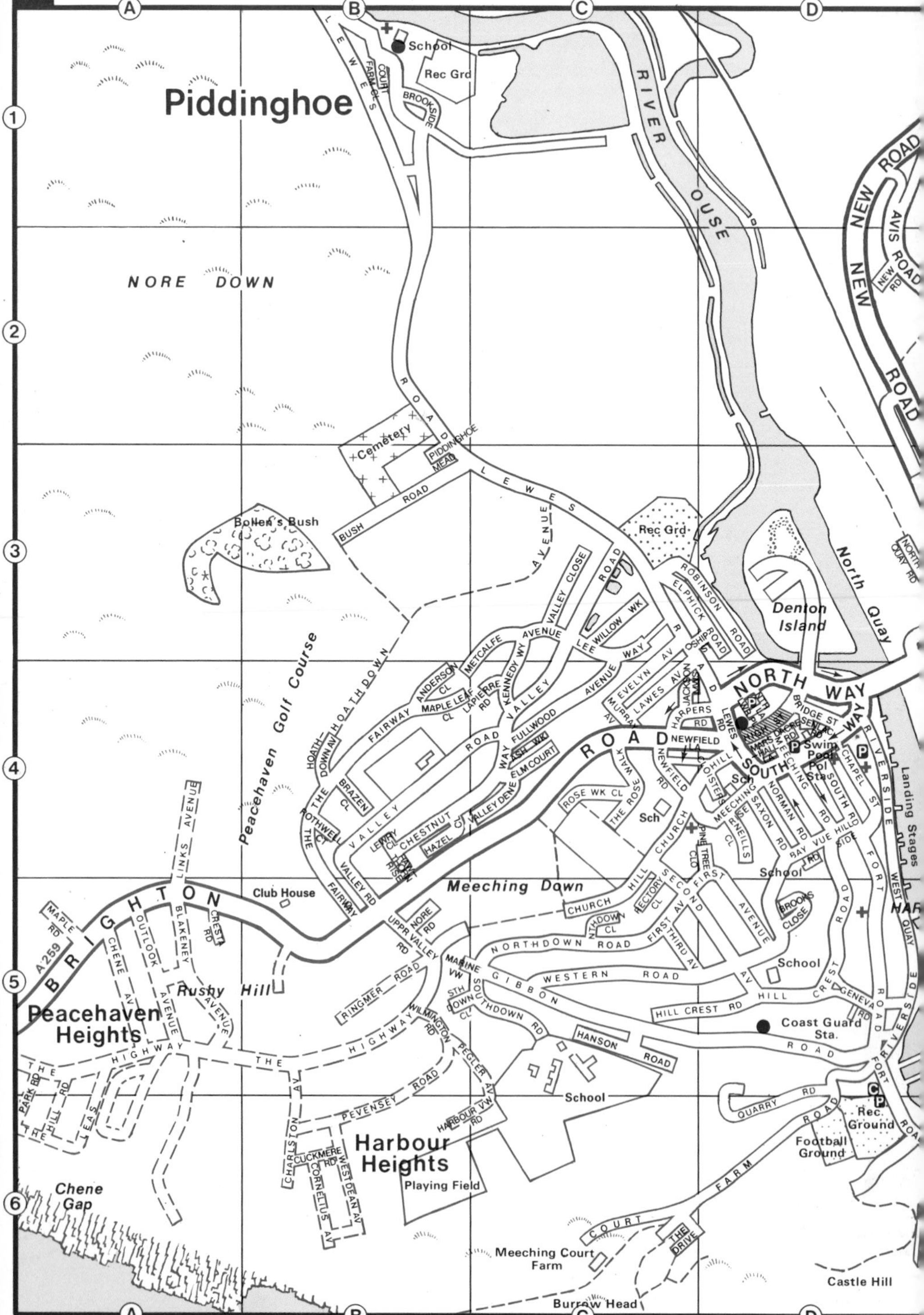

Piddinghoe

NORE DOWN

Bollen's Bush

Peacehaven Golf Course

Meeching Down

Peacehaven Heights

Rushy Hill

Harbour Heights

Chene Gap

RIVER OUSE

Denton Island

North Quay

NORTH WAY
SOUTH WAY

Coast Guard Sta.

Football Ground

Rec. Ground

Meeching Court Farm

Burrow Head

Castle Hill

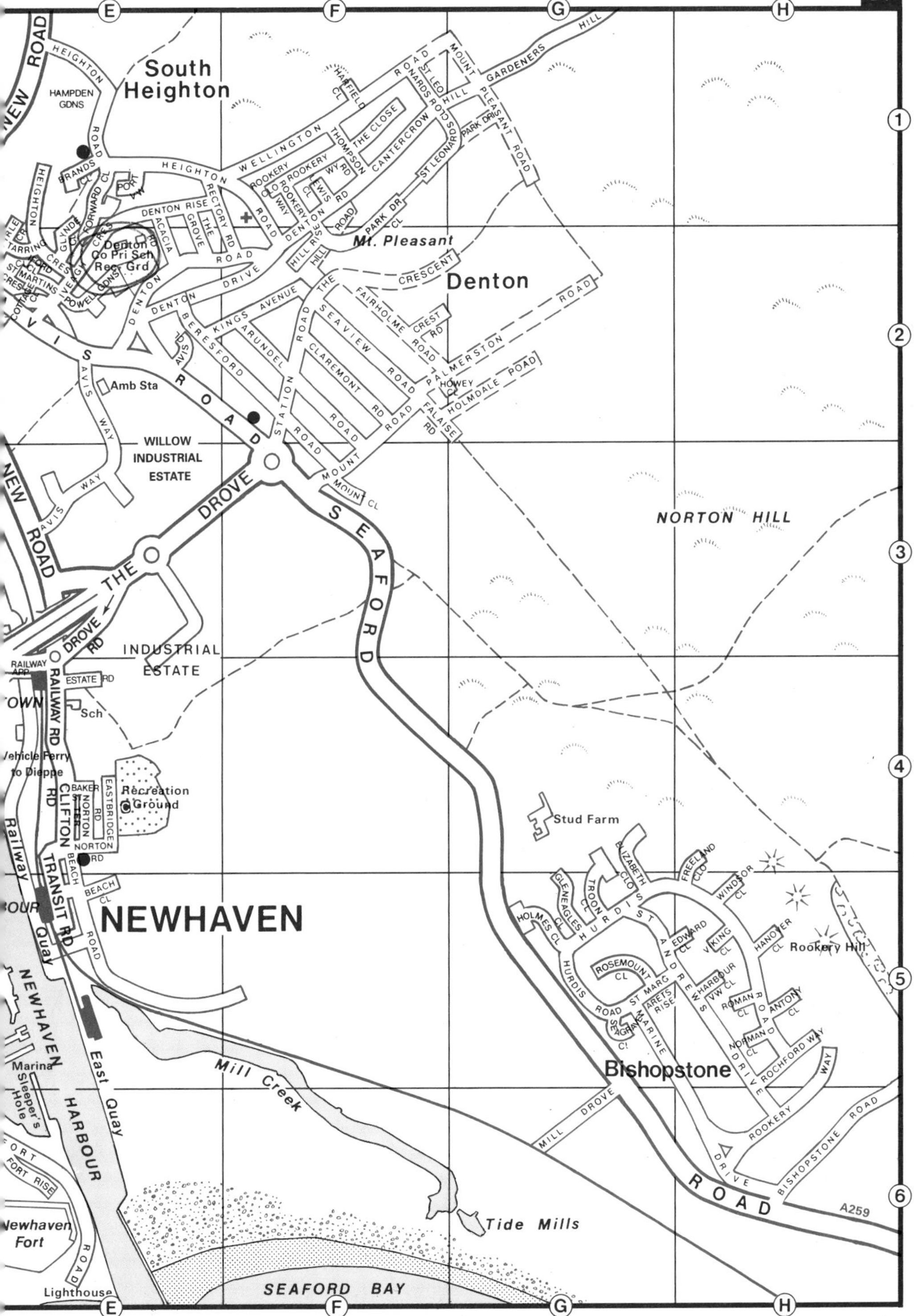
South Heighton
Heighton Road
Hampden Gdns
New Road
Brands Cl
Forward Cl
Port Vw
Heighton Road
Wellington Road
Rookery Cl
Rookery Way
Thompson Rd
Lewis Cl
Wy Rd
The Close
Cantercrow Hill
Harfield Cl
St Leonards Road
St Leonards Cl
Mount Pleasant Road
Park Dr
Gardeners Hill
Denton Rise
Rectory Road
The Grove
Acacia Road
Denton Co Pri Sch
Rec Grd
Glynde
Tarring Cl
Cresent
St Martins
Powell Gdns
Denton Drive
Denton Road
Hill Rise
Park Dr Cl
Mt. Pleasant
Crescent
Denton
Kings Avenue
Arundel Road
Beresford Road
Avis Road
Avis Way
The Seaview Road
Claremont Road
Fairholme Road
Crest Rd
Palmerston Road
Howey Cl
Holmdale Road
Falaise Rd
Station Road
Mount Road
Mount Cl
Amb Sta
Willow Industrial Estate
The Drove
Seaford Road
Norton Hill
Drove Rd
Industrial Estate
Estate Rd
Railway App
Railway Rd
Town
Sch
Vehicle Ferry to Dieppe
Baker St
Norton Rd
Eastbridge Rd
Clifton Rd
Norton Rd
Recreation Ground
Beach Rd
Beach Cl
Transit Rd
Railway
Harbour
Quay
NEWHAVEN
Newhaven Harbour
Marina
Sleeper's Hole
East Quay
Fort Rd
Fort Rise
Newhaven Fort
Lighthouse
Mill Creek
Tide Mills
Seaford Bay
Stud Farm
Elizabeth Clo
Freeland Clo
Troon Cl
Gleneagles Cl
Hurdis Road
Windsor Cl
St Andrews Road
Holmes Cl
Edward Cl
Viking Cl
Hanover Cl
Rookery Hill
Rosemount Cl
St Margarets Rise
Marine Cl
Harbour Vw Cl
Roman Cl
Antony Cl
Norman Cl
Rochford Way
Seagrave Cl
Bishopstone
Drive
Mill Drove
Rookery Way
Bishopstone Road
A259
E
F
G
H
1
2
3
4
5
6

NEWICK

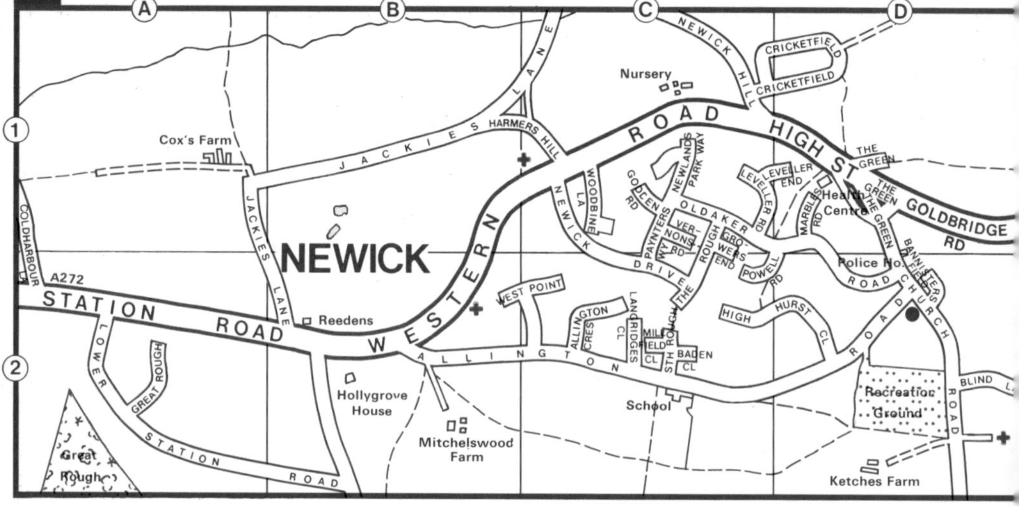

A
B
C
D
1
2
NEWICK
Nursery
NEWICK HILL
CRICKETFIELD
CRICKETFIELD
Cox's Farm
JACKIES LANE
HARMERS HILL
ROAD
HIGH ST
THE GREEN
GOLDBRIDGE RD
COLDHARBOUR
JACKIES LANE
WOODBINE LA
NEWICK
GODDEN RD
NEWLANDS PARK WAY
OLDAKER
LEVELLER RD
LEVELLER END
MARBLES RD
Health Centre
THE GREEN
A272
STATION ROAD
WESTERN
PAYNTERS WAY
VERNONS RD
ROUGH
GROWERS END
DRIVE
POWELL RD
Police Ho.
BANNISTERS FIELD
ROAD
CHURCH
WEST POINT
LANGRIDGES CL
ALLINGTON CRES
MILL FIELD CL
THE ROUGH
STH ROUGH
BADEN CL
HIGH HURST CL
Reedens
ALLINGTON
ROAD
LOWER
GREAT ROUGH
Hollygrove House
School
Recreation Ground
BLIND
ROAD
Mitchelswood Farm
STATION ROAD
Great Rough
Ketches Farm

NORTHIAM

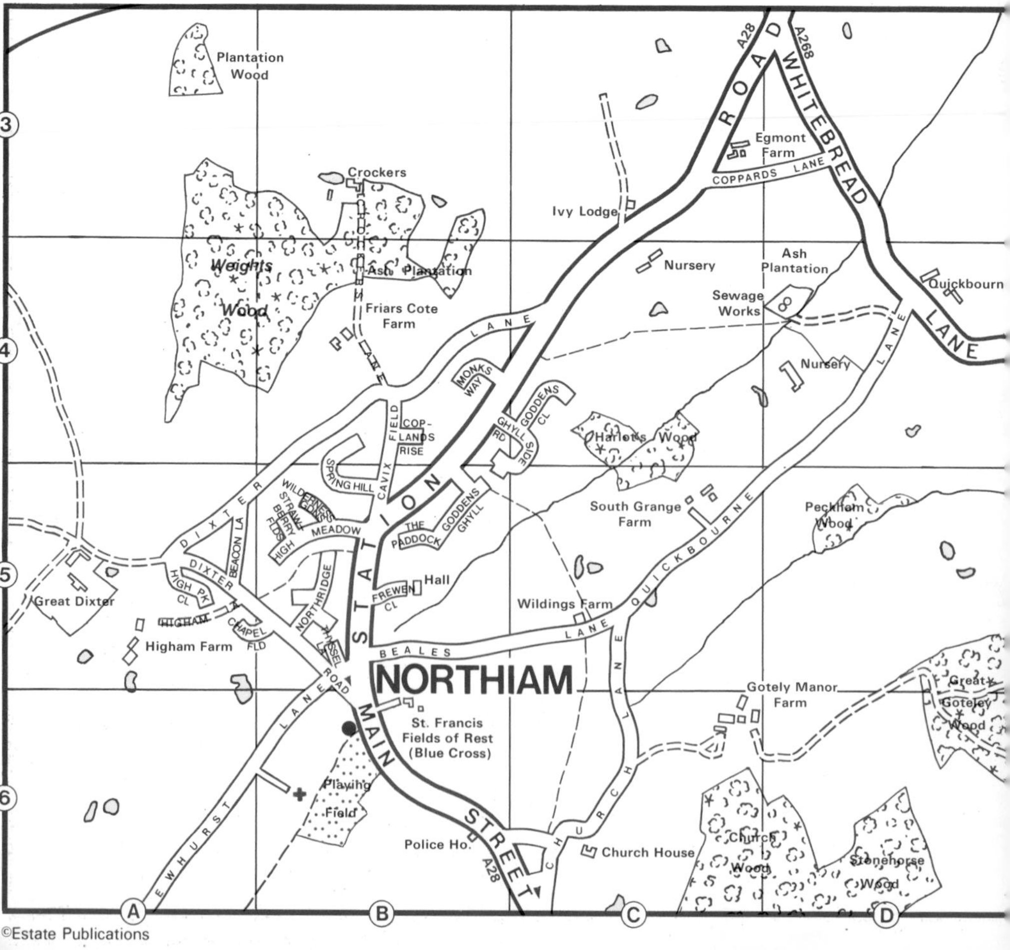

A28
ROAD
A268
WHITEBREAD
Plantation Wood
3
Egmont Farm
COPPARDS LANE
Crockers
Ivy Lodge
Weights Wood
Ash Plantation
Nursery
Ash Plantation
Sewage Works
Quickbourn
LANE
Friars Cote Farm
LANE
4
LANE
Nursery
MONKS WAY
GODDENS CL
GHYLL RD
GHYLL SIDE
COPLANDS RISE
CAVIX FIELD
Harlots Wood
SPRING HILL
STATION
WILDERNESS GDNS
STRAWBERRY FLDS
DIXTER
BEACON LA
MEADOW
HIGH
THE PADDOCK
GODDENS GHYLL
South Grange Farm
Peckham Wood
QUICKBOURNE
5
DIXTER
HIGH PK CL
Great Dixter
NORTHRIDGE
FREWEN CL
Hall
Wildings Farm
HIGHAM
CHAPEL FLD
THISSEL
LANE
Higham Farm
BEALES
NORTHIAM
ROAD
LANE
Gotely Manor Farm
Great Gotely Wood
MAIN
St. Francis Fields of Rest (Blue Cross)
CHURCH
EWHURST
6
Playing Field
STREET
A28
Police Ho.
Church House
Church Wood
Stonehorse Wood
A
B
C
D

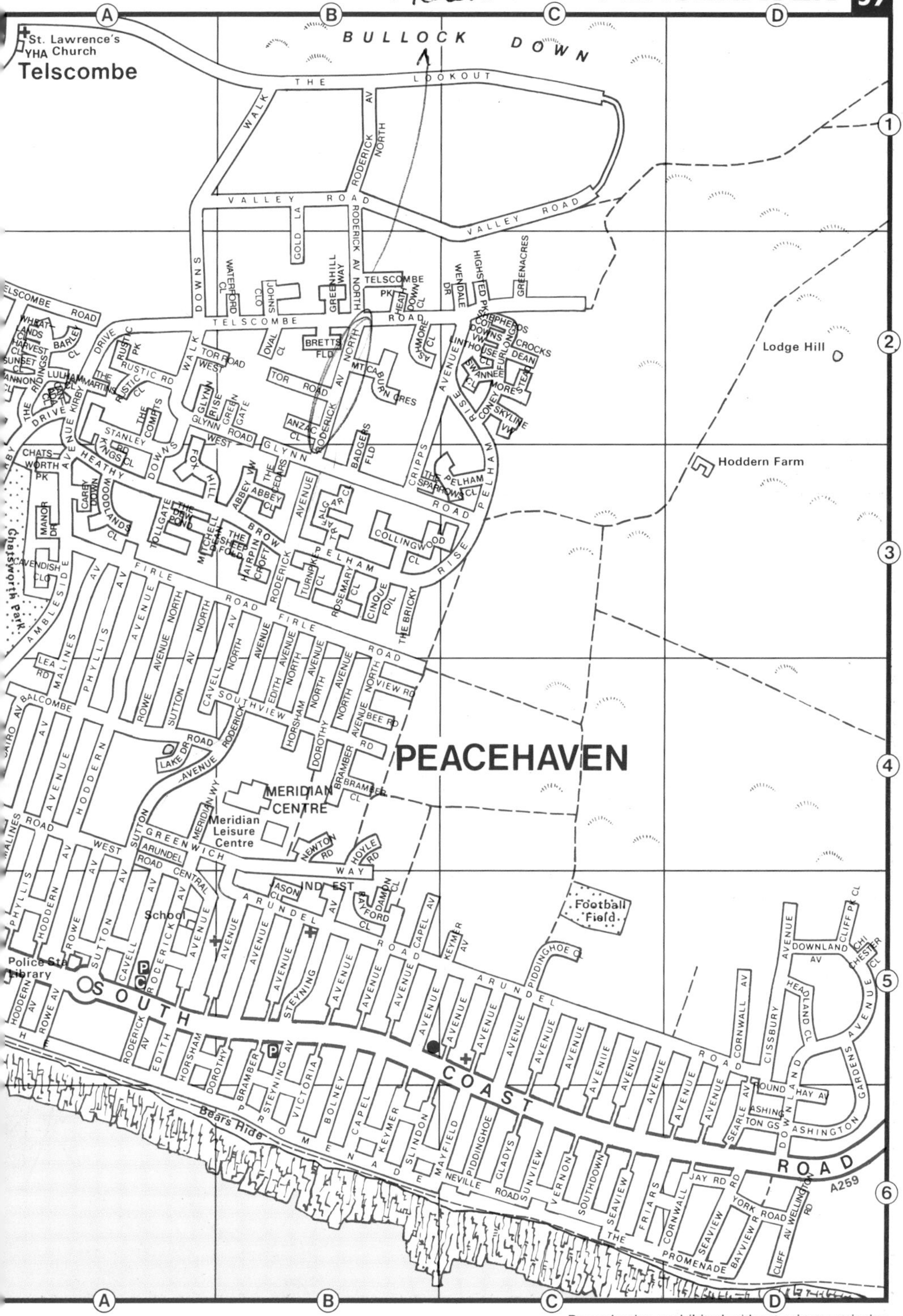

Meridian, Peacehaven

BULLOCK DOWN

St. Lawrence's
YHA Church
Telscombe

THE LOOKOUT

VALLEY ROAD

VALLEY ROAD

Lodge Hill

Hoddern Farm

PEACEHAVEN

MERIDIAN
CENTRE

Meridian
Leisure
Centre

Football
Field

School

Police Stn
Library

SOUTH

COAST

Bears Hide

ROAD

A259

THE PROMENADE

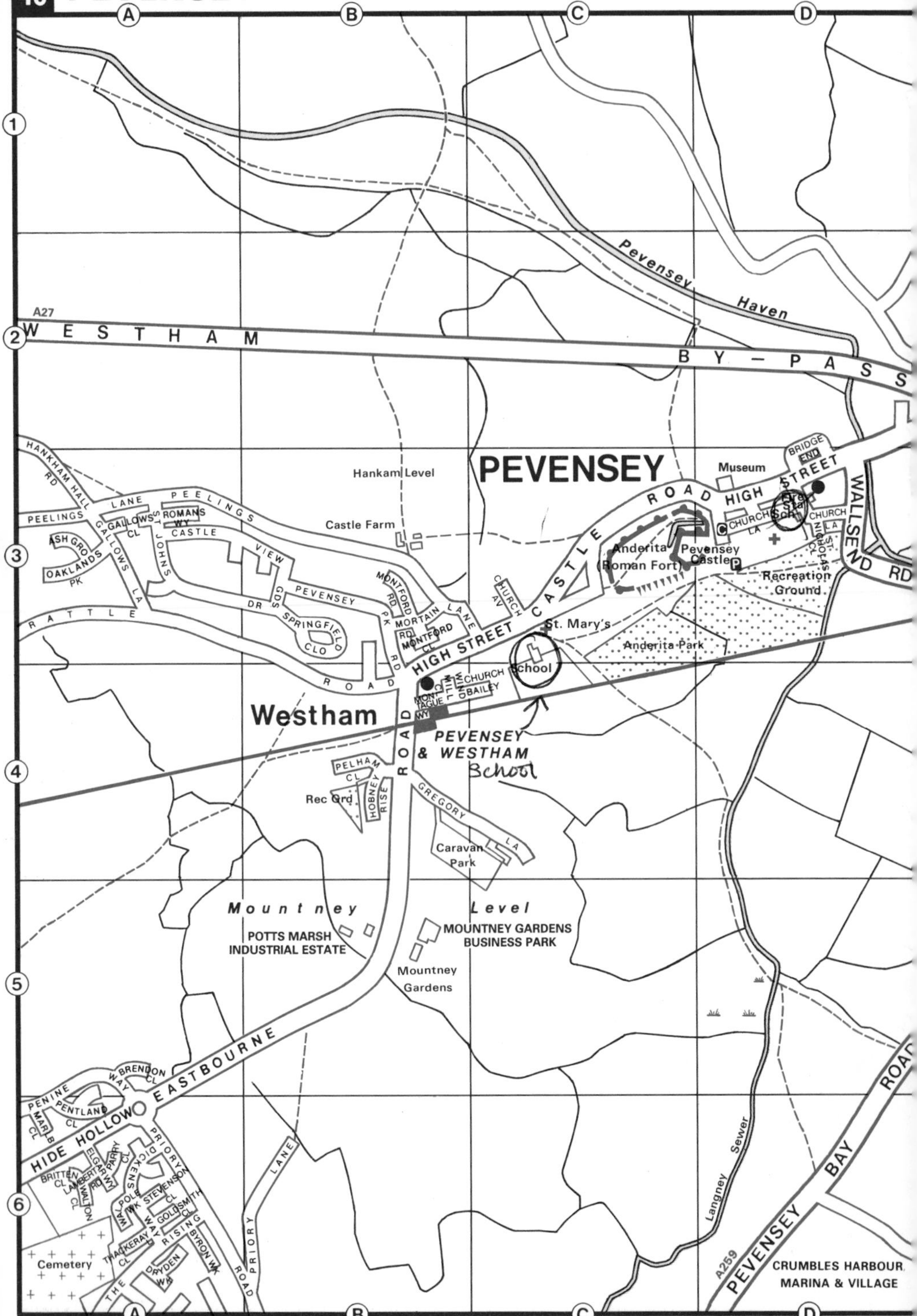
A
B
C
D
1
2
3
4
5
6
A27
WESTHAM BY-PASS
Pevensey Haven
PEVENSEY
Hankam Level
Castle Farm
HANKHAM HALL RD
PEELINGS LANE
GALLOWS CL
ROMANS WY
ST JOHNS
CASTLE VIEW
ASH GRO
OAKLANDS PK
GALLOWS LA
RATTLE ROAD
PEVENSEY GDS
PEVENSEY PK RD
SPRINGFIELD CLO
MONTFORD RD
MORTAIN LANE
MONTFORD CL
CHURCH AV
HIGH STREET
CASTLE ROAD
St. Mary's
School
Museum
BRIDGE END
HIGH STREET
CHURCH LA
Anderita (Roman Fort)
Pevensey Castle
Recreation Ground
Anderita Park
ST NICHOLAS CL
CHURCH LA
WALLSEND RD
Westham
MONTAGUE WY
MILL CL
WIND MILL
CHURCH BAILEY
PEVENSEY & WESTHAM
PELHAM CL
HOBNEY RISE
Rec Grd
ROAD
GREGORY LA
Caravan Park
Mountney Level
POTTS MARSH INDUSTRIAL ESTATE
MOUNTNEY GARDENS BUSINESS PARK
Mountney Gardens
EASTBOURNE
BRENDON CL
WAY
PENINE
PENTLAND CL
MARLB CL
HIDE HOLLOW
PRIORY
PRIORY LANE
PRIORY ROAD
ELGAR WY
PARRY CL
DICKENS WAY
STEVENSON CL
BRITTEN CL
LAMBERT RD
WALTON CL
WALPOLE WK
GOLDSMITH
RISING
BYRON WK
THACKERAY CL
DRYDEN WK
THE
Cemetery
Langney Sewer
A259
PEVENSEY BAY ROAD
CRUMBLES HARBOUR, MARINA & VILLAGE

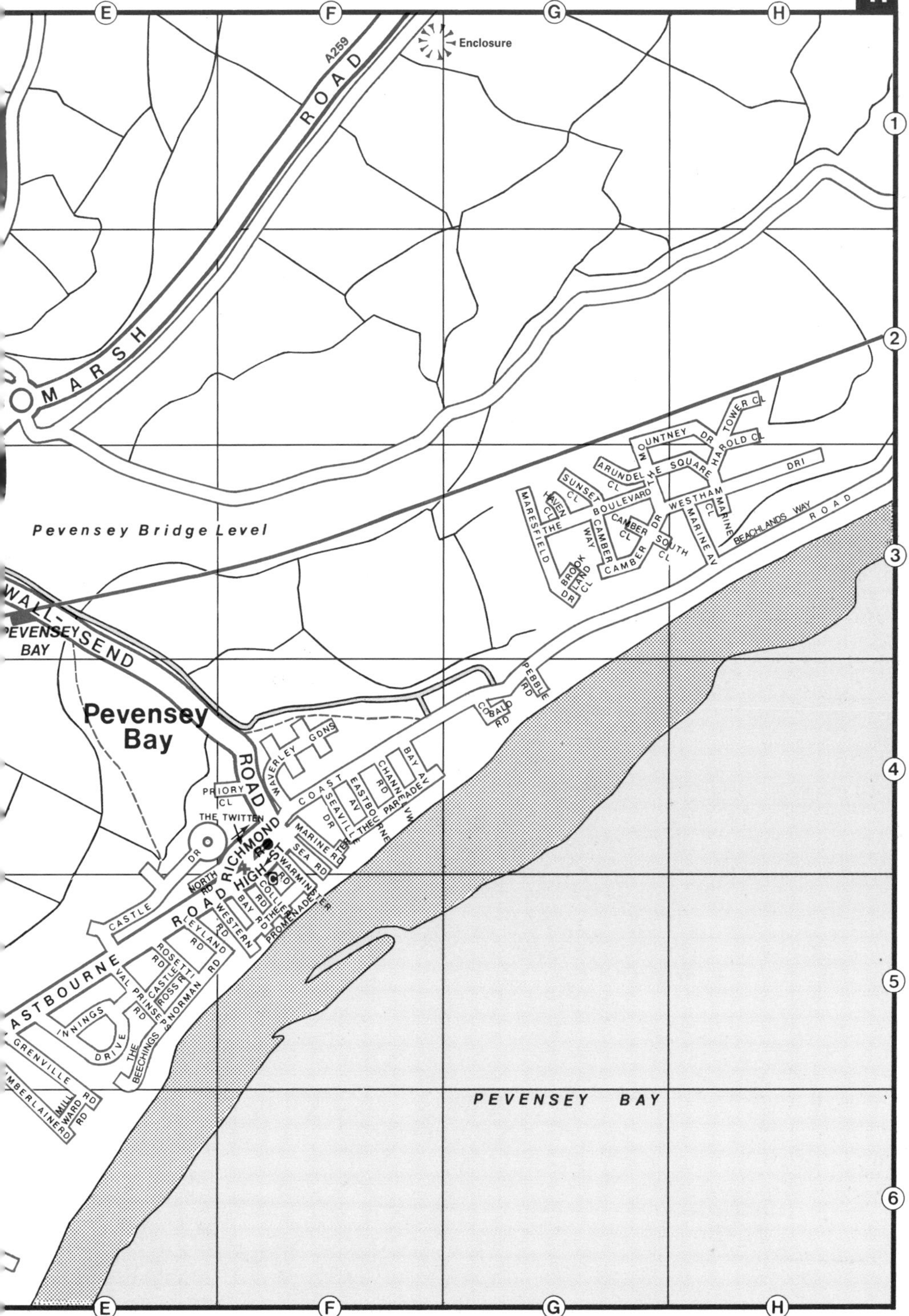
E
F
G
H
1
2
3
4
5
6
Enclosure
A259
MARSH ROAD
Pevensey Bridge Level
WALLSEND
PEVENSEY BAY
Pevensey Bay
ROAD
PRIORY CL
THE TWITTEN
WAVERLEY GDNS
COAST RD
SEAVILLE DR
EASTBOURNE AV
CHANNEL VW
BAY AV
THE PARADE
MARINE RD
SEA RD
RICHMOND RD
HIGH ST
NORTH RD
WARMINSTER RD
COLLIER RD
BAY RD
THE PROMENADE
WESTERN RD
LEYLAND RD
CASTLE DR
ROAD
EASTBOURNE
ROSETTI RD
CASTLE RD
ROSS RD
NORMAN RD
PRINSEP RD
VAL
INNINGS DRIVE
THE BEECHINGS
GRENVILLE RD
MILLWARD RD
COBALD RD
PEBBLE RD
MARESFIELD DR
THE HAVEN CL
SUNSET CL
ARUNDEL CL
MOUNTNEY DR
TOWER CL
HAROLD CL
THE SQUARE
THE BOULEVARD
WESTHAM DR
MARINE CL
MARINE AV
CAMBER WAY
CAMBER CL
CAMBER DR
CAMBER
SOUTH CL
BROOKLAND CL
BEACHLANDS WAY
MARINE ROAD
PEVENSEY BAY

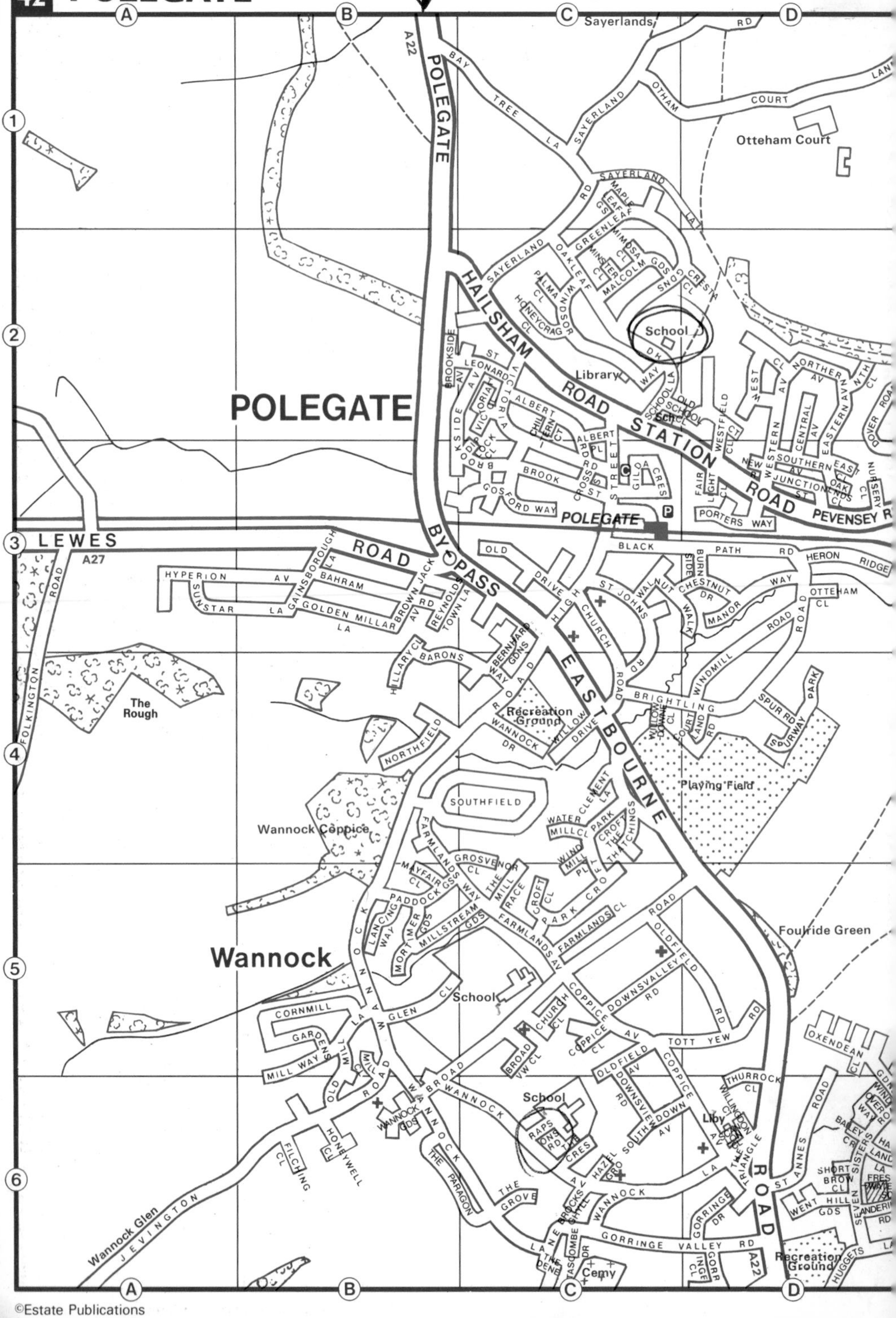
POLEGATE
Wannock
Sayerlands
Otteham Court
School
Library
Schl
POLEGATE
LEWES ROAD
A27
A22
POLEGATE BY-PASS
HAILSHAM ROAD
STATION ROAD
PEVENSEY R
EASTBOURNE ROAD
The Rough
Recreation Ground
Playing Field
Wannock Coppice
Foulride Green
Wannock Glen
SOUTHFIELD
Liby
Cemy
Recreation Ground

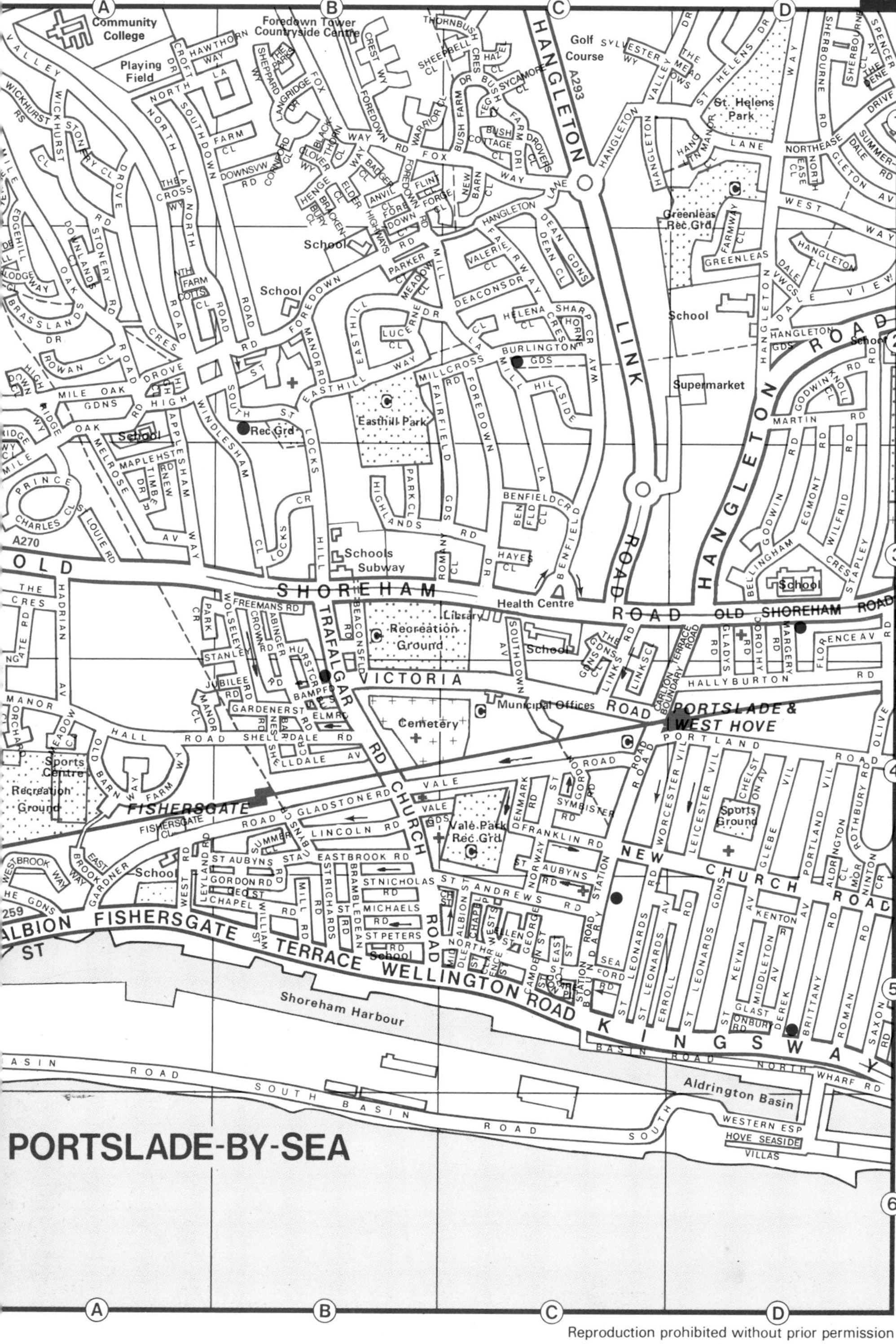
PORTSLADE-BY-SEA
Community College
Playing Field
Foredown Tower Countryside Centre
Golf Course
HANGLETON
A293
HANGLETON LINK ROAD
St. Helens Park
Greenleas Rec.Grd
School
Supermarket
HANGLETON ROAD
Easthill Park
Rec.Grd
Schools
Subway
Health Centre
Library
Recreation Ground
OLD SHOREHAM ROAD
A270
VICTORIA ROAD
Municipal Offices
Cemetery
PORTSLADE & WEST HOVE
FISHERSGATE
Sports Centre
Recreation Ground
Vale Park Rec.Grd
Sports Ground
TRAFALGAR RD
CHURCH ROAD
NEW CHURCH ROAD
GLADSTONE RD
PORTLAND ROAD
ALBION ST
FISHERSGATE TERRACE
WELLINGTON ROAD
KINGSWAY
A259
Shoreham Harbour
BASIN ROAD
SOUTH BASIN ROAD
BASIN ROAD NORTH
WHARF RD
Aldrington Basin
WESTERN ESP
HOVE SEASIDE VILLAS

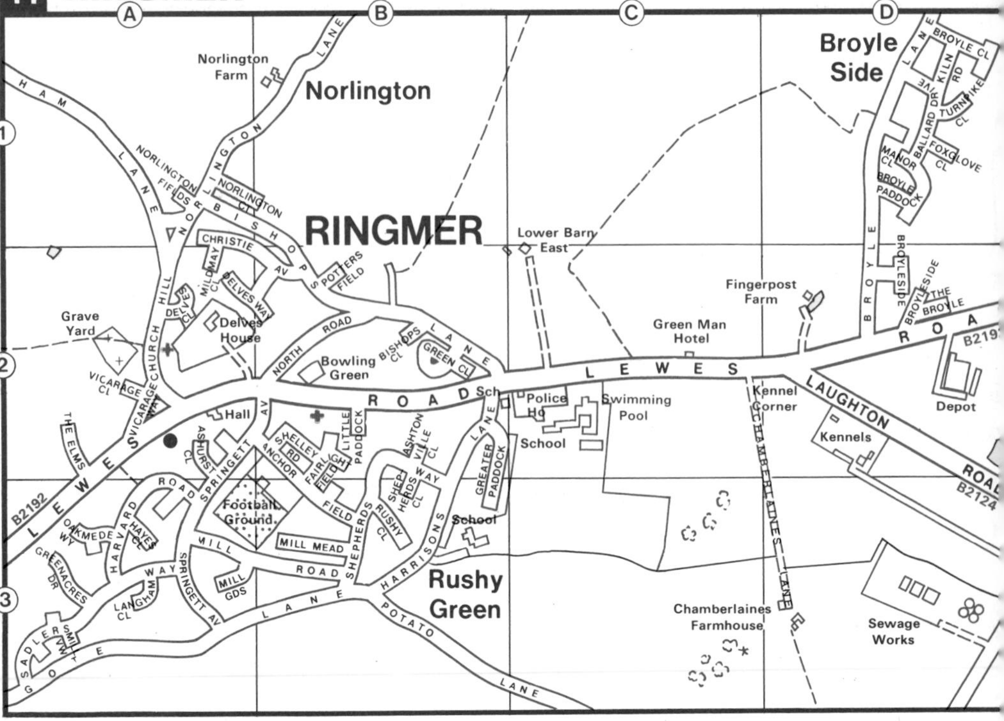

RINGMER

Norlington

Norlington Farm

Broyle Side

BROYLE CL
KILN
TURNPIKE
BROYLE DR
BALLARD DR
FOXGLOVE CL
MANOR CL
BROYLE PADDOCK

Lower Barn East

Fingerpost Farm

Green Man Hotel

BROYLE
BROYLESIDE
THE BROYLE
ROAD
B219

CHRISTIE AV
ELVES WAY
POTTERS FIELD
DEL
Delves House
Bowling Green
BISHOPS LANE
GREEN CL

Grave Yard

VICARAGE CL
VICARAGE
CHURCH HILL
NORTH ROAD
MILDMAY

L E W E S R O A D

Police Ho
Swimming Pool
Sch
School

Kennel Corner

LAUGHTON ROAD B2124

Kennels

Depot

THE ELMS
Hall
B2192
L E W E S
ROAD
ASHURST
SPRINGETT
ANCHOR
SHELLEY RD
FAIRLIGHT
FIELD
LITTLE PADDOCK
ASHTON VILLE CL
SHEP
HERDS WAY
GREATER PADDOCK
LANE

School

OAKMEDE
HARVARD
HAYES
ROAD
MILL LANE
SPRINGETT AL
Football Ground
MILL MEAD
SHEPHERDS
RUSHY CL
HARRISONS LANE

GREENACRES
SADLERS
SMITH
GROVE
LANGHAM CL
SPRINGAM WAY
MILL GDS

Rushy Green

POTATO LANE

Chamberlaines Farmhouse

Sewage Works

ROBERTSBRIDGE

Pound Platt

Northbridge Street

A21
ROTHERVIEW
ANDREWS WAY
CHURCH
KEMPS ROAD
RD

Bugsell Farm

Mill

NORTHBRIDGE
ST RUMLEY CL

River

Bugsell Wood

Beech Farm

LANE

Playing Field

THE CLAPPERS
Rec Grd
Cricket Grd

FAIR LANE

Fair Ridge Wood

ROBERTSBRIDGE

FAYRE MEADOW

Fair Ridge

School

KNELLE
BELLHURST
GLENLEIGH WLK
ROAD
MILL RD

Works
Factory

FAIR LANE
HIGH STREET

Sewage Works

LANGHAM
BRIGHTLING

Willow Cottage Farm

ROBERTSBRIDGE

STATION ROAD

Police Ho
MILL RISE
BISHOPS
MILL RISE
WILLOW MEWS
WILLOWBANK
BLENHEIM CT
Grove Farm

Park Wood

Brown's Bridge

BISHOPS CROFT
GEORGE GDS
HEATHFIELD LANE
A21

Darvell

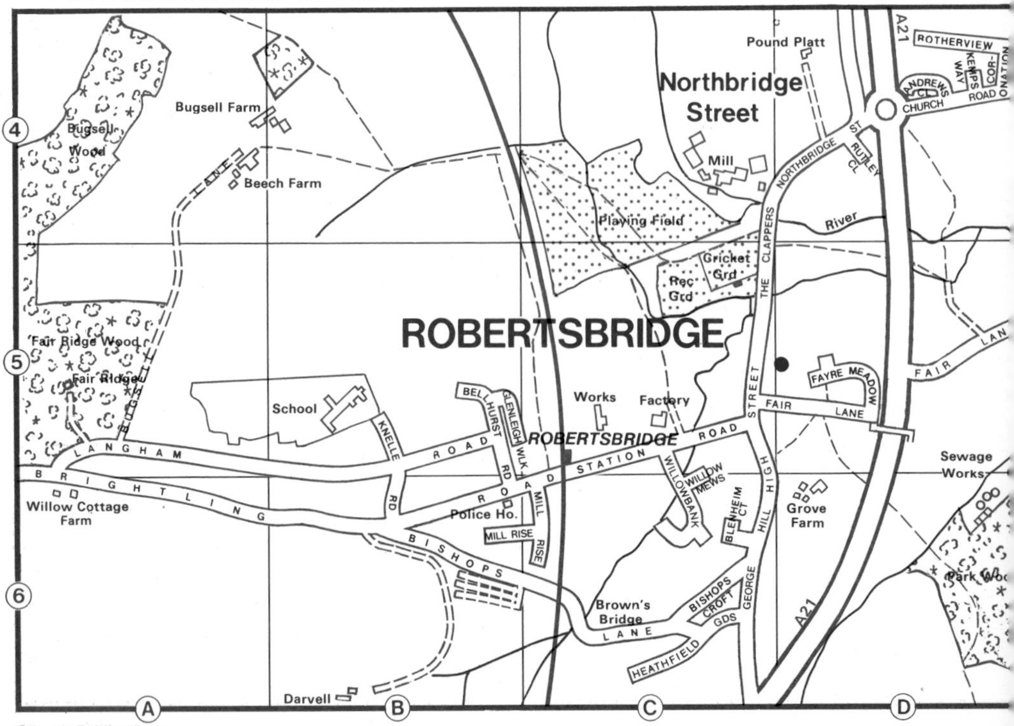

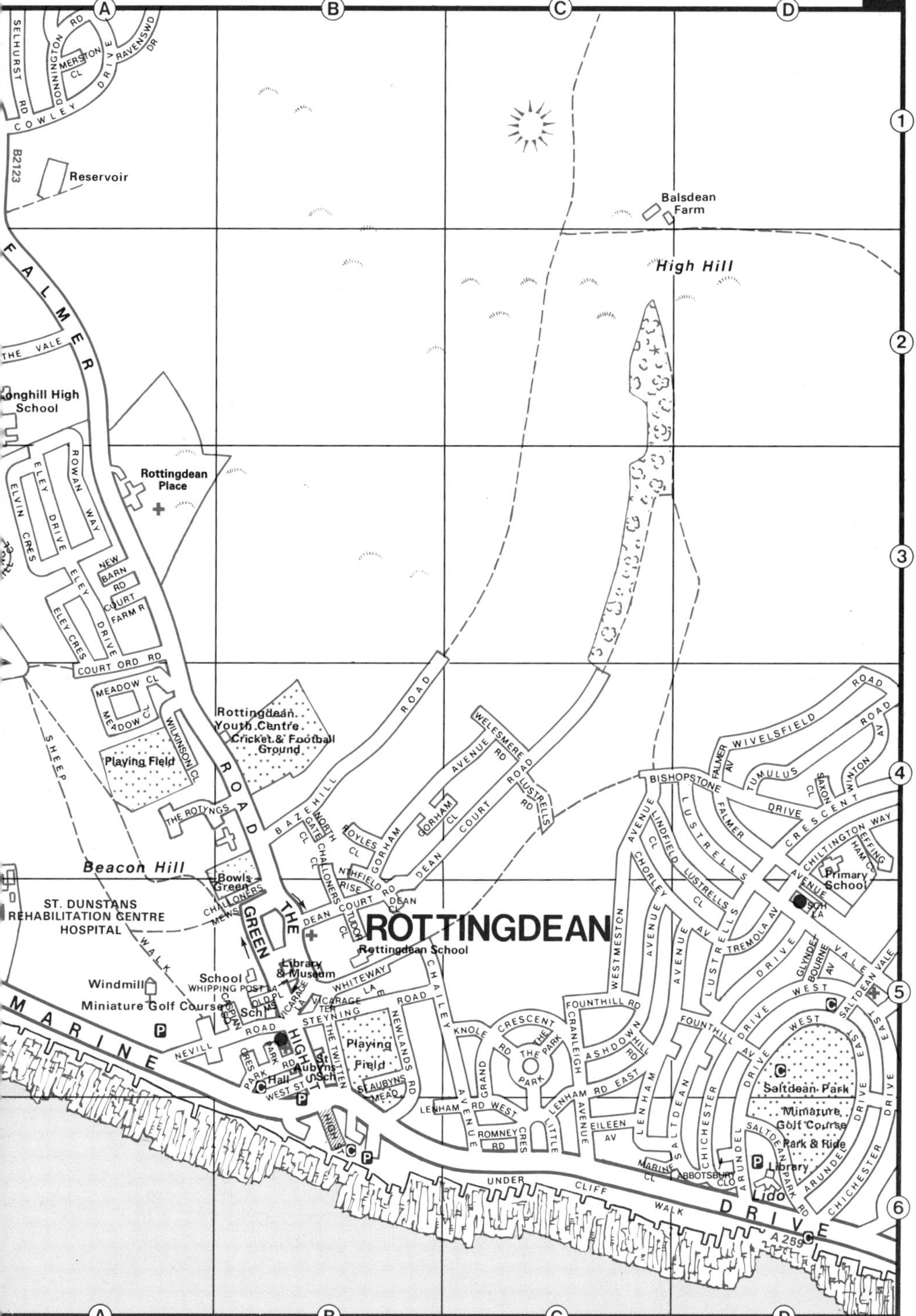
A
B
C
D
1
2
3
4
5
6
SELHURST RD
DONNINGTON RD
MERSTON CL
DRIVE
RAVENSWD DR
COWLEY
B2123
Reservoir
Balsdean Farm
High Hill
FALMER ROAD
THE VALE
Longhill High School
ELEY DRIVE
ROWAN WAY
ELVIN CRES
Rottingdean Place
NEW BARN RD
COURT FARM R
ELEY CRES
COURT ORD RD
MEADOW CL
WILKINSON CL
Playing Field
SHEEP WALK
Rottingdean Youth Centre
Cricket & Football Ground
THE ROTYNGS
Beacon Hill
Bowls Green
CHALLONERS MEWS
ST. DUNSTANS REHABILITATION CENTRE HOSPITAL
THE GREEN
Library & Museum
School
WHIPPING POST LA
Windmill
Miniature Golf Course
MARINE
NEVILL ROAD
CASPIAN SQ
OLD PL
Sch
VICARAGE LA
VICARAGE TER
HIGH ST
PARK CRES
PARK RD
Hall
WEST ST
St Aubyns Sch
THE TWITTEN
Playing Field
STEYNING ROAD
NEWLANDS RD
ST AUBYNS MEAD
WHITEWAY LA
BAZEHILL ROAD
NORTH GATE CL
CHALLONERS CL
ROYLES CL
GORHAM AVENUE
GORHAM CL
WELESMERE RD
DEAN COURT ROAD
LUSTRELLS RD
NTHFIELD RISE
DEAN COURT RD
DEAN CL
TUDOR CL
ROTTINGDEAN
Rottingdean School
CHAILEY AVENUE
KNOLE RD
CRESCENT
THE PARK
GRAND AVENUE
LENHAM RD WEST
ROMNEY RD
CRES
LITTLE CRES
UNDER CLIFF WALK
DRIVE
A 259
WESTMESTON AVENUE
FOUNTHILL RD
CRANLEIGH AVENUE
ASHDOWN RD
HILL RD
LENHAM RD EAST
EILEEN AV
LENHAM AVENUE
SALTDEAN AVENUE
MARINE CL
ABBOTSBURY CLO
CHICHESTER
ARUNDEL
BISHOPSTONE
FALMER AV
WIVELSFIELD ROAD
TUMULUS
SAXON CL
WINTON AV
LUSTRELLS CRESCENT
FALMER DRIVE
CHORLEY AVENUE
LINDFIELD CL
LUSTRELLS AV
TREMOLA AV
CHILTINGTON WAY
EFFINGHAM CL
Primary School
SCH LA
GLYNDE AV
BOURNE AV
SALTDEAN VALE
FOUNTHILL AV
WEST DRIVE
Saltdean Park
Miniature Golf Course
Park & Ride
Library
Lido
SALTDEAN PARK RD
ARUNDEL DRIVE
CHICHESTER DRIVE
EAST DRIVE

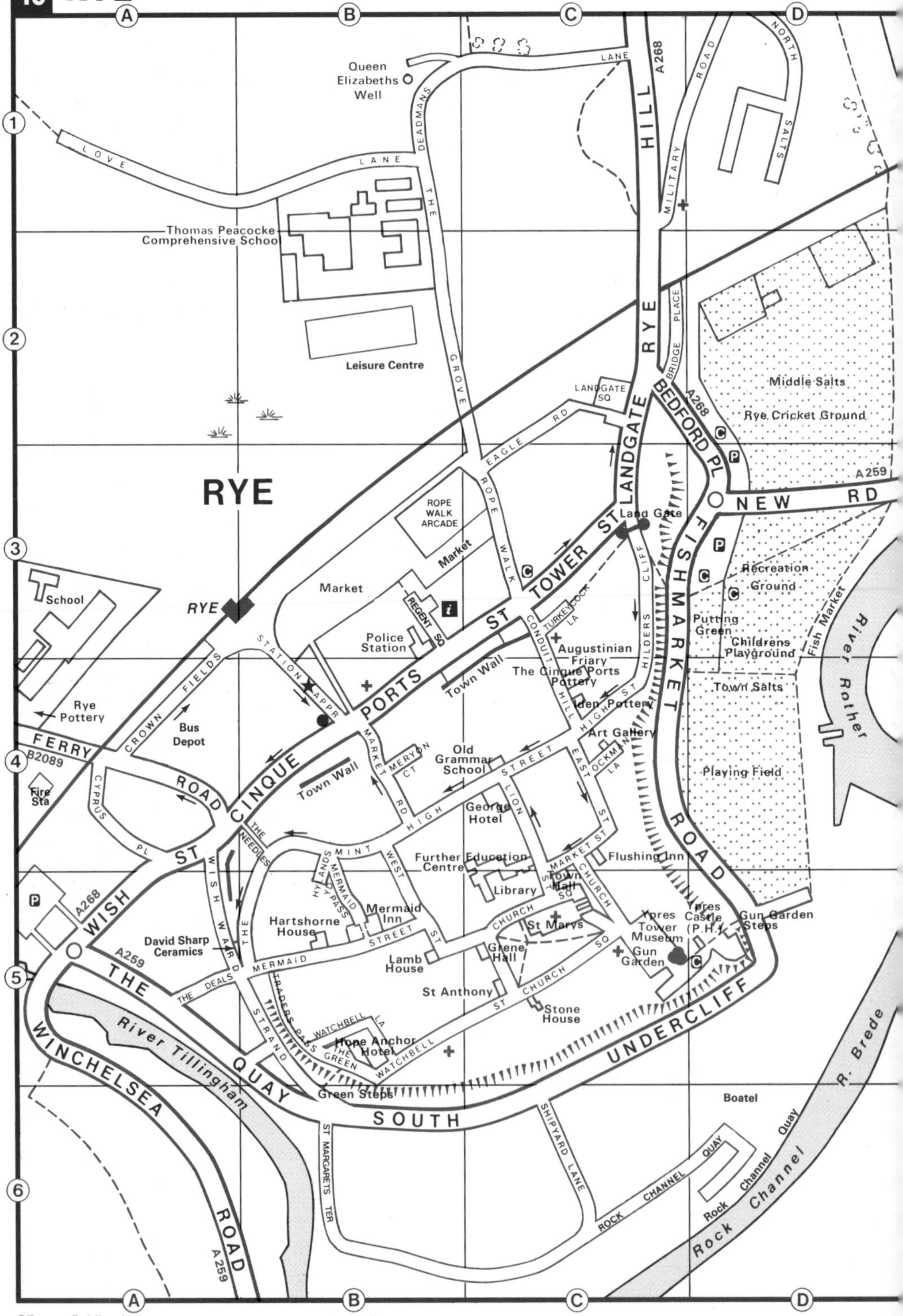
RYE
Queen Elizabeths Well
LOVE LANE
DEADMANS LANE
THE GROVE
Thomas Peacocke Comprehensive School
Leisure Centre
A268
RYE HILL
NORTH SALTS
MILITARY ROAD
BRIDGE PLACE
Middle Salts
Rye Cricket Ground
BEDFORD PL
NEW RD
A259
LANDGATE SQ
LANDGATE
EAGLE RD
ROPE WALK ARCADE
ROPE WALK
Market
Land Gate
TOWER ST
FISHMARKET ROAD
Recreation Ground
Putting Green
Childrens Playground
Fish Market
River Rother
Town Salts
Playing Field
School
RYE
STATION APPR
REGENT SQ
Police Station
TURKEY COCK LA
CONDUIT HILL
HILDERS CLIFF
Augustinian Friary
The Cinque Ports Pottery
Iden Pottery
HIGH ST
Art Gallery
Rye Pottery
CROWN FIELDS
Bus Depot
Town Wall
PORTS
CINQUE
FERRY ROAD
B2089
Fire Sta
CYPRUS PL
MARKET RD
MERYON CT
Old Grammar School
HIGH STREET
EAST ST
OCKMAN LA
LION ST
George Hotel
THE NEEDLES
MINT
WEST ST
Further Education Centre
MARKET ST
Flushing Inn
Library
Town Hall
CHURCH SQ
WISH ST
WISH WARD
THE STRAND
HYLANDS YD
MERMAID PASS
Hartshorne House
Mermaid Inn
MERMAID STREET
CHURCH
St Marys
Ypres Tower Museum
Ypres Castle (P.H.)
Gun Garden Steps
Gun Garden
A268
A259
David Sharp Ceramics
Lamb House
Grene Hall
St Anthony
CHURCH SQ
Stone House
THE DEALS
THE STRAND
TRADERS PASS
WATCHBELL LA
Hope Anchor Hotel
THE GREEN
WATCHBELL ST
UNDERCLIFF
THE QUAY
River Tillingham
WINCHELSEA ROAD
Green Steps
SOUTH
Boatel
ST MARGARETS TER
SHIPYARD LANE
ROCK CHANNEL
QUAY
Rock Channel Quay
Rock Channel
R. Brede
A B C D
1 2 3 4 5 6

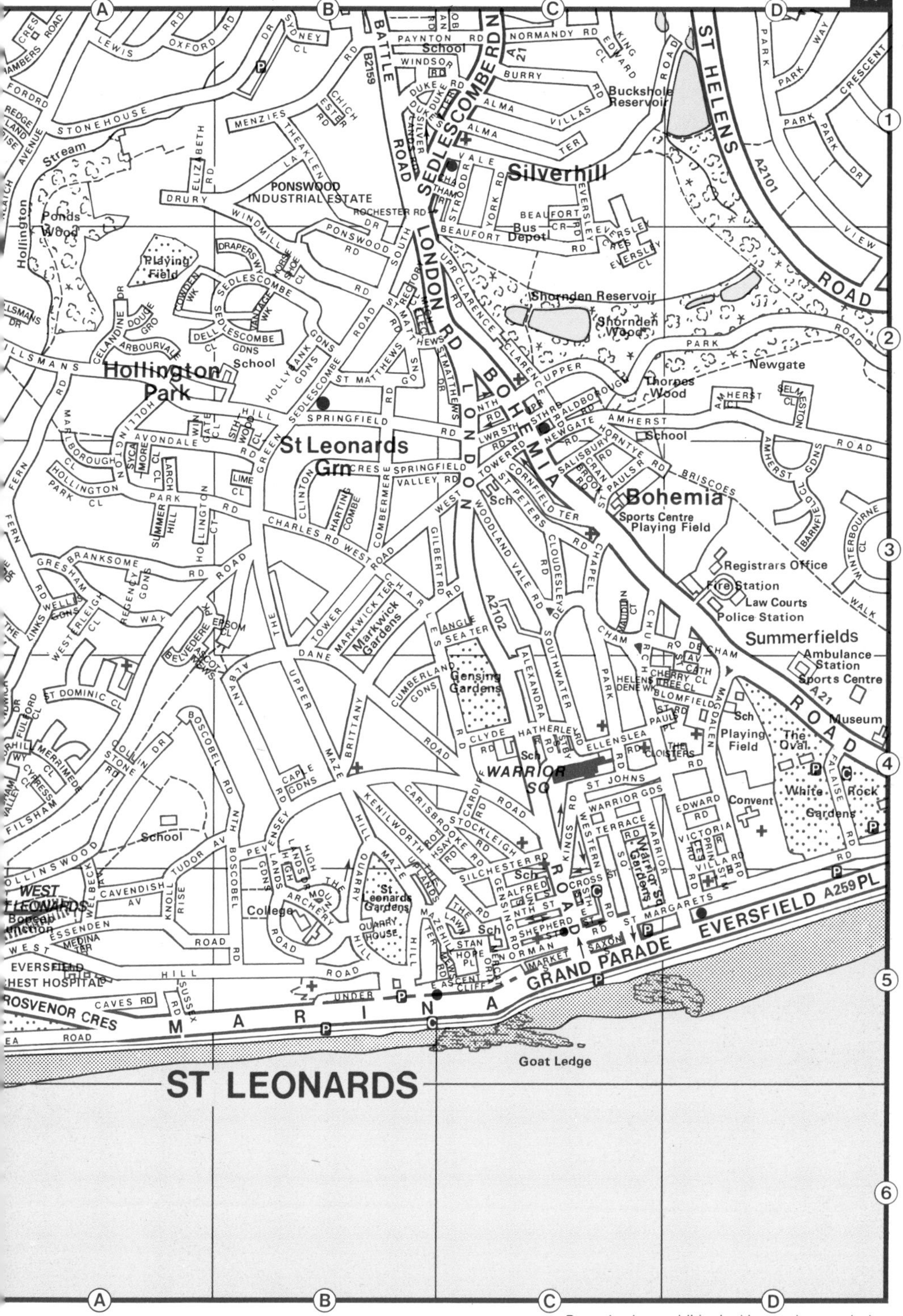
A
B
C
D
1
2
3
4
5
6
ST LEONARDS
Hollington Park
St Leonards Grn
Silverhill
Bohemia
Summerfields
Newgate
WEST ST LEONARDS
PONSWOOD INDUSTRIAL ESTATE
Ponds Wood
Playing Field
School
Stream
Buckshole Reservoir
Shornden Reservoir
Shornden Wood
Thorpes Wood
Bus Depot
Sports Centre Playing Field
Registrars Office
Fire Station
Law Courts
Police Station
Ambulance Station
Sports Centre
Museum
The Oval
White Rock Gardens
Convent
Playing Field
Gensing Gardens
Markwick Gardens
St Leonards Gardens
Quarry House
College
Warrior Sq Gardens
WARRIOR SQ
Goat Ledge
Bopeep Junction
EVERSFIELD CHEST HOSPITAL
BATTLE ROAD
B2159
SEDLESCOMBE RD N
LONDON RD
BOHEMIA ROAD
A21
A2102
A2101
ST HELENS ROAD
GRAND PARADE
EVERSFIELD PL
A259
MARINA
GROSVENOR CRES
STONEHOUSE
HOLLINGTON AVENUE
SPRINGFIELD RD
CHARLES RD WEST
WEST HILL RD
SEDLESCOMBE RD S
UPPER PARK RD
AMHERST RD
BRISCOES WALK
CORNFIELD TER
WOODLAND VALE RD
SOUTHWATER RD
KINGS RD
NORMAN RD
UPPER MAZE HILL
PEVENSEY RD
BOSCOBEL RD
FILSHAM
ST JOHNS RD
UPPER CLARENCE RD
ALMA VILLAS
NORMANDY RD
PAYNTON RD
MENZIES RD
DRURY
WINDMILL DR
PONSWOOD RD
ST MATTHEWS RD
CHARLES RD
CUMBERLAND RD
DANE RD
CARISBROOKE RD
SILCHESTER RD
ST MARGARETS RD
CAVES RD
SUSSEX RD
UNDER CLIFF
EAST ASCENT

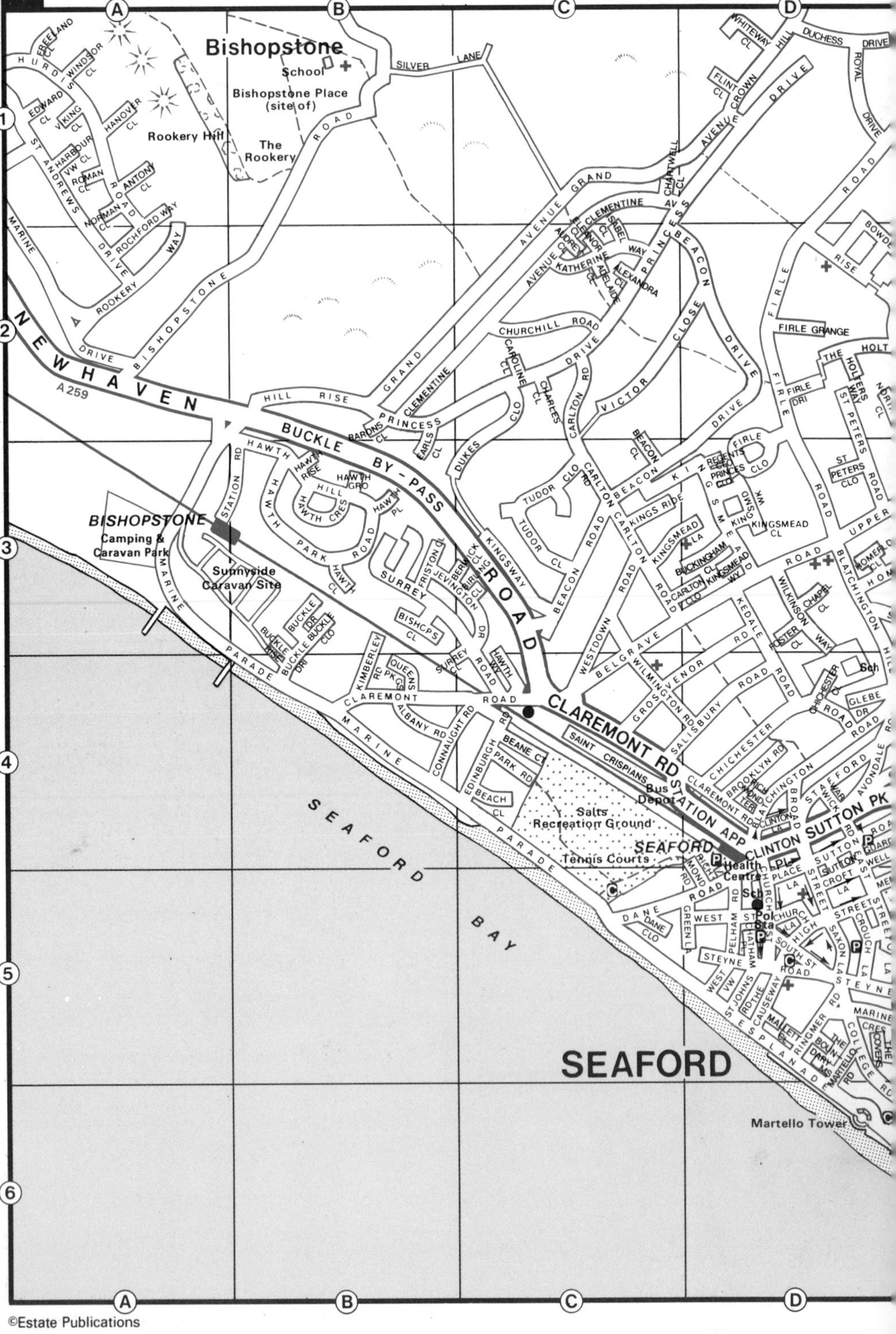
A
B
C
D
1
2
3
4
5
6
Bishopstone
School
Bishopstone Place
(site of)
Rookery Hill
The
Rookery
SILVER LANE
ROAD
FREELAND CL
HURDIS
WINDSOR CL
EDWARD CL
VIKING CL
HANOVER CL
ST ANDREWS
HARBOUR VW
ROMAN CL
ANTONY CL
NORMAN CL
ROCHFORD WAY
DRIVE
ROOKERY
MARINE
BISHOPSTONE
NEWHAVEN
A 259
HILL RISE
GRAND
CLEMENTINE
PRINCESS
BARONS CL
EARLS CL
DUKES
CAROLINE CL
CHARLES
CARLTON RD
VICTOR
CLOSE
DRIVE
BEACON
CHURCHILL ROAD
AVENUE
GRAND
CLEMENTINE AV
CHARTWELL CL
CROWN
AVENUE
WHITEWAY CL
FLINT CL
HILL
DUCHESS DRIVE
ROYAL
DRIVE
ROAD
AUDREY CL
ELEANOR CL
ISABEL CL
KATHERINE
ADELAIDE
ALEXANDRA
WAY
BOWDEN
RISE
FIRLE
FIRLE GRANGE
THE HOLT
HOLTERS WAY
FIRLE DRI
ST PETERS
ST PETERS CLO
FIRLE CLO
REGENTS CLO
PRINCES CLO
KINGS MEAD
KINGSMEAD CL
KINGSMEAD WK
KINGS RIDE
KINGSMEAD LA
BUCKINGHAM CL
KINGSMEAD WY
CARLTON CLO
UPPER
ROAD
BLATCHINGTON
HOMEFIELD
WILKINSON WAY
CHAPEL CL
FOSTER CL
TUDOR CLO
TUDOR CL
BEACON CL
CARLTON RD
KINGSWAY
BUCKLE BY-PASS
ROAD
HAWTH
HAWTH RISE
HAWTH GRO
HAWTH HILL
HAWTH CRES
HAWTH PL
HAWTH PARK ROAD
HAWTH CL
STATION RD
BISHOPSTONE
Camping &
Caravan Park
Sunnyside
Caravan Site
SURREY
FRISTON CL
JEVINGTON
BERWICK CL
BIRLING CL
BISHOPS CL
SURREY CL
HAWTH WY
HAWTH ROAD
BUCKLE DR
BUCKLE CLO
BUCKLE RISE
BUCKLE DRI
MARINE
PARADE
KIMBERLEY RD
QUEENS PK
CLAREMONT ROAD
ALBANY RD
CONNAUGHT RD
EDINBURGH PARK RD
BEANE CL
BEACH CL
CLAREMONT RD
SAINT CRISPIANS
STATION APP
Bus Depot
Salts
Recreation Ground
Tennis Courts
SEAFORD
Health Centre
WESTDOWN
BELGRAVE
WILMINGTON RD
GROSVENOR
SALISBURY ROAD
KEDALE RD
CHICHESTER
CHICHESTER CL
CLAREMONT RD
BROOKLYN RD
RICHMOND TER
BLATCHINGTON
CLINTON LA
CLINTON PL
SUTTON PK
STAFFORD WAY
WARWICK
AVONDALE
GLEBE DR
ROAD
Sch
BROAD
SUTTON RD
SUTTON CROFT LA
PLACE
STREET
WELL
EAST
CROUCH LA
SAXON LA
STEYNE
RICHMOND ROAD
DANE RD
DANE CLO
GREEN LA
WEST
PELHAM RD
CHURCH ST
CHURCH LA
Pol Sta
HATHAM
HIGH
SOUTH ST
ROAD
STEYNE
WEST VW
ST JOHNS
ROTHE
CAUSEWAY
MALLETT CL
RINGMER RD
BOUNDARY
MARTELLO
THE COVERS
MARINE CRES
COLLEGE
ESPLANADE
SEAFORD
SEAFORD
BAY
Martello Tower

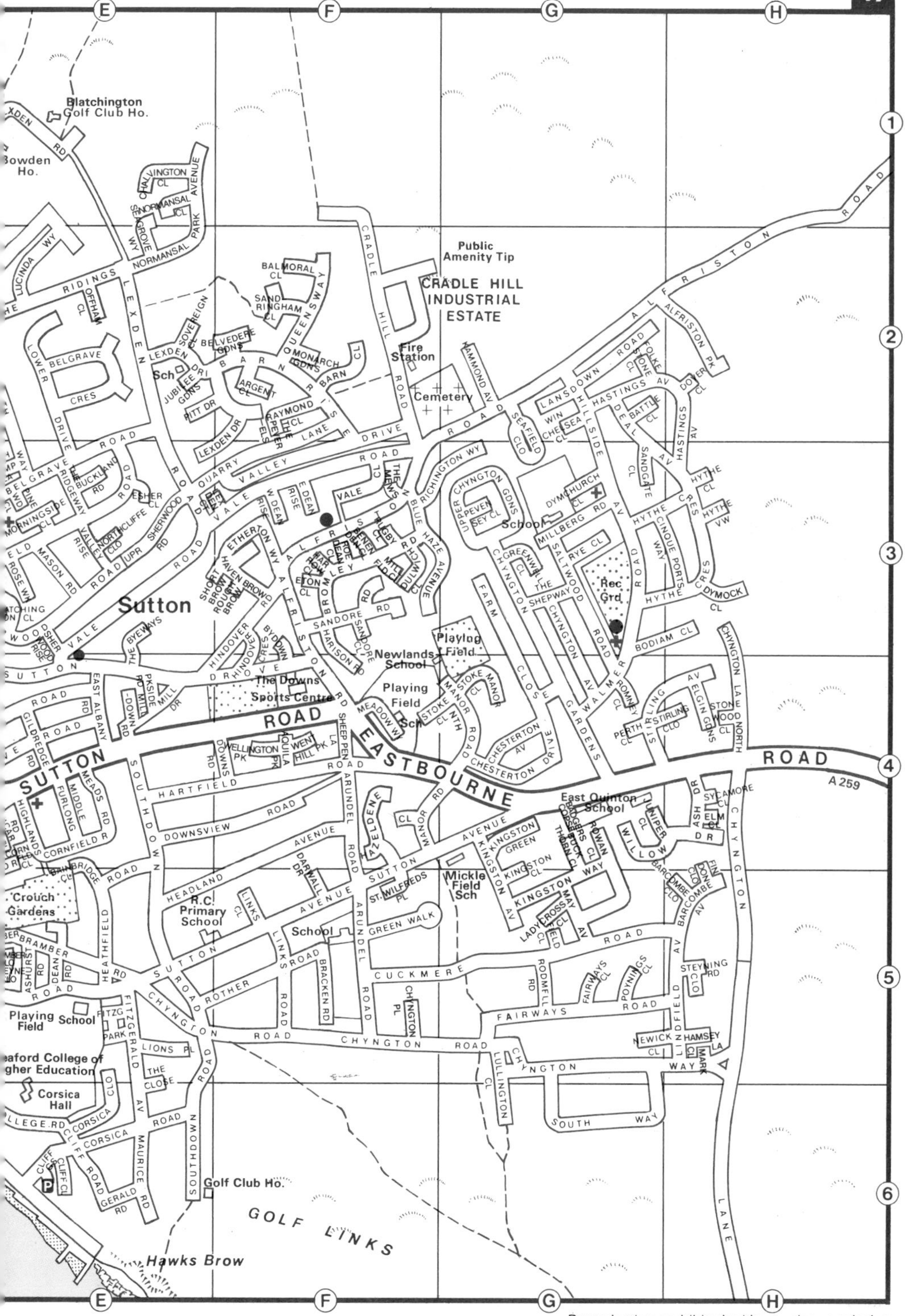
Blatchington Golf Club Ho.
Bowden Ho.
Public Amenity Tip
CRADLE HILL INDUSTRIAL ESTATE
Fire Station
Cemetery
ALFRISTON ROAD
Sutton
School
Rec Grd
Playing Field
Newlands School
The Downs Sports Centre
Playing Field
SUTTON ROAD
EASTBOURNE ROAD
ROAD
A 259
East Quinton School
Mickle Field Sch
R.C. Primary School
School
Crouch Gardens
Playing Field
School
Seaford College of Higher Education
Corsica Hall
Golf Club Ho.
GOLF LINKS
Hawks Brow
E
F
G
H
1
2
3
4
5
6

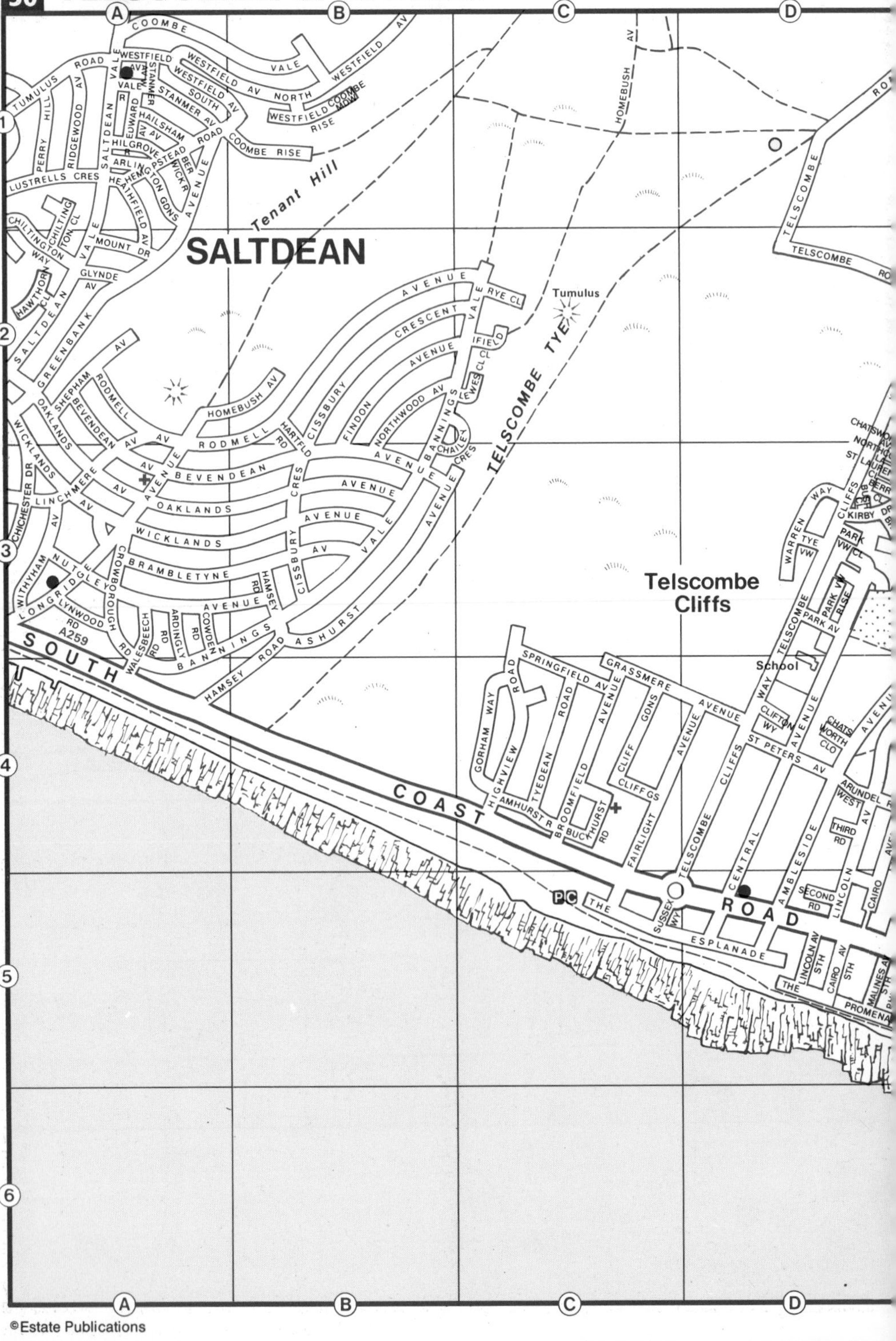
A
B
C
D
1
2
3
4
5
6
SALTDEAN
Telscombe Cliffs
Tenant Hill
Tumulus
TELSCOMBE TYE
School
COOMBE ROAD
WESTFIELD AV
WESTFIELD VALE
WESTFIELD AV NORTH
WESTFIELD RISE
COOMBE MDW
COOMBE RISE
SOUTH
STANMER AV
HAILSHAM AV
HILGROVE
ARLINGTON GDNS
WICKHURST
SALTDEAN VALE
TUMULUS
PERRY HILL
RIDGEWOOD AV
LUSTRELLS CRES
HEATHFIELD AV
MOUNT DR
CHILTINGTON WAY
CHILTINGTON CL
GLYNDE AV
HAWTHORN CL
SALTDEAN
GREENBANK
SHEPHAM AV
RODMELL AV
BEVENDEAN AV
HOMEBUSH AV
OAKLANDS
WICKLANDS
CHICHESTER DR
LINCHMERE AV
WITHYHAM AV
NUTGLEY
LONGRIDGE
LYNWOOD RD
CROWBOROUGH RD
A259
SOUTH COAST ROAD
BEVENDEAN AVENUE
OAKLANDS AVENUE
WICKLANDS
BRAMBLETYNE AVENUE
WALESBEECH RD
ARDINGLY RD
COWDEN RD
HAMSEY RD
BANNINGS VALE
ASHURST ROAD
HAMSEY ROAD
HARTFIELD RD
CISSBURY CRES
CISSBURY AV
FINDON AVENUE
NORTHWOOD AV
CRESCENT
AVENUE
RYE CL
LEWES CL
CHAILEY CRES
HOMEBUSH AV
TELSCOMBE ROAD
TELSCOMBE
GORHAM WAY
HIGHVIEW ROAD
SPRINGFIELD AV
TYEDEAN ROAD
BROOMFIELD AVENUE
AMHURST RD
BUCKHURST RD
GRASSMERE AVENUE
CLIFF GDNS
CLIFF GS
FAIRLIGHT AVENUE
TELSCOMBE CLIFFS WAY
CENTRAL AVENUE
CLIFTON WY
ST PETERS AV
AMBLESIDE AVENUE
SUSSEX WY
THE ESPLANADE
PC
WARREN WAY
TYE VW
PARK VW CL
PARK VW RISE
PARK AV
CHATSWORTH CLO
ARUNDEL RD WEST
THIRD AV
SECOND RD
LINCOLN AV
LINCOLN AV STH
CAIRO AV STH
CAIRO AV
MALINES AV STH
THE PROMENADE
KIRBY DR
CHATSWORTH AV
NORTHCOTE AV
ST LAURENCE AV
BERRY CL
CLIFFS

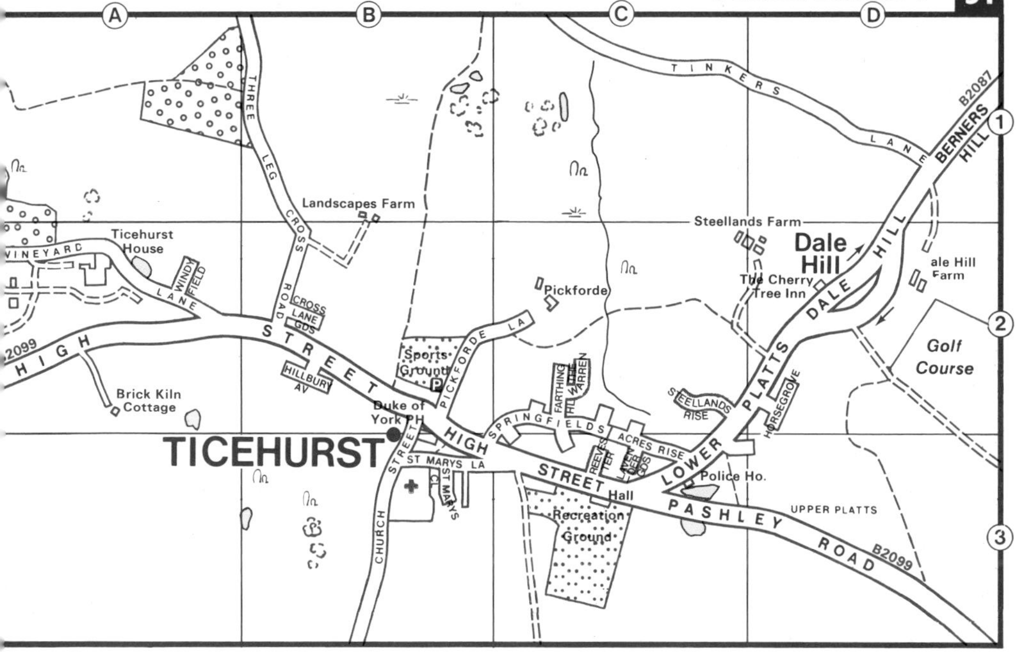
A
B
C
D
1
2
3
THREE LEG CROSS ROAD
Landscapes Farm
TINKERS LANE
B2087
BERNERS HILL
Steellands Farm
Dale Hill
The Cherry Tree Inn
DALE HILL
ale Hill Farm
Golf Course
Ticehurst House
VINEYARD
WINDY FIELD
LANE
CROSS LANE GDS
Pickforde
PICKFORDE LA
B2099
HIGH STREET
HILLBURY AV
Sports Ground
Brick Kiln Cottage
Duke of York PH
TICEHURST
CHURCH STREET
ST MARYS LA
ST MARYS CL
SPRINGFIELDS
FARTHING HILL
THE WARREN
ACRES RISE
REEVES TER
STEELLANDS RISE
LOWER PLATTS
HORSEGROVE
Police Ho.
Hall
Recreation Ground
PASHLEY ROAD
UPPER PLATTS
B2099

WESTFIELD

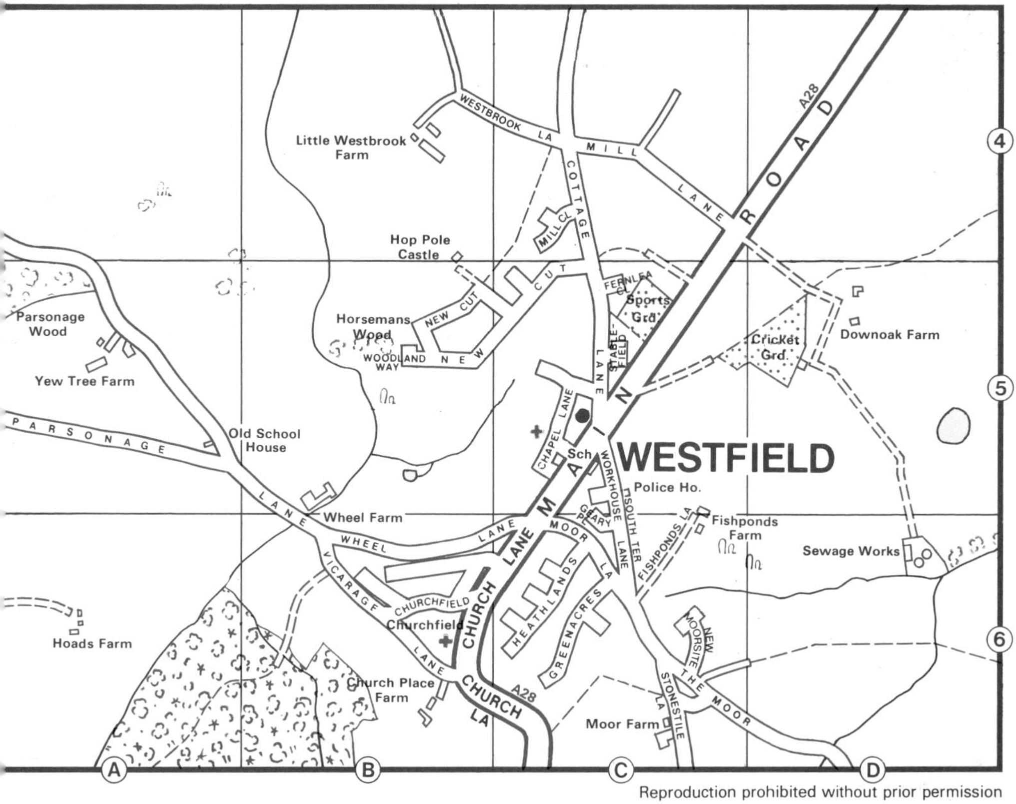
A
B
C
D
4
5
6
WESTBROOK LA
MILL LANE
Little Westbrook Farm
COTTAGE LANE
A28
ROAD
MILL CL
Hop Pole Castle
CUT
NEW CUT
FERNLEA CL
Sports Grd
Horsemans Wood
WOODLAND WAY
NEW
STABLE FIELD
Cricket Grd
Downoak Farm
Parsonage Wood
Yew Tree Farm
PARSONAGE LANE
Old School House
CHAPEL LANE
Sch
MAIN
WESTFIELD
WORKHOUSE LANE
Police Ho.
SOUTH TER
GEARY PL
Wheel Farm
WHEEL LANE
MOOR LA
FISHPONDS LA
Fishponds Farm
Sewage Works
VICARAGE LANE
CHURCHFIELD
Churchfield
CHURCH LANE
HEATHLANDS
GREENACRES
NEW MOORSITE
Hoads Farm
Church Place Farm
CHURCH LA
A28
STONESTILE LA
THE MOOR
Moor Farm

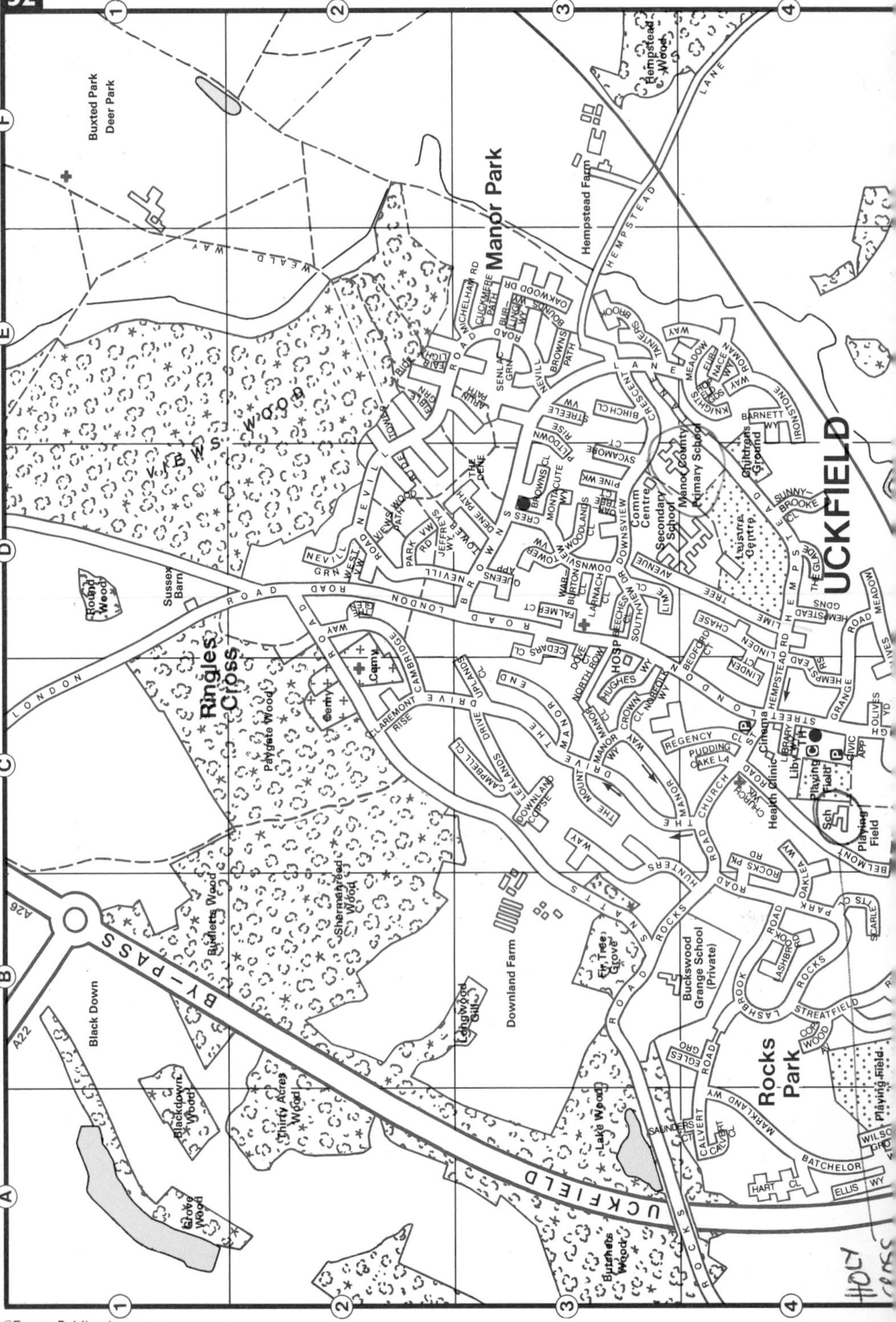
UCKFIELD
Manor Park
Ringles Cross
Rocks Park
Buxted Park Deer Park
VIEWS WOOD
WEALD WAY
Hempstead Farm
Hempstead Wood
HEMPSTEAD LANE
LONDON ROAD
Round Wood
Sussex Barn
Paygate Wood
Budletts Wood
Black Down
Blackdown Wood
Grove Wood
Thirty Acres Wood
Longwood Gill
Downland Farm
Fir Tree Grove
Lake Wood
Butchers Wood
BY-PASS
UCKFIELD
A22
A26
Secondary School
Manor County Primary School
Comm Centre
Leisure Centre
Childrens Ground
Buckswood Grange School (Private)
Health Clinic
Cinema
Library
Playing Field
Cemy

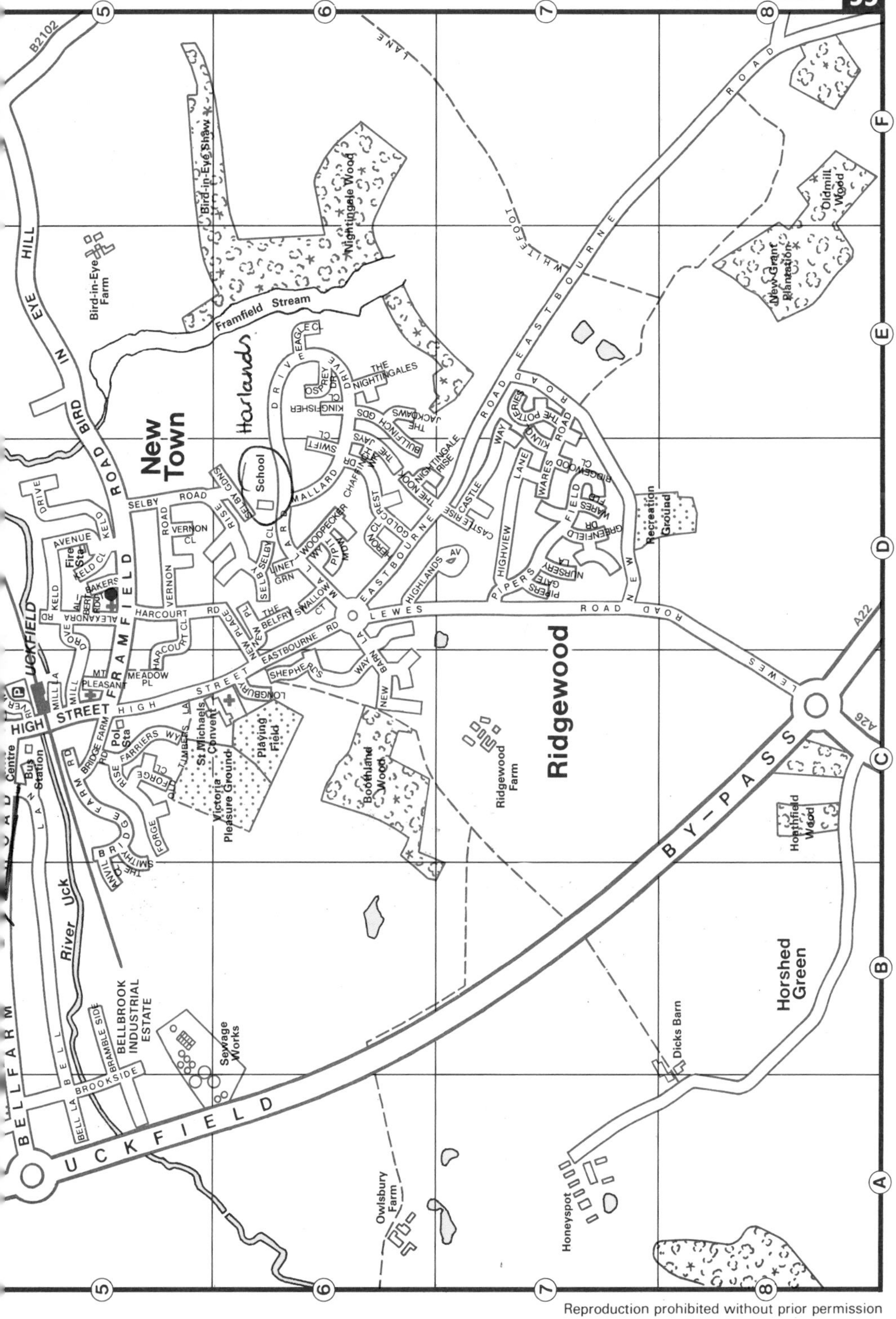

New Town

Harlands

Bird-in-Eye Shaw

Nightingale Wood

Bird-in-Eye Farm

Framfield Stream

Old-Grant Plantation

Oldmill Wood

THE NIGHTINGALES

School

Ridgewood

Recreation Ground

Ridgewood Farm

Boothland Wood

Victoria Pleasure Ground

Playing Field

St Michaels Convent

Pol Sta

Fire Sta

Bus Station

Centre

River Uck

Bellbrook Industrial Estate

Sewage Works

BELLFARM

UCKFIELD

Owlsbury Farm

Dicks Barn

Honeyspot

Horshed Green

Hophfield Wood

BY-PASS

HIGH STREET

FRAMFIELD

EYE HILL

BIRD IN EYE HILL

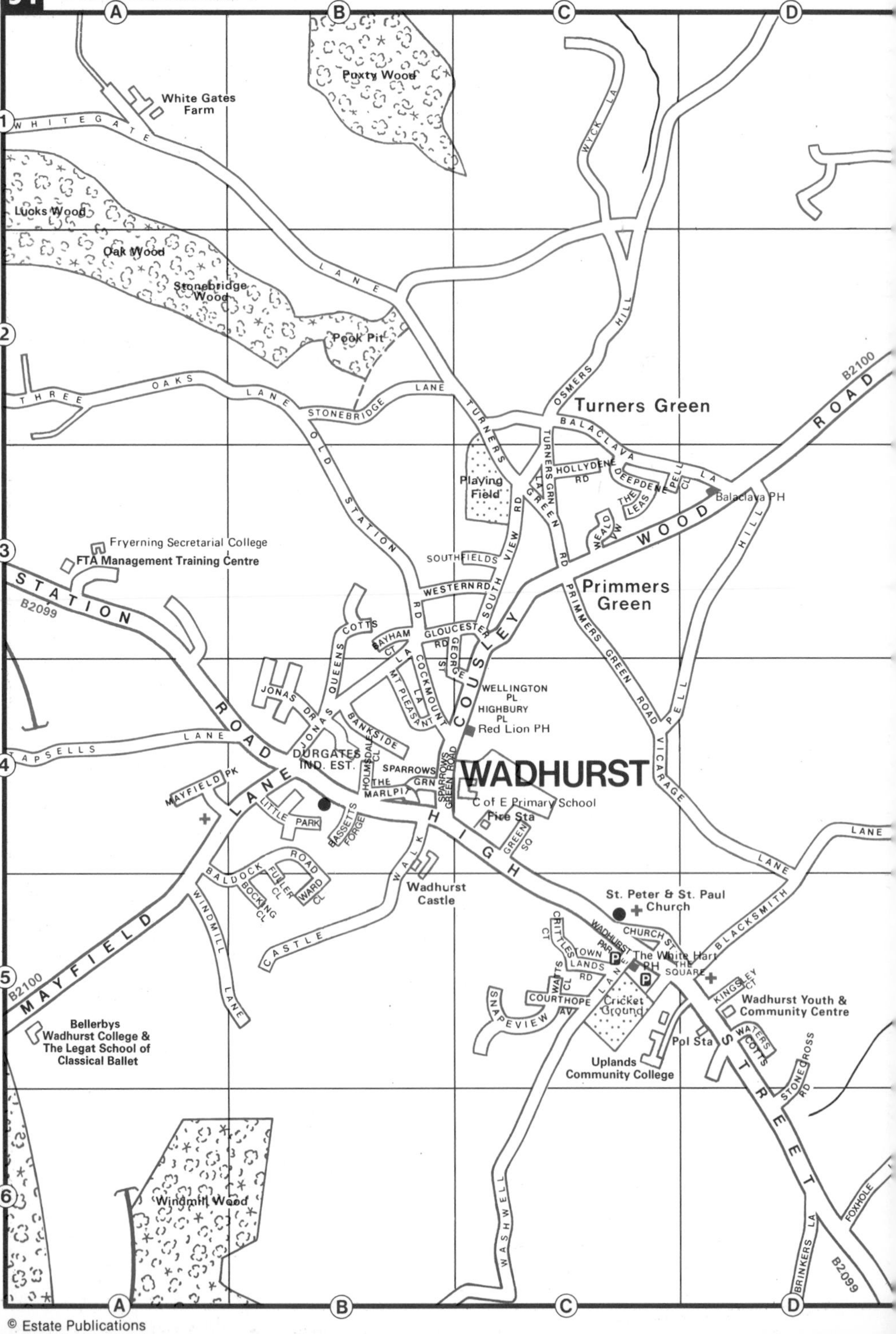
A
B
C
D
1
2
3
4
5
6
White Gates Farm
Puxty Wood
WHITEGATE LANE
Luoks Wood
Oak Wood
Stonebridge Wood
Pook Pit
WYCK LA
HILL
OSMERS
THREE OAKS LANE
STONEBRIDGE LANE
Turners Green
BALACLAVA LA
B2100
ROAD
TURNERS
TURNERS GRN
OLD STATION
Playing Field
RD
HOLLYDENE RD
DEEPDENE
THE LEAS
PELL CL
Balaclava PH
GREEN LA
RD
WEALD VW
WOOD
SOUTH VIEW
SOUTHFIELDS
Fryerning Secretarial College
FTA Management Training Centre
STATION
B2099
WESTERN RD
Primmers Green
HILL
COUSLEY
PRIMMERS GREEN ROAD
RD
GLOUCESTER RD
GEORGE ST
COTTS
BAYHAM CT
LA
QUEENS
JONAS
DR
COCKMOUNT LA
MT PLEASANT
WELLINGTON PL
HIGHBURY PL
Red Lion PH
PELL
BANKSIDE
JONAS LA
ROAD
TAPSELLS LANE
DURGATES IND. EST.
HOLMSDALE CL
SPARROWS
SPARROWS GRN
SPARROWS GREEN ROAD
WADHURST
VICARAGE
THE MARLPIT
C of E Primary School
Fire Sta
GREEN SQ
MAYFIELD PK
LANE
LITTLE PARK
BASSETTS FORGE
HIGH
WALK
Wadhurst Castle
ROAD
BALDOCK
FULLER CL
WARD CL
BOCKING CL
WINDMILL LANE
MAYFIELD
B2100
CASTLE
LANE
LANE
BLACKSMITH
St. Peter & St. Paul Church
CHURCH ST
WADHURST PAR.
CRITTLES CT
TOWN LANDS RD
The White Hart PH
THE SQUARE
KINGSLEY CT
Wadhurst Youth & Community Centre
WATTS CL
LANE
SNAPE VIEW
COURTHOPE AV
Cricket Ground
Pol Sta
WATERS COTTS
STONECROSS RD
Bellerbys Wadhurst College & The Legat School of Classical Ballet
Uplands Community College
STREET
Windmill Wood
WASHWELL
BRINKERS LA
FOXHOLE
B2099

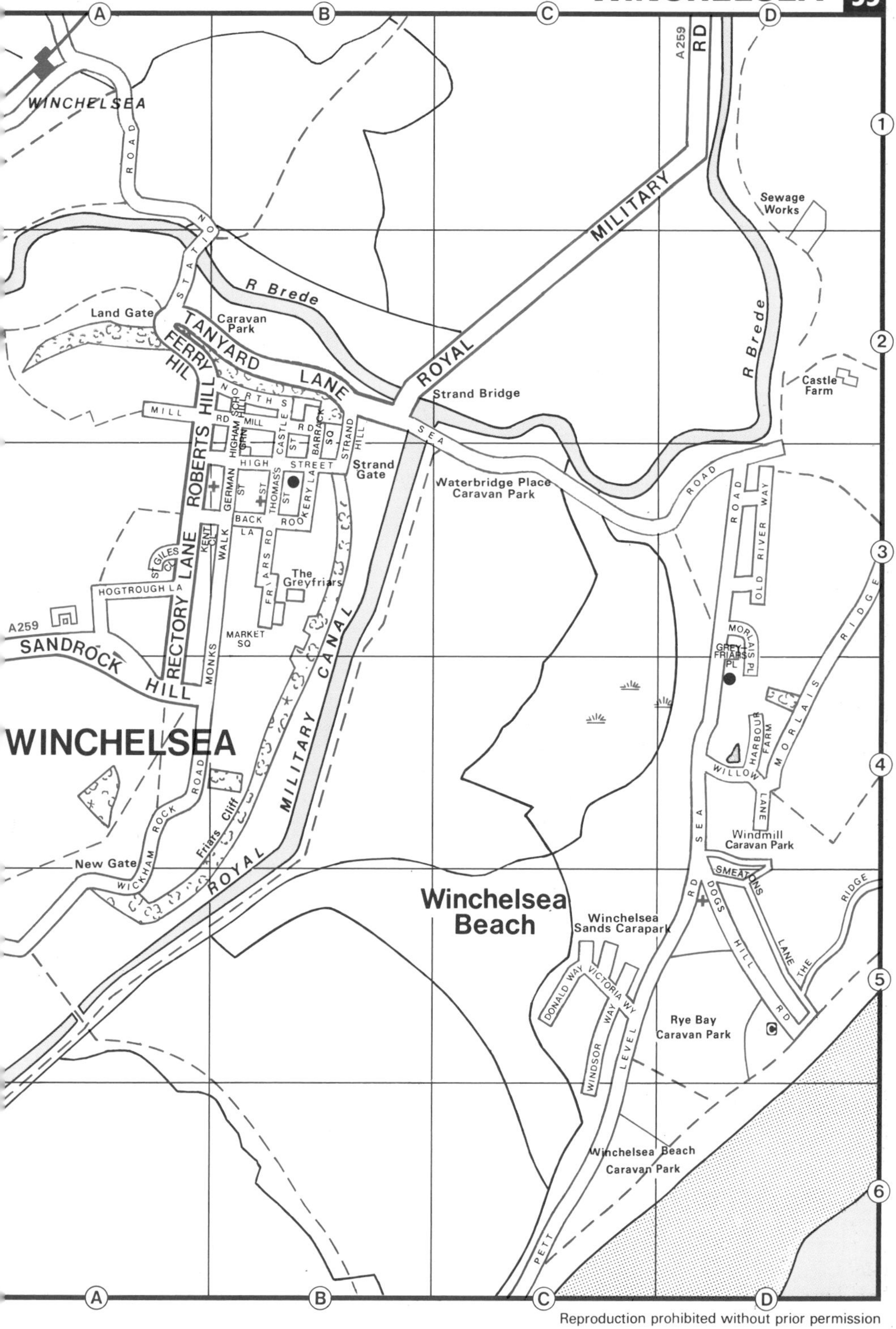
A
B
C
D
1
2
3
4
5
6
WINCHELSEA
A259
RD
ROAD
STATION
MILITARY
ROYAL
R Brede
Sewage Works
Land Gate
Caravan Park
TANYARD
LANE
FERRY HILL
Castle Farm
Strand Bridge
MILL RD
NORTH ST
ROBERTS HILL
HIGHAM GRN
CASTLE ST
BARRACK SQ
STRAND HILL
HIGH STREET
Strand Gate
SEA ROAD
Waterbridge Place Caravan Park
GERMAN ST
ST THOMAS'S ST
ROOKERY LA
BACK LA
KENT CL
WALK
ST GILES CL
FRIARS RD
The Greyfriars
OLD RIVER WAY
HOGTROUGH LA
A259
SANDROCK HILL
RECTORY LANE
MONKS
MARKET SQ
CANAL
MORLAIS PL
GREY-FRIARS PL
RIDGE
MORLAIS
HARBOUR FARM
WINCHELSEA
ROAD
WILLOW LANE
Friars Cliff
New Gate
WICKHAM ROCK
Windmill Caravan Park
SMEATONS
Winchelsea Beach
Winchelsea Sands Carapark
DOGS HILL RD
THE RIDGE
LANE
DONALD WAY
VICTORIA WY
WAY
WINDSOR
LEVEL
Rye Bay Caravan Park
C
Winchelsea Beach Caravan Park
PETT

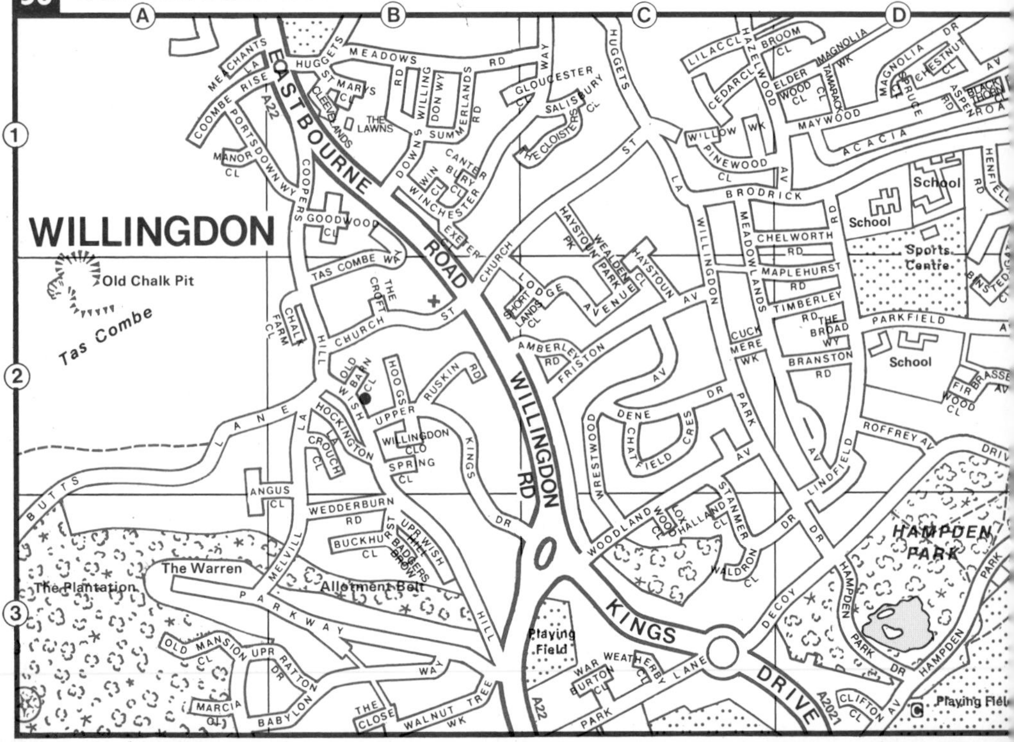

A - Z INDEX TO STREETS
With Postcodes

57

BUXTED

CAMBER

CROWBOROUGH

Whincroft Pk. TN6 18 B6
Whitehill Clo. TN6 18 D5
Whitehill Rd. TN6 18 D5
Wilderness Park. TN6 18 C4
Windsor Pl. TN6 19 G6
Windsor Rd. TN6 19 G6
Winscote Clo. TN6 18 C5
Wolfe Clo. TN6 19 E6
Woodside. TN6 18 C4

DITCHLING

Barnfield Gdns. BN6 35 C6
Beacon Hurst. BN6 35 A5
Beacon Rd. BN6 35 B6
Boddingtons La. BN6 35 B5
Church La. BN6 35 B5
Church Mead. BN6 35 A5
Clayton Rd. BN6 35 A6
Damian Way. BN6 35 A4
Dumbrells. BN6 35 B4
Dumbrells Ct. BN6 35 B4
Dumbrells Ct Rd. BN6 35 B4
East End La. BN6 35 B5
East Gdns. BN6 35 B5
Farm La. BN6 35 C5
Fieldway. BN6 35 C5
High St. BN6 35 B5
Keymer Rd. BN6 35 A5
Lewes Rd. BN6 35 C5
Lodge Hill La. BN6 35 B4
Long Park Cnr. BN6 35 B5
Mulberry Clo. BN6 35 C5
Neville Cotts. BN6 35 B6
Orchard La. BN6 35 B4
Shirleys. BN6 35 D6
Silverdale. BN6 35 A5
South St. BN6 35 B5
Spatham La. BN6 35 D6
The Crescent. BN6 35 A5
The Dymocks. BN6 35 C5
West St. BN6 35 B5

EASTBOURNE

Abbey Rd. BN20 20 A1
Addingham Rd. BN22 21 H1
Albert St. BN21 20 B1
Albion Rd. BN22 21 G1
Alfriston Clo. BN20 20 C3
Arlington Rd. BN21 21 E2
Arundel Rd. BN21 21 E2
Ascham Pl. BN20 20 D4
Ascot Clo. BN20 21 E5
Ashburnham Gdns. BN21 20 D1
Ashburnham Rd. BN21 20 D1
Ashford Rd. BN21 21 F2
Ashford Sq. BN21 21 F2
Avenue La. BN21 21 F2
Avondale Rd. BN22 21 G1
Bakers Rd. BN21 20 D2
Bakewell Rd. BN21 20 C1
Barcombe Clo. BN20 20 B2
Barcombe Walk. BN20 20 B2
Barden Rd. BN22 21 H1
Baslow Rd. BN20 20 C6
Bath Rd. BN21 21 E3
Bay Pond Rd. BN21 20 D2
Bayham Rd. BN22 21 H2
Beachy Head Rd. BN20 20 B6
Beamsley Rd. BN22 21 H1
Beatrice La. BN21 21 E2
Bedford GroS. BN21 21 E1
Bedford Well Rd. BN21 21 F1
Beechwood Cres. BN20 20 D2
Beechy Av. BN20 20 B1
Beechy Gdns. BN20 20 B1
Belmore Rd. BN22 21 G1
Beltring Rd. BN22 21 G1
Beltring Ter. BN22 21 G1
Beristede Clo. BN20 21 E4
Bernards La. BN21 21 E2
Birling St. BN21 20 C1
Blackwater Rd. BN20 21 E4
Bodmin Clo. BN20 20 B2
Bolsover Rd. BN20 21 E5
Bolton Rd. BN21 21 F3
Borough La. BN20 20 D2
Bourne St. BN21 21 G2
Bradford St. BN21 20 C2

Brightland Rd. BN20 20 C2
Brodie Pl. BN21 20 D2
Broomfield St. BN21 20 B2
Burfield Rd. BN22 21 G2
Burlington Pl. BN21 21 F3
Burlington Rd. BN21 21 G3
Burrowdown. BN20 20 A1
Buxton Rd. BN20 20 D5
Calverley Rd. BN21 21 F3
Cambridge Rd. BN22 21 H2
Camden Rd. BN21 21 E3
Carew Rd. BN21 21 E1
Carlisle Rd. BN20 20 C5
Cavendish Av. BN22 21 G2
Cavendish Pl. BN21 21 G2
Ceylon Pl. BN21 21 G2
Chamberlain Rd. BN21 20 C1
Charleston Rd. BN21 20 C1
Chatsworth Gdns. BN20 21 E5
Chawbrook Rd. BN22 21 G2
Cherry Garden Rd. BN20 20 B2
Chesterfield Gdns. BN20 21 E5
Chesterfield Rd. BN20 20 D5
Chiswick Pl. BN21 21 F3
Church La. BN21 20 D2
Church St. BN21 20 C2
Churchill Clo. BN20 20 D2
Clarence Rd. BN22 21 G1
Cliff Rd. BN20 20 D6
College Grn. BN21 20 D1
College Rd. BN21 21 F3
Collington Clo. BN21 21 E5
Colonnade Gdns. BN21 21 G3
Colt Stocks Rd. BN20 20 D5
Commercial Rd. BN21 21 F2
Compton Dri. BN20 20 D2
Compton Place Rd. BN20 20 D2
Compton St. BN21 21 F4
Connaught Rd. BN21 21 F3
Coombe La. BN20 20 C6
Coombe Rd. BN20 20 B1
Cornfield La. BN21 21 F3
Cornfield Rd. BN21 21 F3
Cornfield Ter. BN21 21 F3
Cranborne Av. BN20 20 B5
Crown St. BN21 20 D2
Crunden Rd. BN21 20 B1
Dacre Rd. BN21 20 B2
Dalton Rd. BN20 20 D5
Darley Rd. BN20 20 C5
De Roos Rd. BN21 20 D1
De Walden Mews. BN20 20 D5
Den Hill. BN20 20 A1
Denton Rd. BN20 20 D5
Derwent Rd. BN20 20 D5
Devonshire Pl. BN21 21 F3
Dillingburgh Rd. BN20 20 B1
Dittons Rd. BN21 20 D2
Downside Clo. BN20 20 B2
Dudley Rd. BN22 21 G1
Dursley Rd. BN22 21 G2
East Dean Rd. BN20 20 A4
Edensor Rd. BN20 20 C6
Elms Av. BN21 21 G3
Elms Rd. BN21 21 G3
Enys Rd. BN21 21 E1
Eshton Rd. BN20 21 H1
Eton Mews. BN21 21 F2
Eversfield Rd. BN21 21 E1
Fairfield Rd. BN20 20 D5
Fairway Rd. BN20 20 C3
Firle Rd. BN22 21 G1
Fitzgerald Clo. BN20 21 E5
Foredown Clo. BN20 20 B3
Furness Rd. BN21 21 F3
Garden Mews. BN20 20 D5
Gaudick Clo. BN20 20 D5
Gaudick Rd. BN20 20 D4
Gilbert Rd. BN20 20 D5
Gildredge Rd. BN21 21 F3
Glebe Clo. BN20 20 B3
Glenmore Mews. BN21 21 F2
Gore Park Av. BN21 20 C1
Gore Park Rd. BN21 20 C1
Gorringe Rd. BN22 21 F1
Grand Parade. BN21 21 F4
Grange Rd. BN21 21 E4
Granville Rd. BN20 21 E4
Grassington Rd. BN20 21 E3
Green St. BN21 20 B1
Greenfield Rd. BN21 20 C2

Greys Rd. BN20 20 C2
Grove Rd. BN21 21 E3
Halton Rd. BN22 21 H1
Hanover Rd. BN22 21 H1
Hardwick Rd. BN21 21 F3
Hartfield La. BN21 21 F2
Hartfield Rd. BN21 21 E2
Hartington Pl. BN21 21 F3
Havelock Rd. BN21 21 G1
High St. BN21 20 D2
Hoad Rd. BN21 21 G1
Holbrook Clo. BN20 21 E5
Holywell Clo. BN20 20 D6
Holywell Rd. BN20 20 D6
Howard Sq. BN21 21 F4
Hurst La. BN21 20 D1
Hurst Rd. BN21 20 D1
Hyde Gdns. BN21 21 F3
Hyde Rd. BN21 21 E3
Hyde Tynings Clo. BN20 20 C5
Ivy La. BN21 21 E2
Ivy Ter. BN21 21 F3
Jephson Clo. BN20 21 E5
Jevington Gdns. BN21 21 F4
Junction Rd. BN21 21 F2
Kerrara Ter. BN21 21 G1
Kilda St. BN22 21 G1
King Edwards Par. BN20 21 E6
Kirk Way. BN20 20 A1
Laleham Clo. BN20 20 D1
Langney Rd. BN21 21 G3
Lascelles Ter. BN21 21 F4
Latimer Rd. BN22 21 H2
Lawns Av. BN20 20 D2
Le Brun Rd. BN21 21 E1
Leaf Hall Rd. BN22 21 G2
Leaf Rd. BN21 21 F2
Leslie St. BN22 21 G1
Letheren Pl. BN21 20 C2
Lewes Rd. BN21 21 E1
Lincoln Clo. BN20 20 B5
Lindsay Clo. BN20 20 B3
Link Rd. BN20 20 D4
Lion La. BN21 21 G3
Lismore Rd. BN21 21 F3
Longland Rd. BN20 20 B1
Longstone Rd. BN21 21 F2
Lordslaine Clo. BN20 20 C5
Love La. BN20 20 D2
Lower Rd. BN21 20 D1
Lushington La. BN21 21 F3
Lushington Rd. BN21 21 F3
Manifold Rd. BN21 21 G1
Manvers Rd. BN20 20 B2
Marine Par. BN21 21 G3
Marine Parade Rd. BN22 21 G2
Marine Rd. BN22 21 G2
Mark La. BN21 21 F3
Matlock Rd. BN20 20 D5
Mayfield Pl. BN22 21 F1
Meads Brow Clo. BN20 20 C6
Meads Rd. BN20 20 D5
Meads St. BN20 20 D6
Melbourne Rd. BN22 21 G2
Michel Gro. BN21 20 D2
Mill Gap Rd. BN21 21 E1
Mill Rd. BN21 20 D1
Milnthorpe Rd. BN20 20 D5
Milton Cres. BN21 20 C1
Milton Rd. BN21 20 C1
Moat Croft Rd. BN21 20 D2
Mona Rd. BN22 21 G1
Monceux Rd. BN21 20 C1
Motcombe La. BN21 20 C2
Motcombe Rd. BN21 20 C2
Mount Rd. BN20 21 E5
Mountney Rd. BN21 20 C1
Moy Av. BN21 21 G1
Naomi Clo. BN20 20 D4
Neville Rd. BN22 21 G1
New Pl. BN21 20 C2
New Rd. BN22 21 G2
New Upperton Rd. BN21 20 D2
North St. BN21 21 G3
Northiam Rd. BN20 20 B1
Ocklynge Av. BN21 20 C1
Ocklynge Rd. BN21 20 C1
Okehurst Rd. BN21 20 D1
Old Camp Rd. BN20 20 B3
Old Motcombe Mews. BN21 20 C2
Old Orchard Rd. BN21 21 E3

Old Wish Rd. BN21 21 E4
Osbourne Rd. BN20 20 B2
Oxford Rd. BN21 21 G1
Paradise Clo. BN20 20 C3
Paradise Dri. BN20 20 C4
Park Clo. BN20 20 D2
Parsonage Rd. BN21 20 C2
Pashley Rd. BN20 20 B3
Peppercombe Rd. BN20 20 B2
Pevensey Rd. BN21 21 G2
Prospect Gdns. BN21 20 D1
Queens Gdns. BN21 21 G3
Ratton Rd. BN21 20 D1
Ravenscroft. BN20 21 E5
Rectory Clo. BN20 20 C2
Redoubt Rd. BN22 21 H1
Regency Mews. BN21 21 F5
Richmond Pl. BN21 21 E2
Ridgelands Clo. BN20 20 B3
Roborough Clo. BN21 21 F1
Rochester Clo. BN20 20 B5
Rowsley Rd. BN20 20 C6
Royal Parade. BN22 21 H2
Rylstone Rd. BN21 21 F4
Saffrons Pk. BN20 21 E4
Saffrons Rd. BN21 21 E3
St Annes Rd. BN21 21 E1
St Aubyns Rd. BN22 21 H2
St Georges Rd. BN22 21 G1
St Gregorys Clo. BN20 20 D5
St James Rd. BN22 21 H1
St Johns Rd. BN20 20 D5
St Leonards Pl. BN20 20 C2
St Leonards Rd. BN21 21 F2
St Marys Rd. BN21 20 C1
St Vincents Pl. BN20 20 D4
Salehurst St. BN21 20 C2
Salisbury Rd. BN20 20 C5
Sancroft Rd. BN20 20 B2
Seaside. BN22 21 G2
Seaside Rd. BN21 21 G3
Selby Rd. BN21 20 D1
Selwyn Dri. BN21 20 D1
Selwyn Rd. BN21 20 D1
Sheen Rd. BN22 21 G2
Sheraton Clo. BN21 21 E3
Shortdean Pl. BN21 20 C1
Sidley Rd. BN22 21 H1
Silverdale Rd. BN20 21 E4
South Av. BN20 20 B1
South Cliff. BN20 21 E5
South Cliff Av. BN20 21 F5
South Lynn Dri. BN21 21 E1
South St. BN21 21 E3
Southfields Rd. BN21 21 E2
Spencer Rd. BN21 21 F3
Springfield Rd. BN22 21 G1
Stanley Rd. BN22 21 G1
Stansted Rd. BN21 21 G1
Star Rd. BN21 20 D2
Station St. BN21 21 F3
Staveley Rd. BN20 21 E5
Summerdown Clo. BN20 20 C3
Summerdown Rd. BN20 20 C2
Susans Rd. BN21 21 F2
Sutton Rd. BN21 21 F2
Sydney Rd. BN22 21 G2
Taddington Rd. BN22 21 H1
Terminus Rd. BN21 21 F3
The Avenue. BN21 21 E2
The Conifers. BN21 21 F1
The Dentons. BN20 20 D5
The Goffs. BN21 20 D2
The Greys. BN20 20 C2
The Quadrant. BN20 20 D1
The Sanctuary. BN20 20 A1
The Village. BN20 20 D5
Tideswell Rd. BN21 21 G2
Torfield Rd. BN21 21 E1
Trinity Pl. BN21 21 G3
Trinity Trees. BN21 21 F3
Upland Rd. BN20 20 B3
Upper Avenue. BN21 21 F2
Upper Carlisle Rd. BN20 20 C5
Upper Dukes Dri. BN20 20 C6
Upperton Gdns. BN21 21 E2
Upperton La. BN21 21 E2
Upperton Rd. BN21 20 D1
Upwick Rd. BN20 20 C2
Vicarage Dri. BN20 20 C2
Vicarage La. BN20 20 C2

Vicarage Rd. BN20 20 C2
Victoria Dri. BN20 20 B1
Victoria Gdns. BN20 20 B1
Victoria Rd. BN20 20 B1
Warren Clo. BN20 20 C5
Warren Hill. BN20 20 C5
Warrior Sq. BN21 21 H1
Waterworks Rd. BN22 21 G1
Watts La. BN21 20 D1
Wellcombe Cres. BN20 20 C6
Wellesley Rd. BN21 21 G2
Wells Clo. BN20 20 B5
West St. BN21 21 F3
West Ter. BN21 21 F3
Western Rd. BN22 21 G1
Wharf Rd. BN21 21 E2
Whitley Rd. BN22 21 F1
Willingdon Rd. BN21 20 D1
Willowfield Rd. BN22 21 G1
Willowfield Sq. BN22 21 G2
Wilmington Gdns. BN21 21 F4
Wilmington Sq. BN21 21 F4
Winchcombe Rd. BN22 21 G2
Wish Rd. BN21 21 F3
York Rd. BN21 21 E3

FAIRLIGHT

Battery Hill. TN35 22 B2
Blackthorne Way. TN35 22 E3
Bramble Way. TN35 22 F2
Briar Clo. TN35 22 F2
Broad Way. TN35 22 E2
Channel Way. TN35 22 E3
Cliff Way. TN35 22 F2
Clinton Way. TN35 22 F2
Coastguard La. TN35 22 B2
Commanders Walk. TN35 22 E2
Fairlight Gdns. TN35 22 E2
Fairlight Rd. TN35 22 A3
Farley Way. TN35 22 D3
Fyrs Way. TN35 22 D3
Gorsethorn Way. TN35 22 E3
Heather Way. TN35 22 E3
Hill Rd. TN35 22 E2
Knowle Av. TN35 22 E2
Knowle Rd. TN35 22 D2
Lower Waites La. TN35 22 E3
Meadow Way. TN35 22 C3
New Rd. TN35 22 C3
Peter James La. TN35 22 B1
Pett Level Rd. TN35 22 F2
Primrose Hill. TN35 22 F2
Rockmead Rd. TN35 22 F2
Rosemary La. TN35 22 E2
Sea Rd. TN35 22 E3
Shepherds Way. TN35 22 E3
Smugglers Way. TN35 22 E3
Stream La. TN35 22 F1
The Avenue. TN35 22 E2
The Close. TN35 22 B3
Waites La. TN35 22 F2
Warren Rd. TN35 22 B3
Woodland Way. TN35 22 D2

FOREST ROW

Allens Clo. RH19 23 B1
Ashdown Clo. RH19 23 D5
Ashdown Rd. RH18 23 C5
Balfour Gdns. RH18 23 C6
Beeches. RH19 23 A1
Blacklands Cres. RH18 23 D5
Blenheim Field. RH18 23 C4
Box La. RH19 23 B1
Broadstone. RH18 23 D5
Cage Ridge. RH18 23 B5
Cansiron La. RH19 23 C1
Card Hill. RH18 23 C6
Chapel La. RH19 23 B1
Chapel La RH18 23 D5
Chequer Grange. RH18 23 C6
Colchester Vale. RH18 23 B5
Dale Rd. RH18 23 C5
Dirty La. RH18 23 B1
Freshfield Bank. RH18 23 B5
Gilhams La. RH18 23 C6
Hammerwood Rd. RH19 23 B1
Hartfield Rd. RH18 23 C4

HAILSHAM

HASTINGS

Hill St. TN34 26 D5
Hillside Rd. TN34 26 A1
Hillyglen Clo. TN34 26 A5
Hoads Wood Rd. TN34 26 C2
Hole Farm Clo. TN34 26 A3
Holmesdale Gdns. TN34 26 A5
Hopgarden Clo. TN34 26 A4
Hughenden Pl. TN34 26 C3
Hughenden Rd. TN34 26 C3
Hurrell Rd. TN34 26 D3
Kenwood Clo. TN34 26 D1
Keppel Rd. TN34 26 B2
Kildare Clo. TN34 26 D1
Lancing Clo. TN34 26 A2
Langham Clo. TN34 26 B1
Langham Rd. TN34 26 B1
Laton Rd. TN34 26 B3
Linley Clo. TN34 26 C2
Linley Dri. TN34 26 C2
Linton Cres. TN34 26 A5
Linton Rd. TN34 26 A4
Lodge Rd. TN35 27 F3
London Rd. TN37 27 F1
Lower Park Rd. TN34 26 A4
Lyndhurst Av. TN34 26 C1
Malvern Way. TN34 26 D2
Manhatten Gdns. TN35 27 F1
Mann St. TN34 26 B5
Manor Rd. TN34 26 C4
Manston Way. TN34 26 B3
Marianne Pk. TN35 27 E3
Marine Par. TN34 26 C5
Mayne Way. TN34 26 D1
Mendip Gdns. TN34 27 E1
Middle Rd. TN35 27 E1
Middle St. TN34 26 B5
Mill Clo. TN35 27 G1
Mill La. TN35 27 G1
Milward Cres. TN34 26 C5
Milward Rd. TN34 26 C5
Moscow Rd. TN35 27 F2
Mount Pleasant Cres. TN34 26 C3
Mount Pleasant Rd. TN34 26 C3
Mount Rd. TN35 27 E2
Nelson Rd. TN34 26 C4
New Rd. TN35 27 F3
Newmans Way. TN35 27 G1
Nook Clo. TN35 27 F1
North Ter. TN34 27 E3
Oakfield Rd. TN35 27 E2
Oakwood Clo. TN34 26 B1
Ochiltree Rd. TN34 26 C1
Offa Rd. TN35 27 F2
Old House Gdns. TN34 26 C1
Old Humphrey Av. TN35 26 D5
Old London Rd. TN35 27 E4
Old Top Rd. TN35 27 F1
Oliver Clo. TN34 26 A6
Orchard Clo. TN34 26 C2
Osborne Clo. TN34 26 B2
Park Av. TN34 26 A2
Park Clo. TN34 26 A2
Park Cres. TN34 26 A2
Park Dri. TN34 26 A2
Park View. TN34 26 A2
Park Way. TN34 26 A2
Parker Rd. TN34 26 C3
Parkstone Rd. TN34 26 A1
Pegwell Clo. TN34 26 B3
Pelham Cres. TN34 26 C5
Pelham Pl. TN34 26 C5
Pelham St. TN34 26 B5
Pennine Rise. TN34 27 E1
Percy Rd. TN35 27 E1
Pilot Rd. TN34 26 D1
Piltdown Clo. TN34 26 B4
Pinders Rd. TN35 27 F3
Pinders Walk. TN35 27 F2
Pine Av. TN34 26 D2
Playden Gdns. TN34 26 D1
Plynlimmon Rd. TN34 26 C5
Portland Pl. TN34 26 C5
Portland Steps. TN34 26 C5
Priory Av. TN34 26 B4
Priory Clo. TN34 26 B4
Priory Rd. TN34 26 C5
Priory St. TN34 26 B5
Prospect Pl. TN34 26 B6
Quantock Gdns. TN34 27 E1
Quarry Cres. TN34 26 C3
Quarry Rd. TN34 26 C3
Queens Rd. TN34 26 B5
Queens Sq. TN34 26 B4
Ravine Clo. TN34 26 C2
Redlake Ter. TN35 27 F1
Redmayne Dri. TN34 26 A5
Richland Clo. TN35 27 G1
Robert Tressell Clo. TN34 26 B4
Robertson St. TN34 26 B6
Robertson Ter. TN34 26 B6
Robertsons Hill. TN34 27 E3
Rock A Nore Rd. TN34 26 D5
Rock La. TN35 27 F1
Rocklands La. TN35 27 F4
Roebuck St. TN34 26 D5
Rotherfield Av. TN34 26 D3
Russell St. TN34 26 C5
Rye Rd. TN35 27 F1
St Andrews Sq. TN34 26 C5
St Georges Rd. TN34 26 C4
St Helens Av. TN34 26 B1
St Helens Court. TN34 26 B3
St Helens Cres. TN34 26 B3
St Helens Downs. TN34 26 C1
St Helens rk Rd. TN34 26 B2
St Helens Rd. TN34 26 A3
St James Rd. TN34 26 C4
St Margarets Rd. TN37 26 A6
St Marys Rd. TN34 26 C4
St Marys Ter. TN34 26 C4
St Thomas's Rd. TN34 26 D4
Salters La. TN34 26 D4
San Jose Clo. TN35 27 E3
Sandown Rd. TN35 27 E2
Saunders Clo. TN34 26 C4
Saxon Rd. TN35 27 F2
School Rd. TN35 27 E2
Scutes Clo. TN34 26 C2
Sedgebrook Gdns. TN34 26 A3
Selmeston Clo. TN34 26 A4
Seymour Villas. TN34 26 C2
Sherwood Clo. TN34 26 C3
South Ter. TN35 26 B5
Southdown Rd. TN34 26 D2
Stanley Rd. TN34 26 B4
Starwell Clo. TN34 26 A2
Station Approach. TN34 26 B5
Stone St. TN34 26 C5
Stonefield Rd. TN34 26 C5
Streamside Clo. TN34 26 B2
Swan Ter. TN34 26 D5
Tackleway. TN34 26 D5
Tenterden Rise. TN34 26 A2
Thanet Way. TN34 26 A3
The Bourne. TN34 26 D5
The Broadway. TN35 26 F1
The Byway. TN34 26 C1
The Cheviot. TN34 27 E1
The Coppice. TN34 26 B4
The Courtyard. TN34 26 A4
The Croft. TN34 26 D5
The Glebe. TN34 26 D3
The Heights. TN35 27 G1
The Ridge. TN35 27 E1
The Spinney. TN34 26 A4
Tilekiln La. TN35 27 G1
Torfield Clo. TN34 26 D4
Trinity St. TN34 26 B5
Upper Broomgrove Rd. TN34 26 D2
Upper Park Rd. TN37 26 A3
Valley Side Rd. TN35 27 E2
Vicarage Rd. TN34 26 C4
Victoria Av. TN35 27 E1
View Bank. TN35 27 F3
Waldegrave St. TN34 26 C5
Waldene Clo. TN34 26 C2
Watermens Clo. TN34 26 B2
Waterside Clo. TN35 27 E2
Waterworks Rd. TN34 26 C4
Wellington Mws. TN34 26 C5
Wellington Pl. TN34 26 B5
Wellington Rd. TN34 26 C5
Wellington Sq. TN34 26 C5
West St. TN34 26 D5
West View. TN34 26 D3
Westminster Cres. TN34 26 D1
White Rock. TN34 26 A6
White Rock Gdns. TN34 26 B6
White Rock Rd. TN34 26 A6
Whitefriars Rd. TN34 26 C4
Whittingtons Way. TN34 26 D1
Willow End. TN34 26 C1
Wilmington Rd. TN34 26 C2
Winchelsea Rd. TN35 27 F1
Winterbourne Clo. TN34 26 A4
Woodbrook Rd. TN34 26 B2
Woodcombe. TN34 26 B1
Wykeham Rd. TN34 26 A4
York Gdns. TN34 26 B5

HEATHFIELD

Alder Clo. TN21 28 C4
Alexandra Rd. TN21 28 D3
All Saints Gdns. TN21 28 B2
Ash Tree Clo. TN21 28 C2
Ashdown Pl. TN21 28 D3
Oakleigh Dri. TN21 28 D3
Aspen Walk. TN21 28 D4
Battle Rd. TN21 28 E1
Baytree Clo. TN21 28 D4
Beechwood La. TN21 28 E4
Beeches Clo. TN21 28 D2
Birch Way. TN21 28 C4
Browning Rd. TN21 28 C2
Burwash Rd. TN21 28 D1
Cherry Gdns. TN21 28 D4
Cherwell Rd. TN21 28 C1
Church App. TN21 28 F4
Churchill Rd. TN21 28 D3
Collingwood Av. TN21 28 C2
Collingwood Rise. TN21 28 C2
Coppice View. TN21 28 D3
Cuckmere Rise. TN21 28 C2
Cuckoo Dri. TN21 28 C3
Davenport Pk. TN21 28 C2
Downsview. TN21 28 D2
Edge Hill. TN21 28 B2
Elm Way. TN21 28 D3
Fairoak Clo. TN21 28 C2
Firwood Clo. TN21 28 C1
Firwood Rise. TN21 28 C1
Frenches Farm Dri. TN21 28 C4
Geers Wood. TN21 28 B3
Ghyll Rd. TN21 28 B3
Gibraltar Rise. TN21 28 C2
Green La. TN21 28 D3
Hailsham Rd. TN21 28 C4
Halley Rd. TN21 28 F2
Harley La. TN21 28 C3
Hawthorn Clo. TN21 28 D3
High St. TN21 28 A2
Highcroft Cres. TN21 28 C2
Holly Clo. TN21 28 C3
Holly Dri. TN21 28 C3
Idens La. TN21 28 F1
Kennedy Clo. TN21 28 D3
Larch Clo. TN21 28 D4
Leeves Clo. TN21 28 C3
Leeves Way. TN21 28 C3
Lennox Ct. TN21 28 C1
Lime Way. TN21 28 D3
Longview. TN21 28 C4
Magnolia Clo. TN21 28 D4
Marklye La. TN21 28 D1
Marshlands La. TN21 28 C1
Meadow Way. TN21 28 C3
Mileston. TN21 28 C1
Mill Clo. TN21 28 B2
Mill Rise. TN21 28 C1
Mill Rd. TN21 28 B2
Mulberry Way. TN21 28 D4
Mutton Hall Hill. TN21 28 C1
Mutton Hall La. TN21 28 C1
New Rd. TN21 28 C4
Newick La. TN21 28 E1
Newnham Way. TN21 28 C2
Newpond Hill. TN21 28 A2
Nursery Way. TN21 28 A2
Old Ghyll Rd. TN21 28 C4
Pages Clo. TN21 28 A2
Pages Hill. TN21 28 A2
Park Rd. TN21 28 D3
Parkside. TN21 28 D3
Pine Tree Rd. TN21 28 C3
Pook Reed Clo. TN21 28 B3
Pook Reed La. TN21 28 A3
Prospect Rd. TN21 28 C3
Ridgeway Clo. TN21 28 C1
Rowan Clo. TN21 28 C4
Sandy Cross Cotts. TN21 28 C4
Sandy Cross La. TN21 28 C4
Sheepsetting La. TN21 28 A2
Spring Bank. TN21 28 D1
Springwood Rd. TN21 28 B1
Star La. TN21 28 F4
Station App. TN21 28 C2
Station Rd. TN21 28 C2
Stonegate Way. TN21 28 D1
Streatfield Gdns. TN21 28 B1
Streatfield Rd. TN21 28 B1
Swaines Way. TN21 28 C3
Sycamore Clo. TN21 28 D3
The Oaks. TN21 28 D3
The Spinney. TN21 28 D3
Theobalds Grn. TN21 28 C4
Tilsmore Rd. TN21 28 B2
Tower St. TN21 28 D1
Upper Station Rd. TN21 28 D3
Vale View Rd. TN21 28 D3
Waldron Thorns. TN21 28 C3
Walnut Clo. TN21 28 D3
Wayside Wk. TN21 28 B3
Wealdview Rd. TN21 28 A2
Windmill Clo. TN21 28 D1
Woodland Mews. TN21 28 D3
Woodland Way. TN21 28 D3
Woodlands Clo. TN21 28 D4
Wren Clo. TN21 28 C2
Yew Tree Clo. TN21 28 C3

HERSTMONCEUX

Bagham La. BN27 29 B2
Buckwell Rise. BN27 29 A2
Chapel Row. BN27 29 B3
Chestnut Clo. BN27 29 A2
Church Rd. BN27 29 B3
Comphurst La. BN27 29 D3
Coombe Clo. BN27 29 D2
Dacre Rd. BN27 29 A2
Dales Clo. BN27 29 D3
Elmhurst Gdns. BN27 29 A2
Fairfield. BN27 29 A1
Fairlawns Dri. BN27 29 A2
Fiennes Rd. BN27 29 A2
Gardner St. BN27 29 B2
Hailsham Rd. BN27 29 A3
Highview Clo. BN27 29 D3
Hurst La. BN27 29 D2
James Av. BN27 29 A1
Joes La. BN27 29 D2
Middle Way. BN27 29 D2
Monceux Rd. BN27 29 A1
Nursery La. BN27 29 D2
Queens Rd. BN27 29 A2
The Ridgeway. BN27 29 A2
Victoria Rd. BN27 29 D2
West End. BN27 29 A1
Windmill Hill. BN27 29 C2

HORAM

Beauford Rd. TN21 29 B5
Bridge Clo. TN21 29 C5
Downline Clo. TN21 29 C5
Grange Clo. TN21 29 B6
Hailsham Rd. TN21 29 B6
Highfield Rd. TN21 29 B5
Hillside Dri. TN21 29 B5
Horam Park Clo. TN21 29 C5
Horebeech La. TN21 29 B5
Little London Rd. TN21 29 A4
Manor Clo. TN21 29 B5
Manor Rd. TN21 29 B4
Millbrook Clo. TN21 29 C5
Paynsbridge Way. TN21 29 C5
The Avenue. TN21 29 B4
The Rise. TN21 29 B5
Toll Wood Rd. TN21 29 B5
Vines Cross Rd. TN21 29 C5

HOVE

Acacia Av. BN3 30 B3
Albany Mews. BN3 30 D6
Albany Vil. BN3 30 D6
Albert Mews. BN3 30 D6
Albert St. BN3 30 C4
Aldrington Av. BN3 30 B3
Alpine Rd. BN3 30 B4
Amberley Clo. BN3 30 A1
Amberley Dri. BN3 30 A1
Amesbury Cres. BN3 30 A4
Amherst Cres. BN3 30 B3
Applesham Av. BN3 30 A2
Arthur St. BN3 30 B4
Ashlings Way. BN3 30 A1
Aymer Rd. BN3 30 C5
Beeding Av. BN3 30 B1
Belfast St. BN3 30 C5
Benett Av. BN3 30 D1
Benett Dri. BN3 30 D1
*Benham Ct, Kings Esp. BN3 30 C6
Benson Ct. BN3 30 A4
Berriedale Av. BN3 30 A6
Blatchington Rd. BN3 30 C5
Bolsover Rd. BN3 30 A4
Braemore Rd. BN3 30 A6
Bramber Av. BN3 30 A1
Brooker Pl. BN3 30 C5
Brooker St. BN3 30 C5
Byron St. BN3 30 C4
Carlisle Rd. BN3 30 B6
Chartfield. BN3 30 C2
Church Rd. BN3 30 C5
Clarendon Rd. BN3 30 C4
Clarendon Villas. BN3 30 C4
Clarke Av. BN3 30 A1
Clayton Way. BN3 30 B1
Cobton Dri. BN3 30 C1
Coleman Av. BN3 30 A5
Coleridge St. BN3 30 C4
Connaught Rd. BN3 30 C5
Connaught Ter. BN3 30 C5
Conway Pl. BN3 30 C4
Conway St. BN3 30 C4
Court Farm Rd. BN3 30 B1
*Courtenay Ter, Kingsway. BN3 30 C6
Cowper St. BN3 30 B4
Cranmer Av. BN3 30 B3
Cromwell Rd. BN3 30 D4
Dale Vw. BN3 30 A2
Dallington Rd. BN3 30 A4
Denmark Villas. BN3 30 D5
Downland Cres. BN3 30 B1
Eaton Gdns. BN3 30 D5
Eaton Grove. BN3 30 D4
Eaton Rd. BN3 30 D5
Eaton Villas. BN3 30 D5
Edward Av. BN3 30 C1
Edward Clo. BN3 30 C1
Elizabeth Av. BN3 30 C1
Elizabeth Clo. BN3 30 C1
Ellen St. BN3 30 C4
Elm Dri. BN3 30 A3
English Clo. BN3 30 A3
Eridge Rd. BN3 30 C2
Ethel St. BN3 30 D4
Fallowfield Clo. BN3 30 B1
Fallowfield Cres. BN3 30 A2
Findon Clo. BN3 30 B1
Fonthill Rd. BN3 30 D4
Fourth Av. BN3 30 D6
Frant Rd. BN3 30 C1
Frith Rd. BN3 30 C3
George St. BN3 30 D5
Glendor Rd. BN3 30 A6
Goldstone Clo. BN3 30 C1
Goldstone Cres. BN3 30 B1
Goldstone La. BN3 30 D3
Goldstone Rd. BN3 30 C4
Goldstone St. BN3 30 D4
Goldstone Villas. BN3 30 D4
Goldstone Way. BN3 30 B1
Grand Av. BN3 30 D6
Grange Rd. BN3 30 A4
Haddington St. BN3 30 D5
Hangleton Rd. BN3 30 A2
Hartington Villas. BN3 30 D3
Henfield Way. BN3 30 B1
Hill Dri. BN3 30 D1
Hogarth Rd. BN3 30 A5
Holmes Av. BN3 30 B3
Hova Ter. BN3 30 D5
Hova Villas. BN3 30 D5
Hove Park Gdns. BN3 30 D3
Hove Park Rd. BN3 30 D3
Hove Park Villas. BN3 30 D4
Hove Park Way. BN3 30 D2
Hove Pl. BN3 30 C6
Hove St. BN3 30 C6

INDUSTRIAL ESTATES:
Sackville Ind Est. BN3 30 C3
Ingram Ct. BN3 30 A4
Ingram Cres East. BN3 30 A4
Ingram Cres West.
BN3 30 A4
Isabel Cres. BN3 30 A3
Jesmond Rd. BN3 30 B4
Kendal Rd. BN3 30 B4
Kings Esplanade. BN3 30 C6
Kings Gdns. BN3 30 D6
Kings Mews. BN3 30 D6
Kingsthorpe Rd. BN3 30 D6
Kingston Clo. BN3 30 A2
Kingsway. BN3 30 A6
Laburnum Av. BN3 30 A2
Landseer Rd. BN3 30 C3
Langdale Gdns. BN3 30 A6
Langdale Rd. BN3 30 B6
Lark Hill. BN3 30 A1
Lawrence Rd. BN3 30 B5
Leighton Rd. BN3 30 C3
Lennox Rd. BN3 30 B4
Linton Rd. BN3 30 B4
Lion Mews. BN3 30 B5
Livingstone Rd. BN3 30 C4
Lovegrove Ct. BN3 30 A4
Lullington Av. BN3 30 B3
Mainstone Rd. BN3 30 B4
Malvern St. BN3 30 C5
Mansfield Rd. BN3 30 A4
Maple Gdns. BN3 30 A3
Marine Av. BN3 30 A5
Marmion Rd. BN3 30 B4
Marshall Way. BN3 30 A2
Maytree Walk. BN3 30 A2
Meadow Clo. BN3 30 D1
Meadway Cres. BN3 30 A2
Medina Pl. BN3 30 C6
Medina Rd. BN3 30 C6
Medina Ter. BN3 30 C6
Medina Villas. BN3 30 C6
Milcote Av. BN3 30 B3
Mill Dri. BN3 30 C1
Milnthorpe Rd. BN3 30 A4
Modena Rd. BN3 30 B5
Molesworth St. BN3 30 B4
Monmouth St. BN3 30 C5
Montgomery St. BN3 30 B4
Mortimer Rd. BN3 30 B4
Moyne Clo. BN3 30 A2
Namrik Mews. BN3 30 C6
Nevill Av. BN3 30 A2
Nevill Clo. BN3 30 B1
Nevill Gdns. BN3 30 B1
Nevill Pl. BN3 30 C2
Nevill Rd. BN3 30 B1
Nevill Way. BN3 30 C1
New Church Rd. BN3 30 A5
Newtown Rd. BN3 30 C3
Norman Rd. BN3 30 A5
North Ease Dri. BN3 30 A1
Norton Clo. BN3 30 D5
Norton Rd. BN3 30 D5
Old Shoreham Rd. BN3 30 A3
Orchard Av. BN3 30 C3
Orchard Gdns. BN3 30 C3
Orchard Rd. BN3 30 C3
Osborne Villas. BN3 30 C6
Park Av. BN3 30 A5
Park Clo. BN3 30 A1
Park Rise. BN3 30 A1
Park View Rd. BN3 30 C3
*Parnell Ct,
Medina Pl. BN3 30 C6
Payne Av. BN3 30 B4
Pembroke Av. BN3 30 C5
Pembroke Cres. BN3 30 C5
Pembroke Gdns. BN3 30 C5
Pendragon Ct. BN3 30 C4
Poplar Av. BN3 30 A1
Poplar Clo. BN3 30 A1
Portland Av. BN3 30 A5
Portland Rd. BN3 30 A4
Poynter Rd. BN3 30 B4
Princes Av. BN3 30 C6
Princes Cres. BN3 30 B6
Princes Sq. BN3 30 C6
Prinsep Rd. BN3 30 C3
Ranelagh Villas. BN3 30 D3
Raphael Rd. BN3 30 B5
Reynolds Rd. BN3 30 B5
Richardson Rd. BN3 30 B5
Rowan Av. BN3 30 A2
Ruskin Rd. BN3 30 B5
Rutland Gdns. BN3 30 B5
Rutland Rd. BN3 30 B4

Sackville Gdns. BN3 30 B6
Sackville Rd. BN3 30 C3
St Aubyns. BN3 30 C6
St Aubyns Sth. BN3 30 C6
*St Catherines Ter,
Victoria Ter. BN3 30 C6
St Heliers Av. BN3 30 A4
St Josephs Clo. BN3 30 C3
St Patricks Rd. BN3 30 C4
St Peters Clo. BN3 30 B1
St Philips Mews. BN3 30 B5
School Rd. BN3 30 B4
Scott Rd. BN3 30 B4
Seafield Rd. BN3 30 C6
Shakespeare St. BN3 30 C4
Shelley Rd. BN3 30 B4
Sheridan Ter. BN3 30 B4
Shirley Av. BN3 30 D1
Shirley Dri. BN3 30 D1
Shirley St. BN3 30 C4
Stanford Clo. BN3 30 D2
Station App. BN3 30 D4
Stevens Ct. BN3 30 A4
Steyning Av. BN3 30 B1
Stirling Pl. BN3 30 C5
Stoneham Rd. BN3 30 B4
Storrington Clo. BN3 30 A1
Suffolk St. BN3 30 B4
Sunninghill Av. BN3 30 A1
Sunninghill Clo. BN3 30 A1
Sussex Rd. BN3 30 C6
Tamworth Rd. BN3 30 B4
Tandridge Rd. BN3 30 A5
Tennis Rd. BN3 30 A5
The Drive. BN3 30 D5
The Droveway. BN3 30 D2
Third Av. BN3 30 D6
Thorn Hill Clo. BN3 30 A1
Tisbury Rd. BN3 30 D5
Titian Rd. BN3 30 B5
Tongdean Rd. BN3 30 D1
Torrance Clo. BN3 30 B3
Tredcroft Rd. BN3 30 D2
Tudor Clo. BN3 30 B2
Vallance Gdns. BN3 30 C6
Vallance Rd. BN3 30 C5
Ventnor Villas. BN3 30 D5
Victoria Cotts. BN3 30 C6
Walsingham Rd. BN3 30 B6
Wayfield Av. BN3 30 B3
Wayfield Clo. BN3 30 A2
Weald Av. BN3 30 A6
Welbeck Av. BN3 30 A6
West Way. BN3 30 A2
Westbourne Gdns. BN3 30 B5
Westbourne Pl. BN3 30 B6
Westbourne St. BN3 30 B5
Westbourne Villas.
BN3 30 B6
Western Esplanade.
BN3 30 A6
Wilbury Av. BN3 30 D4
Wilbury Gdns. BN3 30 D4
Windmill Clo. BN3 30 B1
Wish Rd. BN3 30 A6
Woodhouse Rd. BN3 30 A4
Woodland Av. BN3 30 C1
Woodland Clo. BN3 30 C1
Woodland Dri. BN3 30 C2
Woodruff Av. BN3 30 D2
Wordsworth St. BN3 30 B4
Wynne Mews. BN3 30 B4

ICKLESHAM

Brede Valley Vw. TN36 31 B2
Goldhurst Grn. TN36 31 B2
High Fords. TN36 31 B2
High Fords Clo. TN36 31 B2
Laurel La. TN36 31 C3
Main Rd. TN36 31 C2
Manor Clo. TN36 31 C2
Oast House Field. TN36 31 C2
Oast House La. TN36 31 C2
Parsonage La. TN36 31 C1
Peartree Field. TN36 31 C1
Watermill La. TN36 31 A3
Workhouse Rd. TN36 31 D2

LEWES

Abergavenny Rd. BN7 32 C3

Abinger Pl. BN7 33 E3
Albion St. BN7 33 E3
Annes Path. BN7 32 D5
Antioch St. BN7 32 D4
Arundel Green. BN7 32 D2
Barn Hatch Clo. BN7 32 B5
Barn Rd. BN7 33 F1
Barons Walk. BN7 32 B4
Barons Down Rd. BN7 32 B5
Baxter Rd. BN7 32 C2
Beckett Way. BN7 33 F1
Bell La. BN7 32 C5
Berkeley Row. BN7 32 C5
Bishops Dri. BN7 32 B4
Blois Rd. BN7 32 B1
Boughey Pl. BN7 33 E1
Bradford Rd. BN7 32 D4
Bridgewick Clo. BN7 33 E1
Brighton Rd. BN7 32 A5
Brook St. BN7 33 F2
Brooks Clo. BN7 33 F2
Brooks Rd. BN7 33 F2
Broomans La. BN7 33 E4
Buckhurst Clo. BN7 33 E1
Buckwell Ct. BN7 32 B1
Bull La. BN7 33 E4
Caburn Cres. BN7 32 B2
Castle Bank. BN7 33 E4
Castle Ditch La. BN7 33 E4
Castle Precinct. BN7 33 E4
Chapel Hill. BN7 33 G3
Christie Rd. BN7 32 C3
Church La,
Lewes. BN7 32 D4
Church La,
South Malling. BN7 33 E2
Church Row. BN7 33 E3
Church Twitten. BN7 33 E4
Churchill Rd. BN7 32 C1
Clare Rd. BN7 32 C2
Cleve Ter. BN7 32 D5
Cliffe High St. BN7 33 F3
Cluny St. BN7 32 D5
Cockshut Rd. BN7 32 D5
Coombe Rd. BN7 33 F2
Court Rd. BN7 33 F4
Cranedown. BN7 32 C6
Cranmer Clo. BN7 32 F2
Crisp Rd. BN7 32 C1
Cross Way. BN7 32 B3
Dale Rd. BN7 32 C5
Daveys La. BN7 33 F3
De Grey Clo. BN7 33 F2
De La Ware Rd. BN7 32 B5
De Montfort Rd. BN7 32 C4
De Warrenne Rd. BN7 32 C3
Deanery Clo. BN7 33 F1
Dorset Rd. BN7 33 E5
Downs Clo. BN7 32 B2
Downside. BN7 32 B4
Dunvan Clo. BN7 33 E1
Earls Gdns. BN7 33 E3
East St. BN7 33 E3
Eastgate St. BN7 33 F3
Eastgate Wharf. BN7 33 F3
Eastport La. BN7 33 E5
Eastway. BN7 32 A2
Edward St. BN7 33 E4
Eleanor Clo. BN7 32 D3
Elm Gro. BN7 33 E4
English Passage. BN7 33 F3
Eridge Green. BN7 32 C2
Evelyn Rd. BN7 32 C2
Farncombe Rd. BN7 33 F4
Ferrers Rd. BN7 32 C3
Firle Cres. BN7 32 A2
Fisher St. BN7 33 E4
Fitzgerald Rd. BN7 33 F1
Fitzjohn Rd. BN7 32 C1
Fitzroy Rd. BN7 32 C1
Foundry La. BN7 33 F4
Friars Walk. BN7 33 F4
Fuller Rd. BN7 32 C1
Garden St. BN7 32 E4
Glebe Clo. BN7 32 B5
Godfrey Rd. BN7 32 D5
Grange Rd. BN7 33 E4
Green La. BN7 33 E4
Green Wall. BN7 33 F3
Greyfriars Ct. BN7 33 F4
Gundreda Rd. BN7 32 C2
Ham La. BN7 33 F5
Hamsey Cres. BN7 32 B2
Harvard Clo. BN7 33 E1
Harveys Way. BN7 33 F3
Hawkenbury Way. BN7 32 B3

Hayward Rd. BN7 32 C1
Hereward Way. BN7 33 F2
High St. BN7 32 D4
Highdown Rd. BN7 32 B2
Hill Rd. BN7 32 B2
Hillyfield. BN7 32 C5
Hoopers Clo. BN7 33 E1
Horsfield Rd. BN7 32 C1
Houndean Clo. BN7 32 B4
Houndean Rise. BN7 32 A5
INDUSTRIAL ESTATES:
Cliffe Ind Est. BN7 33 H5
Malling Brook Ind Est.
BN7 33 F2
Phoenix Ind Est. BN7 33 E3
Irelands La. BN7 32 D4
Juggs Rd. BN7 32 A6
Keere St. BN7 33 E4
King Henry Rd. BN7 32 C2
Kingsley Rd. BN7 32 C2
Kingston Rd. BN7 32 C6
Lambert Pl. BN7 33 E1
Lancaster St. BN7 33 E3
Landport Rd. BN7 32 C1
Lansdown Pl. BN7 33 E4
Lee Rd. BN7 32 C2
Leicester Rd. BN7 32 C3
Lewes Southern By Pass.
BN7 32 A6
Little East St. BN7 33 E3
Lodge Clo. BN7 32 B5
Love La. BN7 32 B5
Malling Clo. BN7 33 F1
Malling Down. BN7 33 F1
Malling Hill. BN7 33 F1
Malling St. BN7 33 G3
Mantell Clo. BN7 33 E1
Market La. BN7 33 E4
Market St. BN7 33 E4
Mayhew Way. BN7 33 E2
Mealla Cl. BN7 33 E1
Meridian Rd. BN7 32 C2
Middle Way. BN7 32 B3
Mildmay Rd. BN7 32 C3
Mill Rd. BN7 33 F1
Monks La. BN7 33 F5
Monks Way. BN7 33 E1
Montacute Rd. BN7 32 A5
Morley Clo. BN7 32 D5
Morris Rd. BN7 33 F4
Mount Harry Rd. BN7 32 B2
Mount Pl. BN7 33 E4
Mount Pleasant. BN7 32 E3
Mount St. BN7 33 E5
Mountfield Rd. BN7 33 E5
Nevill Cres. BN7 32 B3
Nevill Rd. BN7 32 B2
New Rd. BN7 33 E4
Newton Rd. BN7 32 D2
North Ct. BN7 33 F3
North St. BN7 33 E3
North Way. BN7 32 B3
Offham Rd. BN7 32 C2
Old Malling Way. BN7 33 E1
Orchard Rd. BN7 33 G2
Ousedale Clo. BN7 32 B4
Paddock La. BN7 32 D4
Paddock Rd. BN7 32 D4
Paines Twitten. BN7 33 E4
Park Rd. BN7 32 D3
Peckham Clo. BN7 33 E1
Pelham Ter. BN7 33 E3
Pellbrook Rd. BN7 32 C1
Phoenix Causeway. BN7 33 F3
Phoenix Pl. BN7 33 F3
Pinwell Rd. BN7 33 E4
Pipe Passage. BN7 32 D4
Potters La. BN7 32 D5
Prince Charles Rd. BN7 33 F1
Prince Edwards Rd.
BN7 32 C3
Priory Court. BN7 33 E5
Priory Cres. BN7 33 E5
Priory St. BN7 33 E5
Queen Anne Clo. BN7 32 D3
Queens Rd. BN7 33 F1
Railway La. BN7 33 F4
Riverdale. BN7 33 E2
Rotten Row. BN7 32 D4
Rufus Clo. BN7 32 D3
Russell Row. BN7 33 E1
Sackville Clo. BN7 32 D3
St Andrews La. BN7 33 E4
St Annes Cres. BN7 32 C4
St James St. BN7 33 E5
St Johns Hill. BN7 33 E3

St Johns St. BN7 33 E3
St Johns Ter. BN7 33 E3
St Martins La. BN7 33 E4
St Michaels Ter. BN7 33 E2
St Nicholas La. BN7 33 E4
St Pancras Gdns. BN7 32 D5
St Pancras Rd. BN7 32 D5
St Peters Pl. BN7 32 D4
St Swithuns La. BN7 33 E4
St Swithuns Ter. BN7 33 E4
School Hill. BN7 33 E4
Segrave Clo. BN7 32 C3
Sheep Fair. BN7 32 B2
Shelley Clo. BN7 32 C3
South Downs Rd. BN7 33 G4
South St. BN7 33 G4
South Way. BN7 32 B3
Southcliffe. BN7 33 G4
Southdown Av. BN7 32 B4
Southdown Pl. BN7 33 G3
Southover High St.
BN7 32 D5
Southover Rd. BN7 33 E3
Spences Field. BN7 33 F2
Spences La. BN7 33 F2
Spital Rd. BN7 32 C4
Spring Gdns. BN7 33 E3
Stansfield Rd. BN7 32 D2
Station Rd. BN7 33 E5
Station St. BN7 33 E4
Stewards Inn. BN7 33 E4
Stoneham Clo. BN7 33 E1
Sun St. BN7 33 E3
Talbot Ter. BN7 33 E3
Tanners Brook. BN7 33 E4
The Avenue. BN7 32 D3
The Course. BN7 32 D5
The Gallops. BN7 32 B4
The Lynchets. BN7 33 G1
The Martlets. BN7 33 F1
The Meadows. BN7 33 F1
The Spinneys. BN7 33 G2
Thomas St. BN7 33 F3
Timber Yd Cotts. BN7 33 G4
Toronto Ter. BN7 33 E3
Ty La. BN7 33 G4
Valence Rd. BN7 32 C3
Valley Rd. BN7 32 C5
Verralls Walk. BN7 32 D5
Waite Clo. BN7 33 F2
Waldshut Rd. BN7 32 B1
Wallands Cres. BN7 32 D3
Walwers La. BN7 33 E4
Warren Clo. BN7 32 C4
Warren Dri. BN7 32 C4
Watergate La. BN7 33 E4
Waterloo Pl. BN7 33 E3
Weald Clo. BN7 32 D3
Wellhouse Pl. BN7 33 E4
Wellington St. BN7 33 E3
West St. BN7 33 E3
Western Rd. BN7 32 C4
Westgate St. BN7 33 E4
Wheatsheaf Gdns. BN7 33 G3
White Hill. BN7 32 D3
Windover Cres. BN7 32 B2
Winterbourne Clo. BN7 32 B5
Winterbourne Hollow.
BN7 32 C4
Winterbourne La. BN7 32 B5
Winterbourne Mews.
BN7 32 C5

MARESFIELD

Batts Bridge Rd. TN22 34 A2
Cobdown La. TN22 34 C2
Field End. TN22 34 A3
Forest Pk. TN22 34 A2
London Rd. TN22 34 A2
Maple Clo. TN22 34 A2
Middle Dri. TN22 34 B1
Millwood Clo. TN22 34 D3
Millwood La. TN22 34 C2
Nursery La. TN22 34 B2
Parklands. TN22 34 A1
Queens Dri. TN22 34 B2
Robian Clo. TN22 34 B2
Straight Half Mile.
TN22 34 B2
The Drive. TN22 34 A1
The Paddock. TN22 34 B2
Uckfield By-Pass. TN22 34 C4
Underhill. TN22 34 B2

MAYFIELD

Alexandra Rd. TN20 35 D1
Ashley Gdns. TN20 35 B2
Dunstans Croft. TN20 35 D1
East St. TN20 35 D2
Fletching St. TN20 35 C2
High St. TN20 35 B2
Knowle Hill. TN20 35 B3
Knowle Park. TN20 35 B3
Little Trodgers La.
TN20 35 C1
Love La. TN20 35 B3
Loxfield Clo. TN20 35 B3
Mayfield By-Pass. TN20 35 A3
Mayfield Clo. TN20 35 A2
Old La. TN20 35 B2
Richmead Gdns. TN20 35 B2
Roselands Av. TN20 35 A3
Rotherfield La. TN20 35 A1
Rothermead. TN20 35 A3
*St Mary in the Fields,
South St. TN20 35 B2
South St. TN20 35 D1
Southmead Clo. TN20 35 D1
Station App. TN20 35 A2
Station Rd. TN20 35 A2
Stone Cross. TN20 35 A3
The Avenue. TN20 35 C2
The Glade. TN20 35 B2
The Warren. TN20 35 D2
Tunbridge Wells Rd.
TN20 35 B1
Vale Rd. TN20 35 C2
Victoria Rd. TN20 35 A2
West St. TN20 35 B2
Woolbridges Rd. TN20 35 A2

NEWHAVEN

Acacia Rd. BN9 37 E1
Anderson Clo. BN9 36 B4
Antony Clo. BN25 37 H5
Arundel Rd. BN9 37 F2
Ash Walk. BN9 36 C4
Avis Clo. BN9 37 E2
Avis Rd. BN9 37 E2
Avis Way. BN9 37 E2
Baker St. BN9 37 E4
Bay Vue Rd. BN9 36 D4
Beach Clo. BN9 37 E4
Beach Rd. BN9 37 E4
Beresford Rd. BN9 37 E2
Bishopstone Rd. BN25 37 H6
Blakeney Av. BN9 36 A5
Brands Clo. BN9 37 E1
Brazen Clo. BN9 36 B4
Bridge St. BN9 36 D4
Brighton Rd. BN9 36 A5
Brookes Clo. BN9 36 D5
Brookside BN9 36 B1
Bush Rd. BN9 36 B3
Cantercrow Hill. BN9 37 F1
Chapel St. BN9 36 D4
Charlston Av. BN9 36 B6
Chene Av. BN9 36 A5
Chestnut Way. BN9 36 B4
Church Hill. BN9 36 C5
Claremont Rd. BN9 37 F2
Clifton Rd. BN9 37 E4
Cornelius Av. BN9 36 B6
Cottage Clo. BN9 37 F2
Court Farm Clo. BN9 36 B1
Court Farm Rd. BN9 36 C6
Crest Rd. BN9 37 F2
Cresta Rd. BN9 36 A5
Cuckmere Rd. BN9 36 B6
Dacre Rd. BN9 36 D4
Denton Dri. BN9 37 E2
Denton Rise. BN9 37 E1
Denton Rd. BN9 37 E2
Drove Rd. BN9 37 E3
Eastbridge Rd. BN9 37 E4
Edward Clo. BN25 37 H5
Elizabeth Clo. BN25 37 G4
Elm Ct. BN9 36 C4
Elphick Rd. BN9 36 C3
Estate Rd. BN9 37 E4
Evelyn Av. BN9 36 C4
Fairholme Rd. BN9 37 F2

Falaise Rd. BN9 37 F2
Firle Cres. BN9 37 E2
First Av. BN9 36 C5
Fort Rise. BN9 37 E6
Fort Rd. BN9 36 D4
Forward Clo. BN9 37 E2
Freeland Clo. BN25 37 H4
Fullwood Av. BN9 36 C4
Gardeners Hill. BN9 37 G1
Geneva Rd. BN9 36 D5
Gibbon Rd. BN9 37 E2
Gleneagles Clo. BN259 37 G5
Glynde Clo. BN9 37 E2
Hampden Gdns. BN9 37 E1
Hanover Clo. BN25 37 H5
Hanson Rd. BN9 36 C5
Harbour View Rd. BN9 36 C5
Harbour View Rd. BN9 36 C6
Harfield Clo. BN9 37 F1
Harpers Rd. BN9 36 C5
Hawthorn Rise. BN9 36 B4
Hazel Clo. BN9 36 B3
Heighton Cres. BN9 37 E1
Heighton Rd. BN9 37 E1
High St. BN9 36 D4
Hill Crest Rd. BN9 36 D5
Hill Rise. BN9 37 F2
Hill Rd, Peacehaven
Heights. BN9 36 A6
Hill Rd,
South Heighton. BN9 37 F2
Hill Side. BN9 36 D4
Hoathdown Av. BN9 36 B4
Holmdale Rd. BN9 37 G2
Holmes Clo. BN9 37 G5
Howey Clo. BN9 37 F2
Hurdis Rd. BN25 37 G5
Iford Clo. BN9 37 E2
INDUSTRIAL ESTATES:
Willow Ind Est. BN9 37 E3
Iveagh Cres. BN9 37 E2
Jackson Mews. BN9 36 C4
Kennedy Way. BN9 36 C4
Kings Av. BN9 37 F2
Lapierre Rd. BN9 36 C4
Lawes Av. BN9 36 C4
Lee Way. BN9 36 C3
Lewes Rd. BN9 36 B1
Lewis Clo. BN9 37 F1
Lewry Clo. BN9 36 B5
Links Av. BN9 36 A4
Lower Pl. BN9 36 D4
Maple Leaf Clo. BN9 37 E4
Maple Rd. BN9 36 A5
Marine Dri. BN9 37 G5
Marine View. BN9 36 B5
Marshall La. BN9 36 D4
Meeching Rise. BN9 36 D4
Meeching Rd. BN9 36 D4
Metcalfe Av. BN9 36 C3
Mill Drove. BN25 37 G6
Mount Clo. BN9 37 F3
Mount Pleasant Rd.
BN9 37 G1
Mount Rd. BN9 37 F3
Murray Av. BN9 36 C4
Neills Clo. BN9 36 D4
New Rd. BN9 36 D1
Newfield La. BN9 36 C4
Newfield Rd. BN9 36 C4
Nore Rd. BN9 36 B5
Norman Clo. BN25 37 H5
Norman Rd. BN9 36 D4
North La. BN9 36 D4
North Quay Rd. BN9 36 D3
North Way. BN9 36 D4
Northdown Clo. BN9 36 C4
Northdown Rd. BN9 36 C4
Norton Rd. BN9 37 E4
Norton Ter. BN9 37 E4
Outlook Av. BN9 36 A5
Palmerston Rd. BN9 37 E2
Park Drive Clo. BN9 37 F1
Park Rd. BN9 36 A6
Pegler Av. BN9 36 B5
Pevensey Rd. BN9 36 B6
Pine Tree Clo. BN9 36 D4
Port View. BN9 37 E1
Powell Gdns. BN9 37 E2
Quarry Rd. BN9 36 D6
Railway App. BN9 37 E5
Railway Rd. BN9 36 D4
Rectory Clo. BN9 37 E1
Rectory Rd. BN9 37 E1
Ringmer Rd. BN9 36 B5

Riverside. BN9 36 D4
Robinson Rd. BN9 36 C3
Rochford Way. BN25 37 H5
Roman Clo. BN9 37 H5
Rookery Clo. BN9 37 F1
Rookery Way,
Bishopstone. BN25 37 H6
Rookery Way
Sth Heighton. BN9 37 F1
Rose Walk Clo. BN9 36 C4
Rosemount Clo. BN25 37 G5
Rothwell Ct. BN9 36 B4
St Andrews Dri. BN25 37 G5
St Leonards Clo. BN9 37 F1
St Leonards Rd. BN9 37 F1
St Margarets Rise.
BN25 37 E2
St Martins Cres. BN9 37 E2
Saxon Rd. BN9 36 D4
Seaford Rd. BN9 37 F3
Seagrave Clo. BN25 37 G5
Seaview Rd. BN9 37 F2
Second Av. BN9 36 C4
Senlac Rd. BN9 36 C4
Ship St. BN9 36 C3
South Rd. BN9 36 D4
South Way. BN9 36 D4
Southdown Clo. BN9 36 B5
Southdown Rd. BN9 36 C5
Station Rd. BN9 37 F2
Tarring Clo. BN9 37 E2
The Cloisters. BN9 36 D4
The Close. BN9 37 F1
The Crescent. BN9 37 F2
The Drive. BN9 36 C6
The Drove. BN9 37 E3
The Fairway. BN9 36 B4
The Grove. BN9 37 E1
The Highway. BN9 36 A5
The Leas. BN9 36 A6
The Rose Walk. BN9 36 C4
Third Av. BN9 36 C5
Thompson Rd. BN9 37 F1
Transit Rd. BN9 37 E4
Troon Clo. BN25 37 G5
Upper Valley Rd. BN9 36 B5
Valley Clo. BN9 36 C3
Valley Dene. BN9 36 C4
Valley Rd. BN9 36 B4
Viking Clo. BN25 37 H5
Wellington Rd. BN9 37 F1
West Quay. BN9 36 D5
Westdean Av. BN9 36 B6
Western Rd. BN9 36 C5
Willow Walk. BN9 36 C3
Wilmington Rd. BN9 36 B5
Windsor Clo. BN25 37 H5

NEWICK

Allington Cres. BN8 38 C2
Allington Rd. BN8 38 B2
Baden Clo. BN8 38 C2
Bannisters Field. BN8 38 D2
Blind La. BN8 38 D2
Church Rd. BN8 38 C1
Coldharbour La. BN8 38 A1
Cricketfield. BN8 38 C1
Godden Rd. BN8 38 C1
Goldbridge Rd. BN8 38 D1
Great Rough. BN8 38 A2
Growers End. BN8 38 B1
Harmers Hill. BN8 38 B1
High Hurst Clo. BN8 38 D2
High St. BN8 38 D1
Jackies La. BN8 38 A1
Langridges Clo. BN8 38 C2
Leveller End. BN8 38 C1
Leveller Rd. BN8 38 C1
Lower Station Rd. BN8 38 A2
Marbles Rd. BN8 38 D1
Millfield Clo. BN8 38 C1
Newick Dri. BN8 38 C1
Newick Hill. BN8 38 C2
Newlands Park Way.
BN8 38 C1
Oldaker Rd. BN8 38 C1
Paynters Way. BN8 38 C1
Powell Rd. BN8 38 C2
South Rough. BN8 38 C1
Station Rd. BN8 38 A2
The Green. BN8 38 D1
The Rough. BN8 38 C2

Vernons Rd. BN8 38 C1
West Point. BN8 38 C2
Western Rd. BN8 38 B2
Woodbine La. BN8 38 C1

NORTHIAM

Beacon La. TN31 38 A5
Beales La. TN31 38 B5
Cavix Field. TN31 38 B5
Chapel Field. TN31 38 A5
Church La. TN31 38 C6
Coplands Rise. TN31 38 B4
Coppards La. TN31 38 C3
Crockers La. TN31 38 B3
Dixter La. TN31 38 A5
Dixter Rd. TN31 38 A5
Ewhurst La. TN31 38 B6
Frewen Clo. TN31 38 B5
Ghyllside Rd. TN31 38 B4
Goddens Clo. TN31 38 C4
Goddens Ghyll. TN31 38 A5
Higham La. TN31 38 A5
High Mdw. TN31 38 B5
High Park Clo. TN31 38 A5
Main St. TN31 38 B6
Monks Way. TN31 38 B4
Northridge. TN31 38 B5
Quickbourne La. TN31 38 C5
Spring Hill. TN31 38 B5
Station Rd. TN31 38 B5
Strawberry Flds. TN31 38 B5
The Paddock. TN31 38 B5
Thyssel La. TN31 38 B5
Whitbread La. TN31 38 D3
Wilderness Gdns. TN31 38 B5

PEACEHAVEN

Abbey Clo. BN10 39 B3
Abbey Vw. BN10 39 B3
Ambleside Av. BN10 39 A3
Anzac Clo. BN10 39 A2
Arundel Rd. BN10 39 B5
Arundel Rd Central.
BN10 39 A4
Arundel Rd West.
BN10 39 A4
Ashington Gdns. BN10 39 D6
Ashmore Clo. BN10 39 D6
Badgers Field. BN10 39 B3
Balcombe Rd. BN10 39 A4
Barley Clo. BN10 39 A2
Bayview Rd. BN10 39 D6
Bee Rd. BN10 39 B4
Bolney Av. BN10 39 B6
Bramber Av. BN10 39 B6
Bramber Av Nth. BN10 39 B4
Bramber Clo. BN10 39 B4
Bretts Field. BN10 39 A2
Cairo Av. BN10 39 A4
Canada Clo. BN10 39 A2
Capel Av. BN10 39 B6
Carey Down. BN10 39 A3
Cavell Av. BN10 39 A4
Cavell Av Nth. BN10 39 A4
Cavendish Clo. BN10 39 A4
Chatsworth Park. BN10 39 A3
Chichester Clo. BN10 39 D5
Cinquefoil. BN10 39 A2
Cissbury Av. BN10 39 C2
Cliff Av. BN10 39 D6
Cliff Park Clo. BN10 39 C2
Collingwood Clo. BN10 39 B3
Coney Furlong. BN10 39 D5
Cornwall Av. BN10 39 D5
Cripps Av. BN10 39 B3
Crocks Dean. BN10 39 C2
Damon Clo. BN10 39 D5
Dorothy Av. BN10 39 A5
Dorothy Av Nth. BN10 39 B4
Downland Av. BN10 39 A3
Downs Walk. BN10 39 C2
Downs Way. BN10 39 C2
Edith Av. BN10 39 A5
Eith Av Nth. BN10 39 A5
Firle Rd. BN10 39 A3
Fox Hill. BN10 39 A3
Friars Av. BN10 39 C6
Gladys Av. BN10 39 C6
Glynn Rise. BN10 39 A2

Glynn Rd. BN10 39 A2
Glynn Rd West. BN10 39 A2
Gold La. BN10 39 B1
Green Gate. BN10 39 B2
Greenacres. BN10 39 C2
Greenhill Way. BN10 39 B2
Greenwich Way. BN10 39 A4
Hairpin Croft. BN10 39 B3
Harvest Clo. BN10 39 A2
Headland Clo. BN10 39 D5
Heath Down Clo. BN10 39 B2
Heathy Brow. BN10 39 A3
Highsted Park. BN10 39 C2
Hoddern Av. BN10 39 A5
Horsham Av. BN10 39 B3
Horsham Av Nth. BN10 39 B4
Hoyle Rd. BN10 39 B4
Jason Clo. BN10 39 B5
Jay Rd. BN10 39 D6
Johns Clo. BN10 39 B6
Keymer Av. BN10 39 B6
Kings Clo. BN10 39 A3
Kirby Dri. BN10 39 A4
Lake Dri. BN10 39 A4
Lea Rd. BN10 39 A4
Linthouse Clo. BN10 39 C2
Lulham Clo. BN10 39 A5
Malines Av. BN10 39 A4
Manor Dri. BN10 39 A3
Mayfield Av. BN10 39 B6
Mitchell Dean. BN10 39 A3
More Stead. BN10 39 C2
Mount Caburn Cres.
BN10 39 B2
Neville Rd. BN10 39 C6
Newton Rd. BN10 39 B4
Oval Clo. BN10 39 B2
Pelham Clo. BN10 39 B3
Pelham Rise. BN10 39 B3
Phyllis Av. BN10 39 A5
Piddinghoe Av. BN10 39 C6
Piddinghoe Clo. BN10 39 C5
Rayford Clo. BN10 39 B5
Roderick Av. BN10 39 A5
Roderick Av Nth. BN10 39 B2
Rosemary Clo. BN10 39 B3
Roundhay Av. BN10 39 D6
Rowe Av. BN10 39 A5
Rowe Av Nth. BN10 39 A4
Rustic Clo. BN10 39 A2
Rustic Pk. BN10 39 A2
Rustic Rd. BN10 39 A2
Searle Av. BN10 39 D6
Seaview Av. BN10 39 C6
Seaview Rd. BN10 39 D6
Shannon Clo. BN10 39 A2
Shepherds Cot. BN10 39 C2
Skyline Vw. BN10 39 C2
Slindon Av. BN10 39 B6
South Coast Rd. BN10 39 A5
Southdown Av. BN10 39 C6
Southview Rd. BN10 39 A2
Stanley Rd. BN10 39 A2
Steyning Av. BN10 39 B5
Sunset Clo. BN10 39 C6
Sunview Av. BN10 39 A4
Sutton Av. BN10 39 A4
Sutton Av Nth. BN10 39 A4
Swanee Clo. BN10 39 C2
Telscombe Pk. BN10 39 B2
Telscombe Rd. BN10 39 A2
The Bricky. BN10 39 B3
The Cedars. BN10 39 B3
The Compts. BN10 39 B3
The Dew Pond. BN10 39 A3
The Lookout. BN10 39 B1
The Martins. BN10 39 A2
The Promenade. BN10 39 A5
The Ridings. BN10 39 B3
The Sheepfold. BN10 39 B3
The Sparrows. BN10 39 B3
Tollgate. BN10 39 A3
Tor Rd. BN10 39 A2
Tor Rd West. BN10 39 A2
Trafalgar Clo. BN10 39 B3
Turnpike Clo. BN10 39 B3
Valley Rd. BN10 39 B1
Vernon Av. BN10 39 B6
Victoria Av. BN10 39 B6
View Rd. BN10 39 B4
Waterford Clo. BN10 39 B2
Wellington Rd. BN10 39 D6
Wendale Dri. BN10 39 A3
Wheatlands Clo. BN10 39 A2
Woodlands Clo. BN10 39 A3
York Rd. BN10 39 A2

St Aubyns Rd,. BN41 43 C4
St Aubyns Rd,
Fishersgate. BN41 43 B4
St Helens Dri. BN3 43 D1
St Keyna Av. BN3 43 D5
St Leonards Av. BN3 43 C5
St Leonards Gdns. BN3 43 D5
St Leonards Rd. BN3 43 C5
St Louie Rd. BN42 43 A3
St Michaels Rd. BN41 43 B5
St Nicholas Rd. BN41 43 D5
St Peters Rd. BN41 43 B5
St Richards Rd. BN41 43 B5
Saxon Rd. BN3 43 D5
Seaford Rd. BN3 43 C5
Sharpthorne Cres.
BN41 43 C2
Sheepbell Clo. BN41 43 C3
Shelldale Av. BN41 43 B4
Shelldale Cres. BN41 43 B4
Shelldale Rd. BN41 43 B4
Sheppard Way. BN41 43 B1
Sherbourne Clo. BN3 43 D1
Sherbourne Rd. BN3 43 D1
Sidehill Dri. BN41 43 A2
South St. BN41 43 B2
Southdown Av. BN41 43 C4
Southdown Rd. BN41 43 A1
Spencer Av. BN3 43 D5
Springate Rd. BN42 43 A4
Stanley Rd. BN41 43 B3
Stapley Rd. BN3 43 D3
Station Rd. BN41 43 C5
Stonery Clo. BN41 43 A1
Stonery Rd. BN41 43 A2
Summer Clo. BN41 43 D1
Summerdale Rd. BN3 43 D1
Sycamore Clo. BN41 43 C1
Sylvester Way. BN41 43 C1
Symbister Rd. BN41 43 C4
Teg Clo. BN41 43 C1
The Crescent. BN42 43 A3
The Crossway. BN41 43 A1
The Dene. BN3 43 D1
The Gardens,
Fishersgate. BN41 43 A5
The Gardens,
Portslade. BN41 43 C3
The Meadows. BN3 43 D1
The Parks. BN41 43 D1
The Rise. BN41 43 A1
Thornbush Cres. BN41 43 C1
Trafalgar Rd. BN41 43 B3
Vale Gdns. BN41 43 B4
Vale Rd. BN41 43 B4
Valerie Clo. BN41 43 C2
Valley Rd. BN41 43 A1
Victoria Rd. BN41 43 B4
Warrior Clo. BN41 43 B1
Wellington Rd. BN41 43 B5
West Rd. BN41 43 A5
West St. BN41 43 C5
West Way. BN3 43 D1
Westbrook Way. BN41 43 A4
Western Esplanade.
BN3 43 D6
Wharf Rd. BN3 43 D1
Wickhurst Clo. BN41 43 A1
Wickhurst Rise. BN41 43 A1
Wickhurst Rd. BN41 43 A1
Wilfrid Rd. BN3 43 D3
Williams Rd. BN41 43 B5
Windlesham Clo. BN41 43 A2
Wolseley Rd. BN41 43 B3
Worcester Villas. BN3 43 C4

RINGMER

Anchor Fld. BN8 44 B2
Ashton Ville Clo. BN8 44 D1
Ashurst Clo. BN8 44 A2
Ballard Dri. BN8 44 D1
Bishops Clo. BN8 44 B2
Bishops La. BN8 44 A1
Broyle Clo. BN8 44 D1
Broyle La. BN8 44 D2
Broyle Paddock. BN8 44 D1
Broyleside. BN8 44 D1
Chamberlaines La. BN8 44 C2
Christie Av. BN8 44 A5
Church Hill. BN8 44 D1
Delves Clo. BN8 44 A2
Delves Way. BN8 44 A1
Fairlight Fld. BN8 44 B3

Foxglove Clo. BN8 44 D1
Gote La. BN8 44 A3
Greater Paddock. BN8 44 B2
Green Clo. BN8 44 B2
Greenacres Dri. BN8 44 A3
Ham La. BN8 44 A1
Harrisons La. BN8 44 B3
Harvard Rd. BN8 44 A3
Hayes Clo. BN8 44 A3
Kiln Rd. BN8 44 D1
Langham Clo. BN8 44 A3
Laughton Rd. BN8 44 D2
Lewes Rd. BN8 44 A3
Little Paddock. BN8 44 B2
Manor Clo. BN8 44 D1
Mildmay Clo. BN8 44 A2
Mill Gdns. BN8 44 A3
Mill Mead. BN8 44 B3
Mill Rd. BN8 44 A3
Mill View. BN8 44 A3
Norlington Flds. BN8 44 A1
Norlington La. BN8 44 A1
North Rd. BN8 44 B2
Oakmede Way. BN8 44 A3
Potato La. BN8 44 A3
Potters Fld. BN8 44 B2
Rushy Clo. BN8 44 B3
Sadlers Way. BN8 44 A3
Shelley Rd. BN8 44 B2
Shepherds Clo. BN8 44 B3
Shepherds Way. BN8 44 B3
Springett Av. BN8 44 A3
The Broyle. BN8 44 D2
The Elms. BN8 44 A2
Turnpike Clo. BN8 44 D1
Vicarage Clo. BN8 44 A2
Vicarage Way. BN8 44 A2

ROBERTSBRIDGE

Andrews Clo. TN32 44 D4
Bellhurst Rd. TN32 44 B5
Bishops Croft. TN32 44 C6
Bishops La. TN32 44 B6
Blenheim Ct. TN32 44 A6
Brightling Rd. TN32 44 A6
Bugsell La. TN32 44 A5
Church Rd. TN32 44 D4
Coronation Cotts. TN32 44 D4
Fair La. TN32 44 D5
Fayre Meadow. TN32 44 D5
George Hill. TN32 44 D5
Glenleigh Walk. TN32 44 B5
Heathfield Gdns. TN32 44 C6
High St. TN32 44 C6
Kemps Way. TN32 44 D4
Knelle Rd. TN32 44 B5
Langham Rd. TN32 44 A5
Mill Rise. TN32 44 C6
Northbridge St. TN32 44 D3
Rotherview. TN32 44 D4
Rutley Clo. TN32 44 D4
Station Rd. TN32 44 C5
The Clappers. TN32 44 C5
Willowbank. TN32 44 C5
Willow Ms. TN32 44 C6

ROTTINGDEAN

Abbotsbury Clo. BN2 45 D6
Arundel Drive E. BN2 45 D6
Arundel Drive W. BN2 45 D6
Ashdown Av. BN2 45 C5
Bazehill Rd. BN2 45 C4
Bishopstone Dri. BN2 45 C4
Caspian Sq. BN2 45 B5
Chailey Av. BN2 45 B5
Challoners Clo. BN2 45 B5
Challoners Mews. BN2 45 B5
Chichester Drive E.
BN2 45 D6
Chichester Drive W.
BN2 45 D6
Chiltington Way. BN2 45 D4
Chorley Av. BN2 45 C5
Court Farm Rd. BN2 45 A3
Court Ord Rd. BN2 45 B5
Cowley Dri. BN2 45 A1
Cranleigh Av. BN2 45 B5
Dean Clo. BN2 45 B5
Dean Court Rd. BN2 45 B5
Donnington Rd. BN2 45 A1

Effingham Clo. BN2 45 D4
Eileen Av. BN2 45 C6
Eley Cres. BN2 45 A3
Eley Dri. BN2 45 A3
Elvin Cres. BN2 45 A3
Falmer Av. BN2 45 D4
Falmer Rd. BN2 45 A2
Founthill Av. BN2 45 D5
Founthill Rd. BN2 45 C5
Foyles Clo. BN2 45 B4
Glyndebourne Av. BN2 45 D5
Gorham Av. BN2 45 B4
Gorham Clo. BN2 45 B4
Grand Crescent. BN2 45 C5
High St. BN2 45 B5
Hill Rd. BN2 45 C5
Knole Rd. BN2 45 C5
Lenham Av. BN2 45 C6
Lenham Rd E. BN2 45 C6
Lenham Rd W. BN2 45 C4
Lindfield Clo. BN2 45 C4
Little Cres. BN2 45 C6
Longhill Clo. BN2 45 A3
Lustrells Clo. BN2 45 D5
Lustrells Cres. BN2 45 D5
Lustrells Rd. BN2 45 C4
Lustrells Vale. BN2 45 D4
Marine Clo. BN2 45 C6
Marine Dri. BN2 45 A5
Meadow Clo. BN2 45 A4
Merston Clo. BN2 45 A1
Nevill Rd. BN2 45 A2
New Barn Rd. BN2 45 A3
Newlands Rd. BN2 45 B5
Northfield Rise. BN2 45 B5
Northgate Clo. BN2 45 B4
Old Place Mews. BN2 45 B5
Park Cres. BN2 45 B5
Park Rd. BN2 45 B5
Ravenswood Dri. BN2 45 A1
Romney Rd. BN2 45 C6
Rowan Way. BN2 45 A3
St Aubyns Mead. BN2 45 B5
Salehurst Rd. BN2 45 A1
Saltdean Dri. BN2 45 D6
Saltdean Pk Rd. BN2 45 D6
Saltdean Vale. BN2 45 D5
Saxon Clo. BN2 45 D4
School La. BN2 45 D5
Sheep Walk. BN2 45 A4
Steyning Rd. BN2 45 B5
The Green. BN2 45 C5
The Park. BN2 45 C5
The Rotyngs. BN2 45 B4
The Twitten. BN2 45 B4
The Vale. BN2 45 D5
Tremola Av. BN2 45 D5
Tudor Clo. BN2 45 B5
Tumulus Rd. BN2 45 D4
Under Cliff Walk. BN2 45 C6
Vicarage La. BN2 45 B5
Vicarage Ter. BN2 45 B5
Welesmere Rd. BN2 45 C4
West St. BN2 45 B5
Westmeston Av. BN2 45 C5
Whipping Post La. BN2 45 B5
Whiteway La. BN2 45 A5
Wilkinson Clo. BN2 45 A4
Winton Av. BN2 45 A3
Wivelsfield Rd. BN2 45 D4

RYE

Bedford Pl. TN31 46 C2
Bridge Pl. TN31 46 C2
Church Sq. TN31 46 B4
Cinque Ports St. TN31 46 B4
Conduit Hill. TN31 46 C3
Crown Fields. TN31 46 A4
Cyprus Pl. TN31 46 B1
Deadmans La. TN31 46 B1
Eagle Rd. TN31 46 C3
East St. TN31 46 C3
Ferry Rd. TN31 46 A4
Fishmarket Rd. TN31 46 C3
High St. TN31 46 C3
Hilders Cliff. TN31 46 C3
Hylands Yd. TN31 46 C3
Landgate. TN31 46 C3
Landgate Sq. TN31 46 C2
Lion St. TN31 46 C3
Love La. TN31 46 A1
Market Rd. TN31 46 B4
Market St. TN31 46 C4

Mermaid Pass. TN31 46 B5
Mermaid St. TN31 46 B5
Meryon Ct. TN31 46 B4
Military Rd. TN31 46 C1
New Rd. TN31 46 D3
North Salts. TN31 46 D1
Ockman La. TN31 46 C4
Regent Sq. TN31 46 B3
Rock Channel Quay.
TN31 46 C6
Rope Walk. TN31 46 C3
Rope Walk Arcade.
TN31 46 B3
Rye Hill. TN31 46 C2
St Margarets Ter. TN31 46 B6
Shipyard La. TN31 46 C6
South Undercliff. TN31 46 B6
Station App. TN31 46 B3
Strand. TN31 46 B5
The Deals. TN31 46 A5
The Green. TN31 46 B1
The Grove. TN31 46 B1
The Mint. TN31 46 B5
The Needles. TN31 46 B4
The Quay. TN31 46 A5
Tower St. TN31 46 C3
Traders Pass. TN31 46 B5
Turkeycock La. TN31 46 C3
Watchbell La. TN31 46 B5
Watchbell St. TN31 46 B5
West St. TN31 46 B4
Winchelsea Rd. TN31 46 A5
Wish S.t TN31 46 A5
Wish Ward. TN31 46 A5

ST. LEONARDS

Albany Rd. TN38 47 B4
Aldborough Rd. TN38 47 C2
Alexandra Rd. TN37 47 C4
Alfred St. TN38 47 C5
Alma Ter. TN37 47 C1
Alma Villas. TN37 47 C1
Amherst Rd. TN37 47 D2
Amherst Gdns. TN37 47 D3
Amherst Rd. TN37 47 C2
Anglesea Ter. TN38 47 C3
Arbourvale. TN38 47 A2
Archery Rd. TN38 47 B5
Ascot Mews. TN38 47 A3
Avondale Rd. TN38 47 A2
Barnfield Clo. TN38 47 A3
Battle Rd. TN37 47 B1
Beaufort Cres. TN37 47 C1
Beaufort Rd. TN37 47 C2
Belvedere Pk. TN38 47 A3
Blomfield Rd. TN37 47 D4
Bohemia Rd. TN37 47 C2
Boscobel Rd. TN38 47 B4
Boscobel Rd N. TN38 47 A4
Branksome Rd. TN38 47 A3
Briscoes Walk. TN37 47 D3
Brittany Rd. TN38 47 B4
Burhill Way. TN38 47 A4
Burry Rd. TN37 47 C1
Caple Gdns. TN38 47 A4
Cardiff Rd. TN38 47 C4
Carisbrooke Rd. TN38 47 B4
Cavendish Av. TN38 47 A5
Caves Rd. TN38 47 A5
Celandine Dri. TN38 47 A2
Chambers Cres. TN38 47 A1
Chambers Rd. TN38 47 A1
Chapel Park Rd. TN37 47 C3
Charles Rd. TN37 47 C3
Charles Rd W. TN38 47 B3
Chatham Rd. TN37 47 C1
Cherry Tree Clo. TN37 47 C4
Chichester Rd. TN38 47 B1
Church Rd. TN37 47 C3
Clarence Rd. TN37 47 C2
Clinton Cres. TN38 47 C3
Cloudesley Rd. TN37 47 C3
Clyde Rd. TN38 47 C4
Collinstone Rd. TN38 47 A5
Collinswood Dri. TN38 47 A5
Combermere Rd. TN38 47 B4
Cornfield Ter. TN37 47 C3
Cowden Walk. TN38 47 A5
Cranbrook Rd. TN38 47 C5
Cross St. TN37 47 C5
Cumberland Gdns.
TN38 47 B4
Cypress Clo. TN38 47 A4

Dane Rd. TN38 47 B4
De Cham Av. TN37 47 D3
De Cham Rd. TN37 47 C3
Dell Clo. TN38 47 B2
Douce Gro. TN38 47 A2
Drapers Way. TN38 47 B2
Drury La. TN38 47 A1
Duke Rd. TN37 47 B1
Duke St. TN37 47 B1
Duke Ter. TN37 47 C1
East Ascent. TN38 47 C5
East St. TN38 47 C5
Edward Rd. TN37 47 D4
Elizabeth Rd. TN38 47 A1
Ellenslea Rd. TN37 47 C4
Epsom Clo. TN38 47 B3
Essenden Rd. TN38 47 A5
Eversfield Pl. TN37 47 D5
Eversley Clo. TN37 47 C2
Eversley Cres. TN37 47 C2
Eversley Rd. TN37 47 C1
Falaise Rd. TN37 47 A3
Fern Rd. TN38 47 A3
Filsham Rd. TN38 47 A4
Filsham Valley. TN38 47 A4
Ford Rd. TN38 47 A1
Fulford Clo. TN38 47 A4
Gensing Rd. TN38 47 C5
Gilbert Rd. TN38 47 B3
Gillsmans Dri. TN38 47 A2
Gillsmans Hill. TN38 47 A2
Grand Par. TN38 47 C5
Gresham Way. TN38 47 A3
Grosvenor Cres. TN38 47 A4
Harting Combe. TN38 47 B3
Hatherley Rd. TN37 47 C4
Helensdene Walk. TN37 47 C4
Highlands Dri. TN38 47 B4
Highlands Gdns. TN38 47 B4
Hollington Cts. TN38 47 A3
Hollington Park Clo.
TN38 47 A3
Hollington Park Rd.
TN38 47 A2
Hollybank Gdns. TN38 47 B2
Horntye Rd. TN37 47 C2
Horseshoe Clo. TN38 47 B2
INDUSTRIAL ESTATES:
Ponswood Ind Est.
TN38 47 A1
Ironlatch Av. TN38 47 A1
Kenilworth Rd. TN38 47 B4
King Edward Clo. TN37 47 C1
Kings Rd. TN37 47 C4
Knoll Rise. TN38 47 A5
Larch Clo. TN38 47 A3
Lewis Rd. TN38 47 A1
Lime Clo. TN38 47 B3
London Rd. TN37 47 B2
Lower South Rd. TN37 47 C2
Magdalen Rd. TN37 47 D4
Marina. TN38 47 A5
Market St. TN38 47 C5
Markwick Ter. TN38 47 B3
Marlborough Clo. TN38 47 A3
Maudlin Ct. TN37 47 B3
Maze Hill. TN38 47 B4
Mazehill Ter. TN38 47 B5
Medina Ter. TN38 47 B1
Menzies Rd. TN38 47 C5
Mercatoria. TN38 47 C5
Merrimede Clo. TN38 47 C5
Mews Rd. TN38 47 B2
Michele Clo. TN38 47 B2
Newgate Rd. TN37 47 C2
Norman Rd. TN37 47 C5
Normandy Rd. TN37 47 C2
North Rd. TN37 47 C2
North St. TN38 47 C1
Oban Rd. TN37 47 C1
Oxford Rd. TN37 47 A1
Park Cres. TN37 47 D1
Park Dri. TN37 47 D1
Park View. TN37 47 D1
Park Way. TN37 47 D1
Paynton Rd. TN37 47 B1
Pevensey Rd. TN37 47 C4
Ponswood Rd. TN38 47 B2
Princes Rd. TN37 47 B4
Quarry Hill. TN38 47 B4
Quarry House. TN38 47 B5
Rectory Clo. TN38 47 B4
Redgeland Rise. TN38 47 A1
Regency Gdns. TN38 47 A3
Rochester Rd. TN37 47 B1
Rothsay Rd. TN38 47 B4

St Catherines Clo. TN37 47 D4
St Dominic Clo. TN38 47 A4
St Helens Rd. TN37 47 D1
St Johns Rd. TN37 47 C4
St Margarets Rd. TN37 47 C5
St Margarets Ter. TN37 47 D5
St Matthews Dri. TN38 47 C2
St Matthews Gdns. TN38 47 B2
St Matthews Rd. TN38 47 B2
St Pauls Pl. TN37 47 C4
St Pauls Rd. TN37 47 C3
St Peters Rd. TN37 47 C3
Salisbury Rd. TN37 47 C3
Sandwich Dri. TN38 47 A4
Saxon St. TN37 47 C5
Sea Rd. TN38 47 A5
Sedlescombe Gdns. TN38 47 B2
Sedlescombe Rd Nth. TN37 47 B1
Sedlescombe Rd Sth. TN38 47 B2
Selmeston Clo. TN37 47 B2
Shepherd St. TN38 47 C5
Silchester Rd. TN38 47 C5
Silverlands Rd. TN37 47 B1
South St. TN37 47 C5
Southwater Rd. TN37 47 C3
Southwood Clo. TN38 47 B2
Springfield Rd. TN38 47 B2
Springfield Valley Rd. TN38 47 B3
Stainsby St. TN37 47 C4
Stanhope Pl. TN38 47 C5
Stockleigh Rd. TN38 47 C4
Stonehouse Dri. TN38 47 A1
Strood Rd. TN37 47 C1
Summerhill. TN38 47 A3
Sussex Rd. TN38 47 A5
Sycamore Clo. TN38 47 A3
Sydney Clo. TN38 47 B1
Terrace Rd. TN37 47 C4
The Choice. TN38 47 A1
The Cloisters. TN37 47 D4
The Drive. TN38 47 A3
The Green. TN38 47 B3
The Lawn. TN38 47 A3
The Links. TN38 47 A3
The Mount. TN38 47 B5
The Uplands. TN38 47 A3
Theaklen Dri. TN38 47 B1
Tower Rd. TN37 47 C3
Tower Rd W. TN38 47 A4
Tudor Av. TN38 47 A4
Under Cliff. TN38 47 B5
Union St. TN38 47 C5
Upper Clarence Rd. TN37 47 C2
Upper Maze Hill. TN38 47 B4
Upper Park Rd. TN37 47 C2
Upper South Rd. TN37 47 C2
Vale Rd. TN37 47 C1
Vantage Walk. TN38 47 B2
Victoria Rd. TN37 47 D4
Villa Rd. TN37 47 D4
Warrior Gdns. TN37 47 C4
Warrior Sq. TN37 47 C4
Welbeck Av. TN38 47 A5
Wellis Gdns. TN38 47 A3
West Hill Rd. TN38 47 A5
Westerleigh Clo. TN38 47 A3
Western Rd. TN37 47 C4
Windmill Rd. TN38 47 B1
Windsor Rd. TN37 47 B1
Wingate Clo. TN38 47 A2
Winterbourne Clo. TN37 47 D3
Woodland Vale Rd. TN37 47 C3
York Rd. TN37 47 C1

SEAFORD

Adelaide Clo. BN25 48 C2
Albany Rd. BN25 48 B4
Alexandra Clo. BN25 48 C2
Alfriston Pk. BN25 49 H2
Alfriston Rd. BN25 49 F3
Antony Clo. BN25 48 A1
Aquila Pk. BN25 49 F4
Argent Clo. BN25 49 F2
Arundel Rd. BN25 49 F4

Ash Dri. BN25 49 H4
Ashurst Rd. BN25 49 E5
Audrey Clo. BN25 48 C2
Avondale Rd. BN25 48 C4
Badgers Copse. BN25 49 G4
Bainbridge Clo. BN25 49 E5
Balmoral Clo. BN25 49 F2
Barcombe Av. BN25 49 H5
Barcombe Clo. BN25 49 H5
Barn Clo. BN25 49 F2
Barn Rd. BN25 49 F2
Barons Clo. BN25 48 B2
Battle Clo. BN25 49 G2
Beach Clo. BN25 48 C4
Beacon Clo. BN25 48 C3
Beacon Dri. BN25 48 C3
Beacon Rd. BN25 48 C3
Beame Ct. BN25 48 C4
Belgrave Cres. BN25 49 E2
Belgrave Rd. BN25 48 C4
Belvedere Gdns. BN25 49 F2
Benenden Clo. BN25 49 F3
Berwick Clo. BN25 48 B3
Birling Clo. BN25 48 B3
Bishops Clo. BN25 48 B3
Bishopstone Rd. BN25 48 A2
Blatchington Clo. BN25 49 E3
Blatchington Hill. BN25 48 D3
Blatchington Rd. BN25 48 D4
Blue Haze Av. BN25 49 F3
Bodiam Clo. BN25 49 G3
Bowden Rise. BN25 48 D2
Bracken Rd. BN25 49 F5
Bramber Clo. BN25 49 E5
Bramber La. BN25 48 D5
Bramber Rd. BN25 48 D5
Broad St. BN25 48 D4
Bromley Rd. BN25 49 F3
Brooklyn Rd. BN25 48 D4
Buckingham Clo. BN25 48 D3
Buckland Rd. BN25 49 E3
Buckle By-Pass. BN25 48 B2
Buckle Clo. BN25 48 B3
Buckle Dri. BN25 48 B3
Buckle Rise. BN25 48 B3
Buckthorn Clo. BN25 49 G4
Carlton Clo. BN25 48 C3
Carlton Rd. BN25 48 C3
Caroline Clo. BN25 48 C2
Chalvington Clo. BN25 49 E1
Chapel Clo. BN25 48 D3
Charles Clo. BN25 48 C2
Chartwell Clo. BN25 48 C1
Chatham Pl. BN25 48 C4
Chesterton Av. BN25 49 G4
Chesterton Dri. BN25 49 G4
Chichester Clo. BN25 48 D4
Chichester Rd. BN25 48 D4
Church La. BN25 48 D5
Church St. BN25 48 C2
Churchill Rd. BN25 48 C2
Chyngton Av. BN25 49 G3
Chyngton Gdns. BN25 49 G3
Chyngton La. BN25 49 H4
Chyngton La Nth. BN25 49 H4
Chyngton Pl. BN25 49 F5
Chyngton Rd. BN25 49 F5
Chyngton Way. BN25 49 G5
Cinque Ports Way. BN25 49 G3
Claremont Rd. BN25 48 C4
Clementine Av. BN25 48 B2
Cliff Clo. BN25 49 E6
Cliff Gdns. BN25 49 E6
Cliff Rd. BN25 49 E6
Clinton La. BN25 48 D4
Clinton Pl. BN25 48 D4
College Rd. BN25 48 D5
Connaught Rd. BN25 48 B4
Cornfield Clo. BN25 49 E4
Cornfield Rd. BN25 49 E4
Corsica Clo. BN25 49 E6
Corsica Rd. BN25 49 E6
Cradle Hill Rd. BN25 49 F2
Cricketfield Rd. BN25 48 D5
Crooked La. BN25 48 D5
Crouch La. BN25 48 D5
Crown Hill. BN25 48 D1
Cuckmere Rd. BN25 49 F5
Dane Clo. BN25 48 C5
Dane Rd. BN25 48 C5
Darwall Dri. BN25 49 F5
Deal Av. BN25 49 G2
Dean Rd. BN25 48 C5
Dover Rd. BN25 49 H2
Downs Rd. BN25 49 F4

Downsview Rd. BN25 49 E4
Duchess Dri. BN25 48 D1
Dukes Clo. BN25 48 C2
Dulwich Clo. BN25 49 F3
Dymchurch Clo. BN25 49 G3
Dymock Clo. BN25 49 H3
Earls Clo. BN25 48 B2
East Albany Rd. BN25 49 E4
East Dean Rise. BN25 49 F3
East St. BN25 48 D5
Eastbourne Rd. BN25 49 F4
Edinburgh Rd. BN25 48 C4
Edwards Clo. BN25 48 A1
Eleanor Clo. BN25 48 C2
Elgin Gdns. BN25 49 H4
Elm Clo. BN25 49 H4
Esher Clo. BN25 49 E3
Esplanade. BN25 48 D5
*Esplanade Mews,
 Ringmer Rd. BN25 48 D5
Etherton Way. BN25 49 F3
Eton Clo. BN25 49 F3
Fairways Clo. BN25 49 G5
Fairways Rd. BN25 49 G5
Farm Clo. BN25 49 G3
Field Clo. BN25 49 G5
Findon Clo. BN25 49 H5
Firle Clo. BN25 48 D3
Firle Dri. BN25 48 D2
Firle Grove. BN25 48 D2
Firle Rd. BN25 48 D2
Fitzgerald Av. BN25 49 E5
Fitzgerald Park. BN25 49 E5
Flint Clo. BN25 48 D1
Folkestone Clo. BN25 49 G2
Foster Clo. BN25 48 D3
Freeland Clo. BN25 48 A1
Friston Clo. BN25 48 B3
Gerald Rd. BN25 49 E6
Gildredge Rd. BN25 48 D5
Glebe Dri. BN25 48 D4
Grand Avenue. BN25 48 B2
Green La. BN25 48 D5
Green Walk. BN25 49 F5
Greenwell Clo. BN25 49 G3
Grosvenor Rd. BN25 48 C4
Grove Rd. BN25 48 D4
Guardswell Pl. BN25 48 D4
Hamsey La. BN25 49 H5
Hanover Clo. BN25 48 A1
Harbour Vw Clo. BN25 48 A1
Harrison Rd. BN25 49 F3
Harrow Clo. BN25 49 F3
Hartfield Rd. BN25 49 E4
Hastings Clo. BN25 49 G2
Haven Brow. BN25 49 F3
Hawth Clo. BN25 48 B3
Hawth Cres. BN25 48 B3
Hawth Gro. BN25 48 B3
Hawth Hill. BN25 48 B3
Hawth Park Rd. BN25 48 B3
Hawth Pl. BN25 48 B3
Hawth Rise. BN25 48 B3
Hawth Way. BN25 48 C4
Hazeldene. BN25 49 F4
Headland Av. BN25 49 E5
Heathfield Rd. BN25 49 E5
High St. BN25 48 D5
Highlands Rd. BN25 49 E4
Hill Pk. BN25 49 F4
Hill Rise. BN25 48 B2
Hillside Av. BN25 49 G2
Hindover Cres. BN25 49 F4
Hindover Rd. BN25 49 F3
Holters Way. BN25 48 D2
Homefield Clo. BN25 48 D3
Homefield Rd. BN25 48 D3
Hurdis Rd. BN25 48 A1
Hythe Clo. BN25 49 H3
Hythe Cres. BN25 49 G3
Hythe View. BN25 49 H3

INDUSTRIAL ESTATES:
Cradle Hill Ind Est. BN25 49 G2
Isabel Clo. BN25 49 G2
Jevington Dri. BN25 48 B3
Jubilee Gdns. BN25 49 E2
Juniper Clo. BN25 49 G4
Kammond Av. BN25 49 G2
Katherine Way. BN25 48 C2
Kedale Rd. BN25 48 D3
Kimberley Rd. BN25 48 B4
Kings Ride. BN25 48 C3
Kingsmead. BN25 48 C3
Kingsmead Clo. BN25 48 D3
Kingsmead La. BN25 48 C3

Kingsmead Walk. BN25 48 D3
Kingsmead Way. BN25 48 D3
Kingston Av. BN25 49 G4
Kingston Clo. BN25 49 G5
Kingston Green. BN25 49 G5
Kingston Way. BN25 49 G5
Kingsway. BN25 48 C3
Ladycross Clo. BN25 49 G5
Lansdown Rd. BN25 49 G2
Lexden Ct. BN25 49 F3
Lexden Dri. BN25 49 E2
Lexden Rd. BN25 49 E1
Lindfield Av. BN25 49 H5
Links Clo. BN25 49 F5
Links Rd. BN25 49 F5
Lions Pl. BN25 49 E5
Lower Drive. BN25 49 E2
Lucinda Way. BN25 49 E2
Lullington Clo. BN25 49 G5
Mallett Clo. BN25 48 D5
Manor Clo. BN25 49 F4
Manor Rd. BN25 49 F4
Manor Rd Nth. BN25 49 G4
Marine Cres. BN25 48 D5
Marine Dri. BN25 48 A1
Marine Parade. BN25 48 A3
Mark Clo. BN25 49 H5
*Martello Mews,
 Martello Rd. BN25 48 D5
Martello Rd. BN25 48 D5
Mason Rd. BN25 49 E3
Maurice Rd. BN25 49 E6
May Av. BN25 49 G5
Meadow Way. BN25 49 F4
Meads Rd. BN25 49 E4
Mercread Rd. BN25 48 D5
Middle Furlong. BN25 49 E4
Mill Dri. BN25 49 E4
Millberg Rd. BN25 49 G3
Milldown Rd. BN25 49 E4
Millfield Clo. BN25 49 F3
Monarch Gdns. BN25 49 F2
Morningside Clo. BN25 49 E3
Newhaven Rd. BN25 48 A2
Newick Clo. BN25 49 G5
Norman Clo. BN25 48 A1
Normansal Clo. BN25 49 E1
Normansal Pk Av. BN25 49 E3
North Camp La. BN25 49 E3
North Way. BN25 49 E3
Northcliffe Clo. BN25 49 E3
Northfield Clo. BN25 48 D2
Offham Clo. BN25 48 C4
Park Rd. BN25 48 C4
Parkside Rd. BN25 49 E3
Pelham Rd. BN25 48 D5
Perth Clo. BN25 49 G4
Pevensey Clo. BN25 49 G3
Pinewood Clo. BN25 49 F3
Pitt Dri. BN25 49 E2
Place La. BN25 48 D5
Poynings Clo. BN25 49 G5
Princes Clo. BN25 48 D3
Princess Dri. BN25 48 B2
Quarry La. BN25 48 B2
Queens Park Gdns. BN25 48 B4
Queensway. BN25 49 F2
Raymond Clo. BN25 49 F2
Regents Clo. BN25 48 D3
Richington Way. BN25 49 F3
Richmond Rd. BN25 48 D5
Richmond Ter. BN25 48 D4
Ringmer Rd. BN25 48 D5
Rochford Way. BN25 48 A2
Rodmell Rd. BN25 49 G5
Roedean Clo. BN25 49 F3
Roman Clo. BN25 48 A1
Romney Clo. BN25 49 H2
Rookery Way. BN25 49 A2
Rose Walk. BN25 49 F5
Rother Rd. BN25 49 F5
Rough Brow. BN25 49 G4
Rowan Clo. BN25 49 G4
Royal Dri. BN25 49 D1
Rugby Clo. BN25 49 F3
Rye Clo. BN25 49 G3
St Andrews Dri. BN25 48 A1
St Crispians. BN25 48 C4
St Johns Rd. BN25 48 D5
St Peters Clo. BN25 48 D5
St Peters Rd. BN25 48 D4
St Wilfreds Pl. BN25 48 D5
Salisbury Rd. BN25 48 D4
Saltwood Rd. BN25 49 G3
Sandgate Clo. BN25 49 G3

Sandore Clo. BN25 49 F3
Sandore Rd. BN25 49 F3
Sandringham Clo. BN25 49 F2
Saxon La. BN25 48 D5
Seafield Clo. BN25 49 G2
Seagrove Way. BN25 49 E2
Sheep Pen La. BN25 49 F4
Sherwood Rise. BN25 49 E3
Sherwood Rd. BN25 48 D3
Short Brow. BN25 49 E3
Silver La. BN25 48 B1
South St. BN25 48 D5
South Way. BN25 49 G6
Southdown Rd. BN25 49 E4
Sovereign Clo. BN25 49 E2
Stafford Rd. BN25 48 D4
Station App. BN25 48 C4
Station Rd. BN25 48 B3
Steyne Rd. BN25 49 E5
Steyne Rd. BN25 48 D5
Steyning Clo. BN25 49 H5
Steyning Rd. BN25 49 H5
Stirling Av. BN25 49 G4
Stirling Clo. BN25 49 G4
Stoke Clo. BN25 49 F4
Stoke Manor Clo. BN25 49 G4
Stonewood Clo. BN25 49 H4
Surrey Clo. BN25 48 C3
Surrey Rd. BN25 48 B3
Sutton Av. BN25 49 E5
Sutton Drove. BN25 49 E4
Sutton Park Rd. BN25 48 D4
Sutton Rd. BN25 48 D4
Suttoncroft La. BN25 48 D5
Sycamore Clo. BN25 49 H4
The Boundary. BN25 49 F3
The Bydown. BN25 49 F3
The Byeways. BN25 48 D5
The Causeway. BN25 48 D5
The Close. BN25 48 E5
The Covers. BN25 49 F4
The Holt. BN25 48 D2
The Mews. BN25 49 F3
The Peverels. BN25 49 F2
The Ridgeway. BN25 49 F2
The Ridings. BN25 49 G3
The Shepway. BN25 49 G3
Tudor Clo. BN25 48 C3
Upper Belgrave Rd. BN25 48 D3
Upper Chyngton Gdns. BN25 49 G3
Upper Sherwood Rd. BN25 49 E3
Vale Clo. BN25 49 F3
Vale Rd. BN25 49 E3
Valley Dri. BN25 49 F3
Valley Rise. BN25 49 E3
Vicarage Clo. BN25 49 E4
Victor Clo. BN25 48 C2
Viking Clo. BN25 48 A1
Walmer Rd. BN25 49 G4
Warwick Rd. BN25 48 D4
Wellington Pk. BN25 49 F4
West Dean Rise. BN25 49 F3
West St. BN25 48 D5
West View. BN25 48 D5
Westdown Rd. BN25 48 C4
Whiteway Clo. BN25 48 D3
Wilkinson Way. BN25 48 D3
Willow Dri. BN25 49 G4
Wilmington Rd. BN25 48 C4
Winchelsea Clo. BN25 49 G2
Windsor Clo. BN25 48 A1

TELSCOMBE/SALTDEAN

Ambleside Av. BN10 50 C4
Amhurst Rd. BN10 50 C4
Ardingly Rd. BN2 50 A1
Arlington Gdns. BN2 50 A1
Arundel Rd West. BN10 50 D4
Ashurst Av. BN2 50 B3
Bannings Vale. BN2 50 B3
Berry Clo. BN10 50 D3
Berwick Rd. BN2 50 A1
Bevendean Av. BN2 50 A2
Brambletyne Av. BN2 50 A3
Bridleway. BN10 50 D3
Broomfield Av. BN10 50 C4
Buckhurst Clo. BN10 50 C4

Pinewood Clo. BN22 56 C1
Portsdown Way. BN20 56 A1
Roffrey Av. BN22 56 D2
Ruskin Rd. BN20 56 B2
St Marys Clo. BN22 56 B1
Salisbury Clo. BN22 56 C1
Shortlands Clo. BN22 56 C2
Spring Clo. BN20 56 B2
Spruce Clo. BN22 56 D1
Stanmer Dri. BN22 56 C3
Summerlands Rd. BN22 56 B1
Tamarack Clo. BN22 56 D1
Tas Combe Way. BN20 56 B2
The Broadway. BN22 56 D2
The Cloisters. BN22 56 C1
The Close. BN22 56 B3
The Croft. BN20 56 B2
Timberley Rd. BN22 56 D2
Upper Kings Dri. BN20 56 B2
Upper Ratton Dri. BN20 56 A3
Upper Wish Hill. BN20 56 B3
Waldron Clo. BN22 56 C3
Walnut Tree Clo. BN20 56 B3
Warburton Clo. BN21 56 C3
Wealden Park. BN22 56 C2
Weatherby Clo. BN21 56 C3
Wedderburn Rd. BN20 56 B3
Willingdon Clo. BN20 56 B2
Willingdon Park Dri. BN22 56 C1
Willingdon Rd. BN22 56 B2
Willingdon Way. BN22 56 B1
Willow Walk. BN22 56 C1
Winchester Clo. BN22 56 B1
Winchester Way. BN22 56 B1
Wish Hill. BN22 56 B2
Woodland Av. BN22 56 C3
Wrestwood Av. BN22 56 C2

WINCHELSEA

Back La. TN36 55 B3
Barrack Sq. TN36 55 B3
Castle St. TN36 55 B3
Dogs Hill Rd. TN36 55 D5
Donald Way. TN36 55 C5
Ferry Hill. TN36 55 A2
Friars Rd. TN36 55 B3
German St. TN36 55 B3
Greyfriars Pl. TN36 55 D3
Harbour Farm. TN36 55 D4
High St. TN36 55 B3
Hiham Grn. TN36 55 B2
Hogtrough La. TN36 55 A3
Kent Clo. TN36 55 B3
Market Sq. TN36 55 B3
Mill Rd. TN36 55 A2
Monks Walk. TN36 55 A4
Morlais Pl. TN36 55 D3
Morlais Ridge. TN36 55 D4
North St. TN36 55 B2
Old River Way. TN36 55 D3
Pett Level Rd. TN36 55 C6
Rectory La. TN36 55 A4
Roberts Hill. TN36 55 A3
Rookery La. TN36 55 B3
Royal Military Rd. TN36 55 B2
St Giles Clo. TN36 55 A3
St Thomas's St. TN36 55 B3
Sandrock Hill. TN36 55 A3
School Hill. TN36 55 B2
Sea Rd. TN36 55 D4
Smeatons La. TN36 55 D5
Station Rd. TN36 55 A2
Strand Hill. TN36 55 B3
Tanyard La. TN36 55 B2
The Ridge. TN36 55 D5
Victoria Way. TN36 55 C5
Wickham Rock Rd. TN36 55 A5
Willow La. TN36 55 D4
Windsor Way. TN36 55 C5

Edition 519C 10.99.